This book belongs to
Ms. Vallimont

Jesus of History,

Christ of Faith

Nihil Obstat: Rev. William M. Becker, STD
             Censor Librorum
             24 July 1998

Imprimatur: Rev. Michael J. Hoeppner, JCL
             Administrator, Diocese of Winona
             24 July 1998

The nihil obstat and imprimatur are official declarations that a book or pamphlet is free of doctrinal or moral error. No implication is contained therein that those who have granted the nihil obstat or imprimatur agree with the contents, opinions, or statements expressed.

The publishing team included Jerry Daoust, development editor; Barbara Allaire and Stephan Nagel, consulting editors; Rebecca Fairbank, copy editor; Barbara Bartelson, production editor, page designer, and typesetter; Hollace Storkel, typesetter; Maurine R. Twait, art director; Cindi Ramm, cover designer; Alan S. Hanson, pre-press specialist; Penny Koehler and Genevieve Nagel, photo researchers; Evy Abrahamson and Ken Call, illustrators; Laurie Geisler, designer of opening pages; Mapping Specialists, Ltd., mapmakers; and Patricia Deminna, indexer.

The acknowledgments continue on page 335.

Printed in the United States of America

1131 (PO4172)

ISBN 978-0-88489-530-5

Jesus of History,

Christ of Faith

Thomas Zanzig
Third Edition

saint mary's press

Contents

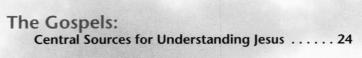

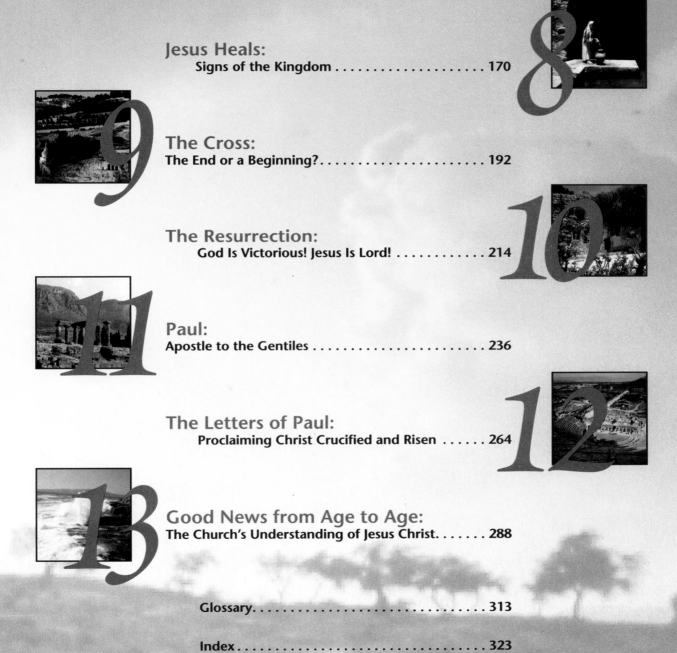

1

Who Is Jesus?

Searching in the New Testament and Beyond

In This Chapter . . .

- "Who Do You Say That I Am?"
- How Do We Learn About Jesus?
- The New Testament

ONCE when Jesus was praying alone, with only the disciples near him, he asked them, "Who do the crowds say that I am?" They answered, "John the Baptist; but others, Elijah; and still others, that one of the ancient prophets has arisen." He said to them, "But who do you say that I am?" Peter answered, "The Messiah of God." [Jesus] sternly ordered and commanded them not to tell anyone. (Luke 9:18–21)

"Who Do You Say That I Am?"

It Begins with the Cross

Jesus hung there, nailed to a cross, dying the death of a common criminal. As life slipped from his body and his last breath left his mouth, some witnesses no doubt cheered. It was the end of him, they thought, and the end as well of the dangerous message he had proclaimed. No more of this subversive challenge to established rules, or this talk of sinners and outcasts being accepted by God, or this call to love even one's enemies. It was also the end of his claim of a unique relationship with God, a relationship that gave him a special kind of authority. If taken seriously, such a claim could lead to a breakdown of the social order, a loss of respect for proper authority. Common people, even from the lowest classes, would begin to think they could make demands of those in power. But there was no need to worry about all of that now. He is dead, they reasoned, and we are finally rid of him.

Others gathered at the foot of that same cross. They, too, watched Jesus cling to the last thread of life. But there was no joy for them, no cheering. For his death spelled not only the end of his life but the end as well of all their dreams. They had loved this man; they had walked with him, sat spellbound by his stories, and felt their hearts freed by his message of hope and love. When he spoke of God and of the meaning of life, he was so convincing, so sure of himself, that they had become sure of their faith in him. They had staked their future on him, convinced that he would lead them to victory over their enemies and return them to a long-lost glory as a people. Now, as the blood drained from his body, it was all over. The end brought only bitter tears and, for some, the fear that they might meet the same brutal end if they did not deny their belief in him.

It Does Not End There

Nearly two thousand years later, people still talk about that man and the meaning of his life. Many claim that Jesus' story did indeed end with his brutal death on that small hill outside Jerusalem. He was clearly a good man, they may claim, maybe even one of the greatest religious leaders of all time—like the Buddha, perhaps, or Moses, or

■
The man named Jesus who walked the shores of the Sea of Galilee two thousand years ago is the same man Christians believe to be Lord of the universe and Savior of the world.

Photo, facing page: **The sun sets over the Sea of Galilee, on whose shores Jesus often walked and taught.** *Background:* **A view of the earth from space.**

Muhammad. He was admittedly a teacher of great wisdom, and parts of his message are worth pondering and even practicing. But he was nothing more than that, certainly not what others claim him to have been—the Messiah, the Son of God, the Lord of the universe. Such claims, they say, are sheer nonsense, illusions, mere superstition.

Others have come to a radically different conclusion about that man and his message. Today they call themselves Christians—"followers of the Christ"—to express their convictions about him. This was no ordinary man, they say. He was not just a great teacher or prophet, not just one more great religious leader. He was much more. He was, Christians claim, the Messiah, one with God. In fact, they boldly state, he was the Son of God and the Lord of the universe. Shocking claims, indeed. If true, those claims not only boggle the mind of the individual but change the entire course of human history.

Who Is This Man?

Nearly two thousand years have passed since the days when "the carpenter's son," the one called Jesus of Nazareth, walked the roads of Palestine, and still we must ask, Who is this man? In his own time he was most often regarded as simply a teacher, yet his "classroom" varied from the formal setting of Jewish houses of prayer and worship to crowded and dusty streets, from peaceful lakeshores to rolling hillsides. His basic message as he delivered it might well fill only a small pamphlet. Yet library shelves today groan under the weight of thousands of books that have attempted to explain that message. He felt his message was so simple that even children—perhaps *only* children—could quickly understand it. It was a message about a good God and a procla-

mation of unlimited love, of generosity, of a world of peace, of brotherhood and sisterhood. It was a message of hope amid despair, of joy beneath the tears and hunger, of freedom from the chains of oppression, of life in the face of death.

The man who proclaimed that message of unbounded hope, of unquenchable joy, of profound liberation and abundant life, was savagely executed on a cross by people he had somehow frightened. His words of love and joy and peace had become for some a threat, even a curse. How could this happen?

No Time to Mourn

Like so many great leaders throughout history, Jesus was fully appreciated only after his brutal death. That in itself is not unusual. We humans often appreciate wonderful gifts only after they have been taken from us; we experience deep love when the ones we love are absent; we recognize great people only when death snatches them from us. Our human inclination in such cases is not only to mourn the loss of what once was but also to ache for what might have been—the promise that might have been fulfilled, the wisdom that might have been shared, the talent that could have been tapped, the songs that could have been sung.

But with *this* person, this man from Nazareth nearly two thousand years ago, the response was strangely, mysteriously different. Following his death there was barely time for grief and no time to write an obituary. All the talk of what might have been had just begun when the shocking message rang out across the land: "The one whom you have crucified has been raised by God and is now alive!" That proclamation changed the course of history, shook the foundation of the world at its roots.

■ *Illustration:* The Christian claim that Jesus is the Son of God and Lord of the universe, if true, changes the entire course of human history.

What Do We Call Him?

Jesus of Nazareth was given many titles during his earthly life—*teacher, rabbi, prophet.* But all references to him changed dramatically in light of what his followers claimed *after* his death: that he was raised from the dead!

The titles Jesus then received—*Lord, Redeemer, Savior, the Christ, Son of God*—come so easily to us now that many of us have lost touch with what they mean. We fail to realize how haltingly these titles must have been uttered by those who first spoke them. We forget that many throughout history have endured torture and execution with these words on their lips and joy in their hearts. Many throughout history have fallen to their knees with the overwhelming realization, "My God . . . he's God!" Yet others remain indifferent, even hostile, to the claims Christians make about that man of long ago.

Jesus of History, Christ of Faith

This is a course about that man, the son of a carpenter from Nazareth, the one called simply Jesus in his own time but who is now recognized by more than a third of all the people in the world as *the Christ,* the anointed one sent by God to redeem the world from sin. Each of the titles applied to Jesus throughout Christian history reflects a different insight into him and his meaning. During this course you will explore some of those titles and their significance for believers. For the purposes of this introduction, however, we must say a few words about the title of this course and its somewhat complex meaning.

Jesus of Nazareth was a genuine historical figure, a Palestinian Jew of two thousand years ago whose life and message profoundly influenced the people of his day. Historical records verify not only that he existed but that he was executed by Roman authorities because of the message he proclaimed and the effect it had on those who followed him. Even those who choose not to believe in Jesus' divinity —that is, in his identity as the Son of God—would generally not deny that he existed. They may even claim that his life and message are worth studying, as are those of other great religious leaders. When such people speak of Jesus, we might say that they are referring to *the historical Jesus.*

When believers speak of Jesus, however, they start with a very different conviction about the one who walked the roads of Palestine two thousand years ago. Christians do not believe that Jesus in some mysterious way *became* divine through his Resurrection from the dead. They believe, rather, that he was divine, that he was one with God, *from the very beginning of time.* They believe that in the person of Jesus, God took on the flesh of humanity and became one with us in

■

Illustration: **The Resurrection of Jesus gives his followers hope that they too can be transformed to new life.**

order to redeem us from our sin. Christians, therefore, do not simply believe in "the historical Jesus" in a conventional sense; he was much, much more than that. To express that reality in this course, we use the term ***Jesus of History.*** By this term we refer to the divine Son of God *as he walked the earth in the person of Jesus.*

The second phrase in the title of this course, ***Christ of Faith,*** recognizes the tremendous Christian conviction that the Jesus of History was raised from the dead by God and that he truly was and is forever Lord and Savior. Here is the key point to grasp: In our discussion of Jesus in this course, we want to avoid any suggestion that the Jesus of History and the Christ of Faith are in some way different or distinct persons. They are, instead, one and the same person understood and experienced in two different ways. When viewing him one way—as the Jesus of History—our focus is on the encounter with Jesus Christ in his earthly ministry up to and including his death. When viewing Jesus the second way—as the Christ of Faith—our focus is on the encounter with Jesus Christ after the Resurrection, especially as that encounter has been experienced, proclaimed, and explained by the community of Christians, the church. But both the titles *Jesus of History* and *Christ of Faith* include the understanding that Jesus was, and is, both human and divine.

The struggle to find language for the realities discussed in this course can seem confusing and, for some, even silly. However, we must remember that countless people throughout history have staked their life—indeed, in many cases, *given* their life—in defense of the realities that such terms attempt to express. As this course unfolds, it will become increasingly clear why these terms carry such power and meaning.

Jesus and You

In the scriptural passage that begins this chapter, Jesus asks two questions of his disciples. His first question is, "Who do the *crowds* say that I am?" The disciples tell him that they have heard many answers: John the Baptist, Elijah, or one of the ancient prophets. Then Jesus makes the question more personal, more direct: "All right, that's what everyone else has been telling you, but now what about you—you as a free individual, you as an adult who must think for yourself? Who do *you* say that I am?" This question posed by the Jesus of History years ago is the same one that Jesus, now recognized by Christians as the Christ of Faith, sets before each new generation.

And what about you? On what basis are you to make judgments or decisions about Jesus? For perhaps fifteen or more years, you have been hearing what the "crowds" have to say about Jesus—from your parents, from the pulpit in your parish, from teachers. You may have been expected, largely because of your age, to accept their conclusions without explanation of how they had arrived at

■
Photo: **Up to this point in your life, many of your ideas about Jesus probably have come from the preaching you have heard in church.**

them. When you asked, "Who is Jesus?" you may have been given a number of answers: the Son of God, who died for our sins; a great miracle worker and healer; a teacher of marvelous truths.

When you were a child, such responses may have been adequate. But that may no longer be the case. As you have grown, you have likely had new questions to ask and new answers to find about Jesus. There comes a time in everybody's life when they must freely choose the values, ideals, and beliefs on which they will base their life. If you are going to make a mature decision about your own response to Jesus, you will likely need more information. The purpose of this course is to provide information so that you can glimpse how credible the Christian faith is and discover for yourself an honest, mature answer to the question, "Who do you say that I am?" **1**

A Look Ahead

In General
This course is an attempt to offer you sound information about Jesus, as clearly and directly as possible. However, it does not begin with the conclusions about Jesus that the Christian church has reached over the process of two thousand years of study, reflection, prayer, and historical experience. Rather, this course begins at the beginning, starting with the earliest sources we have for understanding Jesus: the Christian Scriptures—and more specifically, the four Gospels of the New Testament.

By exploring these basic sources, three main questions can be addressed:

1. Who was the Jesus of History, the man who lived nearly two thousand years ago in a place called Palestine?

2. Why was this man, Jesus, the crucified one, so quickly recognized by the early Christians as the Christ of Faith, the anointed one sent by God to free them from all evil?

3. And perhaps most important of all, how did the church come to the astounding recognition that Jesus was not only the Christ or Messiah awaited by Jews but was and is the divine Son of God, "one in being with the Father," who offers salvation to all humanity?

Only through the perspective of the Christian Scriptures can we begin to get a clearer, fuller picture of Jesus. Only in this light can we understand the early church's teachings about Jesus the Christ, as well as understand how the church's current teachings about Jesus have developed from the early foundations.

For Review

- Jesus' followers responded to his death differently than people have responded to the deaths of other great leaders throughout history. Why was this so?
- Define the following terms: *Jesus of History* and *Christ of Faith.*
- What three main questions will be addressed in this course?

1
Imagine that right now Jesus confronts you with the question, "Who do you say that I am?" Write your honest response to that question. Save your

response for reflection at the end of this course.

■

Photo: Even today Jesus asks each of us, "Who do you say that I am?"

How Do We Learn About Jesus?

At first the question, How do we learn about Jesus? may seem like a fairly easy one, with an obvious answer. But in fact, this initial question is critical in the search for a mature understanding of Jesus. If the sources that provide the foundation of our understanding are shaky and questionable, then everything we build on that foundation will be uncertain and easily disproved or uprooted. If our foundation is solidly and clearly constructed, however, we can pursue a mature understanding of Jesus with confidence. **2**

Faith Sources

How do we, today, come to understand Jesus? A logical response might flow like this:

Many of us first learn about Jesus from our parents and others close to us. But how did those people learn about Jesus, and what makes their understanding acceptable and trustworthy?

They probably learned about Jesus from their own parents, of course, and also from parish communities and their leaders—from pastors and other priests, from teachers, from other laypeople, and so on. But this answer leads to yet another question: Where did all those parish communities, teachers, and others get their information?

A little reflection turns up a good answer: Those parishes and their leaders received their information from the bishops and the pope. But the full answer still eludes us. Where did the bishops and the popes over the last two thousand years get all their information, and how do we know that all the things they have taught about Jesus are reliable and worthy of our acceptance as truth?

The questions seem to be getting tougher, but we can come up with another answer: Church leaders commonly look for guidance from men and women who have devoted their life to the study of church history, the Bible, and other sources of information about Jesus. Those who concentrate on studying the Bible are often referred to as *biblical scholars;* those who study the history, beliefs, and teachings of the church are called *theologians.* But do these people just come up with their own opinions about matters of faith? How do we know they can be trusted?

Throughout the years, scholars and theologians have based their understandings of Jesus on the teachings of the Apostles and the experiences of the early followers of Jesus.

Clearly, we are getting close to the root of the matter. But some final questions still confront us:

- How did the Apostles and those who walked with and learned directly from Jesus pass on information and insights about him to the members of the early church?

2
Before reading further, write a brief response to the following question: *How do we know that what we are taught about Jesus is true and not just made up?*

■
Photo: Many of us first learned about Jesus from our parents.

- How have the information and insights been accurately preserved over the last two thousand years?
- How can we, *today,* get in touch with those very early teachings about Jesus and compare our own understanding with them?

In other words, on what solid information can we reasonably build an understanding of Jesus, so that we can make a mature decision about him?

There is, it seems, only one real answer: We must turn to the same foundation on which all the popes, bishops, scholars, and other believers through the years have ultimately based their own teachings about Jesus and their faith in him: the Christian Scriptures.

The Christian Scriptures

When Christians make reference to the Bible or the **Christian Scriptures,** they mean a whole collection of sacred writings that includes the **Old Testament** and the **New Testament.**

The word *testament* means **covenant,** which is defined as a solemn promise made between people. The Old Testament is all about the covenant, or special relationship, that God made with the people of Israel long before the birth of Jesus. It includes forty-six different books written by different people over a period of about a thousand years. The stories, prayers, and prophecies contained in those books are central to the Jewish faith, and have always been a vital part of the Christian faith as well.

As will become evident in the next several chapters, a full Christian understanding of Jesus is impossible without the Old Testament as a source. Christians believe that everything God promised the people of Israel was promised to Christians, too, and that through Jesus, God fulfilled or made good on those promises. At the same time, God made a new covenant, through Jesus, with all people. The New Testament is all about that new covenant. Its twenty-seven books pertain specifically to the Christian faith.

Catholic Christians believe that the authors of the biblical literature were inspired, or guided, by the Holy Spirit. This does not mean that God spoke to the biblical authors directly, as someone might dictate a letter to a typist. Rather, the Catholic church teaches that **inspired texts** are writings whose authors, prompted by the Holy Spirit, convey God's revealed truth using their own abilities, words, and styles. For Christians, then, God is the ultimate author of the Scriptures, and the truth in them is reliable.

Seen together as the Christian Scriptures, the Old Testament and the New Testament provide what can be called faith sources of information about Jesus. They are **faith sources** because they were written by believers prompted by the Holy Spirit for the purpose of proclaiming the work of God that they found in all aspects of their life. The New Testament, for example, was written specifically to announce God's redeeming, transforming love to all the world in Christ.

The scriptural accounts about Jesus and the early church are therefore different from the kind of reports we might expect to find, say, in a newspaper or a history textbook. As we will see in chapter 2, even though the Scriptures are inspired by the Holy Spirit, understanding their truth requires taking the perspective and intent of their human authors into consideration. In other words, the Scriptures should not be read in the same way we read history textbooks or newspaper accounts.

Ultimately, the Gospels

When it comes to understanding Jesus' ministry and life, we must rely primarily on four short books included in the New Testament: the **Gospels** of Matthew, Mark, Luke, and John.

Just about everything that the Christian church teaches about Jesus comes through the Gospels. The Gospels, in turn, serve as the scale or test of truth and authenticity for everything the church teaches about Jesus. The Gospels are *the* link between Jesus of Nazareth and the people of every age throughout history who have claimed to be his followers. However, faith sources such as the Gospels are not the only sources of information about Jesus. **3**

F • O • C • U • S
Just a Matter of Time

Notice that the dates in this course are identified with the letters B.C.E. and C.E. rather than the more familiar B.C. and A.D. Using B.C.E. and C.E. is becoming more popular in educational publications. The abbreviations B.C. and A.D. refer to the periods before and after the birth of Jesus (B.C. stands for "before Christ," and A.D. stands for *anno Domini,* "in the year of our Lord"). Understandably, some non-Christians find that frame of reference offensive. The new abbreviations use the common era—the calendar system used in most parts of the world—as a frame of reference. So dates are referred to as either before the common era (B.C.E.) or during the common era (C.E.). If a date is not accompanied by an abbreviation, one can assume that the year is during the common era.

Though perhaps somewhat confusing at first, the change in abbreviations is an attempt to show respect for traditions different from our own.

3
Using any complete Bible, compare the size of the Old Testament with the size of the New Testament. Then locate the Gospels and note what percentage of the entire Bible these readings take up. Write your comments on what you discover, considering any factors that might account for the difference in size between the two Testaments.

■
Photo: On a market street in Jerusalem, the old blends with the new.

The Historical Sources in Perspective

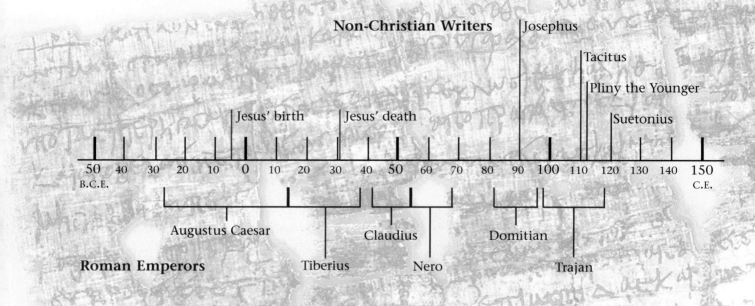

Non-Christian Writers | Josephus

Tacitus

Pliny the Younger

Suetonius

Jesus' birth | Jesus' death

50 B.C.E. 40 30 20 10 0 10 20 30 40 50 60 70 80 90 100 110 120 130 140 150 C.E.

Augustus Caesar | Claudius | Domitian

Roman Emperors | Tiberius | Nero | Trajan

Historical Sources

Several nonbiblical and non-Christian sources are available to help substantiate that Jesus actually did exist as a historical person.

Josephus, a Jewish Historian

Josephus, a Jewish historian, mentioned Jesus in his writings toward the end of the first century C.E., roughly sixty years after Jesus' death. As a non-Christian, Josephus would have had no reason to accept the historical reality of Jesus unless there was some sound basis for it.

In one of his works, Josephus discusses disturbances that were caused by the Jews during the time Pontius Pilate was governor of the region of Judea (26–36 C.E.). These disturbances centered around a man named Jesus and his followers. Josephus identifies Jesus as "a wise man . . . a doer of wonderful works, a teacher of men who receive the truth with pleasure," and he notes that Jesus was later condemned by Pilate to crucifixion. While this mention of Jesus does not suggest that Josephus himself accepted Jesus or the claims made about Jesus by his followers, it does seem clear that Josephus recognized Jesus to be a historical person who had a profound impact on the people he encountered.

Roman Writers

Tacitus. The Roman historian Tacitus referred to Jesus in his account of a fire that burned Rome in the year 64 C.E., for which the emperor Nero supposedly blamed the Christians. Tacitus himself obviously had no great love for that strange group of people called Christians:

Christus, the founder of the name, had undergone the death penalty in the reign of Tiberius, by sentence of . . . Pontius Pilate, and the pernicious [or wicked] superstition [Christianity] was checked for a moment, only to break out once more, not merely in Judaea, the home of the disease, but in the capital [Rome] itself, where all things horrible or shameful in the world collect and find a vogue.

Nero's hideous torture of the Christians, as described below, reflects not only Nero's sick mind but also the extent to which many early followers of Jesus would go rather than deny their faith:

. . . [Christians] were covered with wild beasts' skins and torn to death by dogs; or they were fastened on crosses, and, when daylight failed were burned to serve as lamps by night.

Some historians doubt Tacitus's claim that Nero was responsible for the persecution of many Christians.

Pliny the Younger. Another Roman source, a man named Pliny the Younger, was governor of one of the Roman provinces in Asia Minor about the year 110 C.E. He wrote to the emperor Trajan for advice on what to do about the Christians. The Roman officials were always concerned about the growth of any political or religious sect, and the Christian communities baffled them. Although Pliny's letter mentions Jesus, it offers no new information about him.

Suetonius. Around 120 C.E., the Roman historian and lawyer Suetonius compiled biographies of several Roman emperors. In a discussion of the

■
Illustration: **Emperor Nero was widely accused of persecuting the early Christians.**

emperor Claudius, Suetonius says that Claudius expelled the Jews from Rome because of the riots they were constantly causing, "on the instigation of Chrestus." Though there is some debate over the word *Chrestus,* scholars generally agree that it refers to Christ.

Note that at the time of Suetonius, Christians were still commonly regarded by the Romans as a Jewish sect. That is why Suetonius's account says that Claudius expelled the *Jews* from Rome. (The connections between the Christians and the Jews will become clearer later in this course.)

Though these historical sources do not give us more information about Jesus than we find in the biblical sources, they do support the historical existence of Jesus, and they show **Christianity**—the movement based on Jesus' life and teachings—as worthy of at least brief mention. The fact remains, however, that if we want to know about Jesus to any reasonable degree, we must turn to the Christian Scriptures and, more specifically, to the Gospels.

For Review

- Provide a one-sentence definition of each of these terms: *Christian Scriptures, Old Testament, New Testament, inspired texts.*
- What role do the Gospels play in the church's teaching about Jesus?
- Identify each of the following persons and summarize what they, as a group, contribute to a study of Jesus: *Josephus, Tacitus, Pliny the Younger, Suetonius.*

The New Testament

A Collection of "Books"

The New Testament is composed of twenty-seven separate works, representing not only different authors but also different types of writing. There are personal letters; homilies, or sermons, from early worship services; some highly symbolic and imaginative writings; and of course, the Gospels. These various works are often called the *books* of the New Testament, even though none of them fits the description of a book in the usual sense. **4**

The twenty-seven books of the New Testament developed from roughly twenty years after the death of Jesus (that is, from about 50 C.E.) to about 100 C.E. This period of some fifty years of development may seem quite long, but remember that the development of the Old Testament spanned more than one thousand years!

One principal theme unifies the writings of the New Testament: they all deal in some way with the life, death, and Resurrection of Jesus and the impact he had on the community of those who believed in him—what we now know as the church. Only the four Gospels deal directly with Jesus—his life, his preaching, his wonderful works, and very important, his death and Resurrection. The other writings—the letters of Saint Paul, for example—offer us little information about the historical life of Jesus. They concentrate instead on the happenings within the early community of faith; the meaning of Jesus' life, death, and Resurrection for the individual believer; various difficulties encountered by the first Christians as they moved out into the world; and so on. In that sense, the writings other than the Gospels are about the lives of the Christian

4
Open a copy of the New Testament and leaf through its twenty-seven books (a list of them is included on page 20 of this text). How many pages are in the shortest book? the longest?

Identify two different types of writing that you find, and give an example of each.

■ Jesus was raised in Nazareth, a small city in Galilee. *Photo:* The city of Nazareth today.

The Books of the New Testament

Here is a list of the books of the New Testament in the order in which they appear in the Bible:

Gospels	Acts	Pauline Epistles	Letter to the Hebrews	Catholic Epistles	Book of Revelation
Matthew	Acts	Romans	Hebrews	James	Revelation
Mark	of the	1 Corinthians		1 Peter	
Luke	Apostles	2 Corinthians		2 Peter	
John		Galatians		1 John	
		Ephesians		2 John	
		Philippians		3 John	
		Colossians		Jude	
		1 Thessalonians			
		2 Thessalonians			
		1 Timothy			
		2 Timothy			
		Titus			
		Philemon			

community and the individual Christian more than they are about the life of Jesus himself. In the New Testament, only the Gospels offer us anything like a historical portrait of Jesus.

Writings with Special Authority

As noted earlier, it took some fifty years for the New Testament writings to develop. However, it took even longer for the church to officially recognize these writings as having special importance and authority in the life of the Christian community. Prior to the development of the New Testament, the earliest Christians—many of whom were very devout Jews—had what we now call the Old Testament as their most sacred writings. The Christians commonly used these writings, for example, during community prayer and worship.

The new writings that emerged from the community of Jesus' followers initially came about to meet the needs of that growing, worshiping community. These new writings included short sermons, collections of the sayings of Jesus, hymns to be used during worship, collected stories of Jesus' wondrous works, and so on. Many of these writings were eventually lost, but some were combined into the works we now recognize as the individual books of the New Testament.

By the end of the second century—that is, more than 150 years after Jesus' death and Resurrection

—the church had come to some general agreement about accepting the Gospels of Matthew, Mark, Luke, and John as particularly special and authoritative. Debate continued about many of the other writings that had developed within the community. It was not until the end of the fourth century that the church finally and formally approved the collection of the twenty-seven books of the New Testament.

Because the church believes this collection of writings—known as the Christian **canon**—was inspired by the Holy Spirit, these Scriptures are considered especially authoritative. (The word *canon* comes from the Greek word for "rule" or "standard.")

The Canon of the New Testament

The twenty-seven books that developed out of the faith experiences of the early Christian community can be organized in a variety of ways. The books are summarized below according to the way they appear in most Bibles today.

The Gospels

The Gospels of Matthew, Mark, Luke, and John include information about the life, works, message, death, and Resurrection of Jesus. Each of the Gospels is organized chronologically, which suggests that they are something like historical records of Jesus' life, though we will see that they are not as concerned with the details of Jesus' history as with his message.

The Acts of the Apostles

The **Acts of the Apostles** is Luke's account of the early days of the Christian community under the leadership of Saint Peter. Though Luke does record the initial development of the church in Jerusalem, his main focus in Acts is the spread of the Good News throughout the Roman Empire after the death and Resurrection of Jesus. Acts focuses especially on the missionary work of one of the church's most famous personalities: Saint Paul. The Acts of the Apostles is commonly seen as a companion to Luke's Gospel, and many scholars suggest that the two should be read together as one major work.

Thirteen Pauline Epistles

The Acts of the Apostles is followed by a collection of thirteen **Pauline epistles** (*epistle* means "letter"), either written by or attributed to Saint Paul. Most scholars today agree that only seven of these were actually written by Paul. The other six are thought to have been composed by writers who wanted to honor Paul or who sought special authority in the community by claiming Paul as the author of their letters. The primary purpose of all the Pauline letters was to support and further educate either individual Christians or small communities who believed in Jesus because of the missionary work of Paul and others.

The Letter to the Hebrews

The **Letter to the Hebrews** is another work often attributed to Paul, but scholars now generally believe it was written by an unknown author. Though commonly referred to as a letter, Hebrews does not take the form of a normal letter of the time. Rather, it is a kind of extended sermon to a group of Christians who are in danger of falling away from their belief in Jesus.

The Catholic Epistles

After the Letter to the Hebrews comes a collection of seven epistles attributed to other personalities: James, Peter (two letters), John (three letters), and Jude. Some or all of these are often referred to as **catholic** (which means "universal") or **general epistles,** because they are addressed to believing Christians as a general audience rather than to specific individuals or communities.

The Book of Revelation

The New Testament concludes with a strange and complex work: the **Book of Revelation.** Some Bibles refer to this book as the Apocalypse, based on the Greek word for "revelation." Its highly symbolic and mysterious language reflects a kind of writing that had been popular among the Jews since about two hundred years before Jesus. Most contemporary scholars agree that the Book of Revelation was written for the late-first-century Christians, who were suffering persecution for their beliefs at the hands of the Romans. The book encourages them to remain faithful to Christ. It also deals with their expectation that Jesus will return again in glory at the end of time to fulfill God's work on earth.

Keep in mind throughout this course that the twenty-seven books of the New Testament did not actually develop in the order in which they appear in the Bible. Because the Gospels come first, it might seem that they were written first; however, this was not the case. The fact is that Paul did his missionary work, wrote his profound letters, and likely died before the first Gospel took the form we now recognize. Paul's First Letter to the Thessalonians is generally considered the first book of the New Testament to be written, roughly around the year 50 C.E. The Gospels were written

approximately between the years 70 and 95. The last book written is generally believed to be the Second Letter of Peter, written about the year 100.

The present organization of the New Testament developed for a variety of reasons: the relative popularity of each of the Gospels within the early community of faith, the length of Paul's letters (they are organized from the longest to the shortest), and so on.

For Review

- How many books are in the New Testament? During what years was the New Testament written?
- What is the principal theme that unifies the writings of the New Testament?
- What are the main concerns of the non-Gospel writings of the New Testament?
- Provide a one-sentence description of each of the following: *the Gospels, the Acts of the Apostles, the Pauline epistles, the Letter to the Hebrews, the catholic epistles, the Book of Revelation.*

Turning to the Gospels

This course on Jesus will focus primarily on the portraits of Jesus found in the Gospels. Brief consideration will be given to the understanding of Jesus that emerges from Paul's ministry as it is recorded in the Acts of the Apostles and in Paul's Letters. Only periodically will a few of the other books, for example, the Letters of John, be mentioned. And some of the books of the New Testament will be passed over, only because they tell us very little specifically about Jesus and his message. If this were a course on the New Testament itself, the approach would be quite different. However, the constant concern in this course is, Who is Jesus, and what are we to make of his ministry, message, death, and Resurrection?

With a basic background on the whole New Testament now laid out, the discussion can turn to a more thorough treatment of the biblical writings that will serve as the main sources in this study of Jesus—the Gospels.

■
Photo: **The Hebron Hills, near Jerusalem.**

2
The Gospels:
Central Sources for Understanding Jesus

In This Chapter . . .

- How Do We Read the Gospels?
- The Development of the Gospels
- The Gospels: Four Portraits of Jesus

THIS is the disciple who is testifying to these things and has written them, and we know that his testimony is true. But there are also many other things that Jesus did; if every one of them were written down, I suppose that the world itself could not contain the books that would be written. (John 21:24–25)

How Do We Read the Gospels?

The previous chapter listed the Gospels as part of the faith sources of information about Jesus, meaning that what we learn about Jesus from the Gospels is revealed through the eyes of people who believed him to be the Christ. Before taking a general look at the origins, development, and key characteristics of the four Gospel accounts of Jesus' life, it may be helpful to take a fuller look at what it means to call the Gospels *faith* sources rather than *historical* sources. **1**

Objectivity: The Only Test of Truth?

Some people have the mistaken notion that because the Gospels were written by believers in the risen Jesus, the accounts are unreliable sources of information about Jesus. They think that in order to be acceptable as true, the information that comes to us about Jesus has to be totally accurate and objective.

Other people believe that because the Gospels were written under the inspiration of the Holy Spirit, they are exact factual accounts of the people and events they describe. These people read the Gospels in much the same way they read newspaper reports of current events.

Both of these positions emphasize *objectivity*— the reporting of facts alone, without interpretation through a personal viewpoint—as a measure of the truthfulness of the Gospels. But as will be seen shortly, objectivity is not the only test of the truthfulness of a story. A clearer understanding of what is meant by the term *history* will help to show why this is so.

What Do We Mean by "History"?

History can be viewed as the simple recording of observable facts and events, as if these facts and events were captured accurately by movie cameras or transcribed into words by reporters. This is a simplistic understanding of history, however, because life is too complex for this kind of objective description.

To demonstrate this point, think of one event that happened in the world today and compare the reports of that event as given by two television stations and two newspapers. Obviously all these news stories will share some similarities, but some of the differences in reporting and understanding may be truly startling. Discrepancies might appear

---

■
Understanding the Gospels involves understanding the time, place, and culture of the Gospel authors.
Photo, facing page: **The old city of Jerusalem and the Kidron Valley,**

as seen from the Mount of Olives. *Background:* **A fragment from an ancient Greek papyrus manuscript containing the Lord's Prayer from Matthew's Gospel.**

1
Choose any public figure—for example, an athlete, a musician, or a politician—and list at least ten items of information you would expect to find in a thorough biography of that person.

in the basic details of the reports, and various understandings and opinions on the *meaning of the event* are likely to be presented as well. Why would supposedly "objective" recordings of historical events contain such differences?

All historical information is interpreted through the eyes and perspective of the person doing the recording. For instance, two reporters covering the same event might focus on different details, interview different people, and convey the collected information in different styles. Even the firsthand knowledge we gain through our own experiences is interpreted by us. We see it from a certain perspective, which is influenced by our past experiences, our family and community, the culture we live in, and so forth. No one's perspective is totally objective, because this would require one to be without a point of view, which is impossible! **2**

The Good News, Not the Daily News

A key point to remember when studying the Gospels, then, is that they were written from a certain perspective. That perspective was shaped in part by the culture the early Christians lived in— a culture with a different language, geography,

---

■

Photo: **An alley beside the Church of the Nativity, in Bethlehem. This church is on the site traditionally held as the birthplace of Jesus.**

2
Imagine you are a person from first-century Palestine watching a television show from our time. What expressions, references to contemporary culture, and styles of speaking and behaving might be confusing for you?

technology, history, and religious tradition than our own. (We will explore the culture of Jesus' time in greater detail in chapters 3 and 4.)

Even the literary style in which the Gospels were written differs from what we might expect to find in a modern newspaper account or biography of someone famous. The authors of the Gospels used writing styles and devices common in their own time, such as exaggeration, figures of speech, approximation, and poetry. The authors of the Gospels were writing for the people of their time, a fact that can sometimes make it difficult for us as twenty-first-century readers to understand exactly what they meant.

Furthermore, the Gospels do not include much of the kind of information one would expect to find in a historical account of a person's life. The Gospels do not provide precise dates of Jesus' birth and death, a description of what he looked like, or any detailed information about his childhood and adolescence, his education, or his parents. The authors of the four Gospels selected just some of what had been handed on to them by word of mouth or in writing, as the Gospel quote at the beginning of this chapter indicates. Sometimes they summarized the story of Jesus or combined certain elements. At other times, they explained the Good News in view of the situation of their own faith communities. So, in this sense, the Gospels are not biographies of Jesus.

But if the Gospels are not biographies of Jesus, then what are they? Chapter 1 described the Gospels as faith sources, writings that came out of the community of Jesus' followers. The word *gospel* itself is derived from the Middle English word *godspell,* which means "good news" or "glad tidings." That word, in turn, is a translation of the Greek word *evangelion,* meaning "the proclamation or announcement of good news." (Note also that we call the authors of the Gospels the **Evangelists,** based on the Greek word *evangelion.* The authors of the Gospels are, literally, proclaimers of the Good News.)

So from the origins of the word *gospel* we learn that the purpose of the Gospels is to proclaim a message of faith in Jesus. The Gospels are, in other words, **testimonies of faith.** As such, their primary purpose is not to provide accurate historical accounts of the day-to-day life of Jesus. Rather, they are attempts by the early followers of Christ to share their experiences of Jesus with the world.

What was done by the early Christians in sharing the story of Jesus is not much different from what we do in telling others about a significant happening in our own life. Sharing precisely every last detail is often not our main concern. Instead,

■
Photo: **The Gospels are meant to be "good news" or "glad tidings" for us.**

we want to give whatever information will best help us convey the meaning and significance of the event in our life. Leaving out many of the details does not lessen the truth of our story. **3**

Likewise, the fact that the Gospels are not historical biographies does not automatically make them untruthful. Rather, because the Gospels were written from a certain cultural and faith perspective, understanding them requires more than simply reading them as if they were newspaper or biographical accounts of Jesus. We must keep in mind the perspectives of the people who wrote them.

Searching for Religious Truth

A view of the Gospels that takes the perspective of the Evangelists into consideration does not place too much emphasis on the strict objectivity of their accounts. Instead, such a view focuses on the Gospels' main message, which does not involve looking for historical truth as much as it involves looking for what is called **religious truth.** For Christians, religious truth is the deeper meaning that God intends to reveal to people through historical events.

It is religious truth that the Scriptures—both the Old Testament and the New Testament—are primarily filled with. The authors of the biblical literature were far less concerned with the historical facts, or what an event might have *appeared* to be on the surface. In fact, the biblical writers set out to do precisely what modern reporters supposedly try to avoid: they interpreted events in light of their own faith convictions. Because Christians believe the biblical writers were guided by the Holy Spirit, they are confident that the Scriptures contain the essential truth about Jesus.

■
The Gospels offer a portrait of Jesus from the perspective of the people of his time.
Photo: **An ancient village near the Dead Sea and Jericho.**

3
In a short essay, briefly summarize a favorite story that has been told over and over by one of your relatives. Then respond to the following questions: *To what degree do you think the story has* *been changed or exaggerated over the years? If the story has been changed, does that lessen or cancel out the value or meaning of the story itself? Why or why not?*

The Stories of a Community

Although the Gospels do not provide a totally objective and fully detailed understanding of Jesus as he lived and preached some two thousand years ago, they do offer some basic information about Jesus and his message. Together with the rest of the New Testament, the Gospels also reveal the meaning and significance of Jesus for the people of his time. They tell us the story of the one whom Christians believe to be the Son of God—the one who fully reveals to humanity the very nature of God in his person. Ultimately, is this not of much greater significance to us than mere historical facts? Hearing a person's words firsthand is valuable, but understanding the meaning of those words is far more important.

In seeking the religious truth of the Gospels, Catholic Christians are careful not to rely solely on the interpretations of one person, or even one group of persons, from a particular time. As the

F • O • C • U • S

The Roman Catholic Church's Tradition and Jesus

The Roman Catholic church is often distinguished from other Christian churches by its commitment to both the Scriptures and Tradition as major sources for understanding Jesus and his message.

Many Protestant churches rely almost entirely on the Christian Scriptures as the basis for their teachings and practices. The Catholic church, on the other hand, believes that the same Holy Spirit that guided the authors of the Scriptures continues to guide the church as it moves through history, leading it to clarify, develop, and preserve particular teachings and practices. These official teachings and practices in the Catholic church are known as its **Tradition**, with a capital *T*, and Catholics view Tradition along with the Scriptures as companion, authoritative guides to truth. (The truth contained in the New Testament was actually part of the Tradition of the first generation of Christians before it was written down.)

On the basis of Tradition, Catholics accept as part of God's revelation some things implied, but not mentioned explicitly, in the Scriptures. For example, the commitment to Tradition has guided the Roman Catholic church to have more sacraments than Protestant churches do. Protestant churches generally accept only Baptism and the Eucharist as sacraments because only these two can be found explicitly in the New Testament.

A summary of the development of the Roman Catholic teachings about Jesus will be offered in the last chapter of this textbook.

■
The Roman Catholic church believes that the same Holy Spirit that guided the authors of the Scriptures has continued to guide the church throughout history.

Photo: In Catholic parishes today, priests represent the teaching voice of the church.

earlier discussion of the differences between media accounts of the same event showed, it is important to read more than one newspaper or watch more than one news program. Doing so gives the reader or viewer a more balanced, fuller, and truer understanding of events in the world. Similarly, figuring out religious truth is the responsibility of the whole community of believers, under the guidance of the Holy Spirit. The ongoing task of the Christian church is to reassess the significance of Jesus' life and message for each new age and culture.

A personal and prayerful reading of the entire Bible is encouraged for all Christians. But it is important as well for them to look to the church for guidance in properly understanding the meaning of the Scriptures for today. Even this course, for instance, is not based on the personal opinions of one person. Its information and insights come from a whole host of sources from within the Christian community, including the official teachings of the Catholic church, which were developed with the help of respected biblical scholars and theologians.

For Review

- Is the record of past events that we call history a totally accurate description of the events as they actually happened? Explain your response.
- What do the origins of the word *gospel* suggest about the purpose of the Gospels?
- Briefly explain what is meant by the term *religious truth* and discuss its relationship to the Scriptures.
- What can we gain from the Gospels besides some basic information about Jesus and his message?

The Development of the Gospels

Perhaps the most effective way to understand the Gospels is to look at how they came to be written. Scholars who have studied the New Testament have identified at least three major stages in the Gospels' development:

1. During the time that Jesus lived and worked, he had a profound effect on his disciples.
2. After the death and Resurrection of Jesus, the disciples and the early church proclaimed the Good News throughout the Roman Empire.
3. Later, the Gospels were actually written by the Evangelists, who likely served as editors or collectors of material that had gradually developed through the years.

Stage 1: Jesus of Nazareth and His Disciples

It would seem to go without saying that the Gospels are based on the words and works of Jesus of Nazareth, a historical figure from the land of Palestine who lived some two thousand years ago. However, the recognition and acceptance of this truth is central to our understanding and appreciation of the Gospels. For if the Gospels are not based on historical realities—if Jesus' proclamations and Resurrection never happened—then all that they teach is little more than a flight of fancy or an idealistic vision. It is essential to recognize that the foundation of the events and meaning recorded in the Gospels is Jesus of Nazareth, a man, a historical figure, one whose blood flowed through flesh as truly as does our own.

The Basic Facts

What can we say about Jesus that can be accepted even by those who do not accept him as the **Messiah**, the Christ, the Son of God? From the Gospels and other sources, we are certain of the following points:

- Jesus was born a Jew sometime around the year 5 B.C.E. "in the time of King Herod . . . in Bethlehem of Judea" (Matthew 2:1). He was raised in the small village of Nazareth. As he grew, he learned and practiced the trade of carpentry.

- At about age thirty, Jesus began a public career of preaching and teaching, proclaiming the beginning of a new era, which he called the Kingdom of God. He apparently demonstrated some unusual powers and was referred to by historians of his day as a worker of wonderful deeds.

- Jesus' preaching and actions stirred great interest among the Jewish people, leading some to proclaim him as a great prophet and others to reject him as a sorcerer, a magician, someone who lacked reverence for God, and a threat to

■
We know that Jesus was born a Jew sometime around 5 B.C.E. in Bethlehem of Judea.
Photo: **The town of Bethlehem at sunrise.**

the Roman state. Those in power eventually brought him to trial, found him guilty of crimes under Roman law, and had him executed by crucifixion sometime around the year 30 C.E.

Virtually all people of any religious persuasion or belief could accept this much about Jesus simply by being open to historical records. However, the early Christians—both Jesus' immediate followers and those who had not known him while he walked the earth—clearly believed him to be much more than just a man, more than just Jesus of Nazareth. They also believed him to be the awaited Messiah of Israel and God's only Son.

The Resurrection: The Pivotal Event

That which led the early Christians to believe that Jesus was more than just an extraordinary person was the event that his followers claim to have experienced *after* his death. This event completely and radically changed their understanding of everything Jesus had said and done while he walked the dusty roads of Palestine. What the followers of Jesus claimed was this: He did not remain dead. About three days after he had been savagely executed on the cross, they experienced him alive again and present among them.

Belief in the Resurrection of Jesus became the identifying mark of all those who claimed Jesus as their Lord and Savior. Jesus' rising from the dead made his whole earthly existence—all that he had said and done prior to this event—believable and acceptable as truth. Without the Resurrection, the followers of Jesus would likely have run away in fear of their own execution. But with the experience of the risen Jesus, they burst forth from their places of hiding and began proclaiming that by raising him from the dead "God has made him both Lord and Messiah, this Jesus whom you crucified" (Acts of the Apostles 2:36).

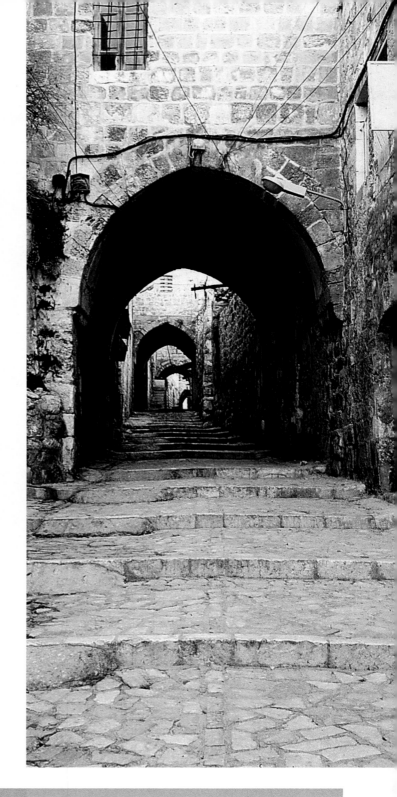

■
Photo: **A stepped street in Jerusalem, leading off the Via Dolorosa, the path believed to have been taken by Jesus on the way to the Crucifixion.**

Calling Jesus "Lord" was a radical expression of the first Christians' belief in the divinity of Jesus. When the Jewish people spoke of God, they used the title *Lord* instead of *Yahweh,* the name revealed to Moses, because God's actual name was considered too sacred to be spoken. So to call Jesus *Lord* was to say that he had a divine identity—a claim that shocked many Jews who heard the first Christians' proclamation. (The uppercase use of the word *Lord,* which is a divine title, should not be confused with the lowercase use of the word *lord,* which is another word for "master.")

The Resurrection and its meaning will be discussed more fully in chapter 10 of this course, but this much can be said now: the belief in Jesus' living presence after death is so central to the lives of Christians that Saint Paul, one of the most influential of all the early Christians, was led to say, "If Christ has not been raised, then our proclamation has been in vain and your faith has been in vain" (1 Corinthians 15:14).

Christ: Not Jesus' Last Name

Some people in Jesus' time immediately rejected the proclamation of the Resurrection. They thought the news foolhardy, ridiculous, insane. For them, Jesus would remain only the carpenter's son who preached a radical message and paid for it with his life. But others were nearly overwhelmed by the conviction that the proclamation of the Resurrection was true—that Jesus had in fact been raised by God from death itself and that he truly was, and would be forever, Lord and Savior. For these people, Jesus was clearly much more than a carpenter's son. For the early Christians, Jesus was also truly the Christ.

Unfortunately, over the years many people have come to think of the title *Christ* as simply a kind of last name or family name for Jesus. In fact,

however, he was never known by that name during his earthly life. The name *Jesus* was a common one for Jewish boys. It is our translation of Jesus' Hebrew name, *Yeshua,* which he would have heard when called by his parents and others. The name *Yeshua* means literally "Yahweh (God) saves" or "Yahweh (God) is salvation." But the title *Christ* means literally "anointed one." It is based on the Greek word *Christos,* which is itself a translation of the Hebrew word *messiah.*

As will be discussed in more detail later, the Jewish people had long awaited the Messiah, "the one sent from God," the one who would save them from all oppression. To those Jews who accepted Jesus as the Messiah after his Resurrection, he became known as Jesus the Christ, which in turn became rather quickly shortened to what we now know as a single name: *Jesus Christ.* This development may have been an unfortunate one, for it clouds to some degree the recognition of a tremendous conviction held by Christians— that the Jesus of History is truly the Christ of

■
Photo: **Jesus' living presence in the world was obvious to those who believed in his Resurrection.**

Stage 2: The Disciples and the Early Community of Faith

What Would You Do?

Try to imagine yourself in the position of an early disciple of Jesus. You, along with the rest of the disciples, walk with Jesus; you hear his inspiring message proclaimed from the synagogues and hillsides; you touch him and are touched by him; and you witness the marvelous effect he has on everyone he meets. Gradually you find yourself captivated by this man and his message. You find in him the answer to all your hopes and dreams, and you are certain that in this man from Nazareth you have discovered true freedom, joy, peace, love, and fullness of life.

But then you see the horror of Calvary: Jesus, whom you so deeply love, stretched out against the sky, nailed to a beam of wood, carrying all your dreams and hopes along with him to his death. You and so many who believed in him run away in fear—shattered, hopeless, convinced that all he promised was a sham, a lie, or at the very least a terrible mistake.

But then comes Easter. Suddenly you have the overwhelming experience of Jesus present again, alive and truly with you—in fact, even more truly with you than he was before. He is risen! Even death is conquered in this man! Incredible joy and peace surge into your heart, and you run from your place of hiding, shouting from the rooftops: "He's alive! Everything he told us is true!"

Now, what will you do next? It is doubtful that you will immediately sit down and begin to write an essay on what you have experienced. For one thing, you need some time just to sort out the significance of the incredible events that have taken place. Also, because of Jesus' promise at the time

Faith. This realization of Jesus as the Christ overwhelmed the disciples, and the whole of their experience of his life, death, and Resurrection marks the first stage of the development of the Gospels.

Photo: **A cross of victory leads the way during an Easter Week procession in Jerusalem.**

Spreading the Word Near and Far

The situation just described is exactly the one the early Christians found themselves in after the Resurrection. Rather than write about their experiences with Jesus, they began an intense missionary campaign to proclaim his life, death, and Resurrection to all people. In a matter of decades, the proclamation of the Good News of Jesus spread like wildfire throughout the Roman Empire—from Palestine, where it had begun, out to Egypt, Syria, Greece, Asia Minor, and ultimately into the capital city of Rome itself (at that time, Rome was often referred to as the ends of the earth).

Though it was clear to the early Christians that preserving their message for the future was not necessary—there was, after all, no "future" expected—they did not lose any of their love for the past. In fact, it was only in terms of history that Jesus' followers could understand him. They began to see how so much of what he had said and done took on meaning only in light of the ideas and past events recorded in the Jewish Bible. As Saint Paul was to say to his fellow Jews, "And we bring you the good news that what God promised to our ancestors he has fulfilled for us, their children, by raising Jesus" (Acts of the Apostles 13:32–33). This idea of the promises of God fulfilled in Jesus became a fundamental part of the preaching of the early Christians as they spread the word across the land.

Words and Deeds to Remember

It was within the context of preaching the Good News throughout the land that the process of picking and choosing what to remember about Jesus was begun. Incidents from his life and lessons from his teaching were used to instruct

of his Ascension into heaven—that he will come again to fully establish God's Kingdom—many of his followers are anticipating the almost certain end of the world as they know it. Perhaps based on a misunderstanding of some of the things Jesus taught, they believe that he will come back soon—within their lifetime. These people believe that they have little time to make up their mind about him. They suppose that either they will turn from their past ways, repent of their sins, and accept Jesus as Lord and Savior, or they will perish. Some Christians are even advising against marriage, and some are refusing to take jobs, feeling that these are silly considerations when the end of the world is right around the corner. With all of this commotion and speculation, writing about your experiences seems to be unnecessary. You have more important things to do.

■
The Good News spread like wildfire throughout the Roman Empire.
Photo: Caesarea, a Mediterranean port in Palestine named after the Roman emperor Augustus Caesar, was a stop in the travels of the church's early missionaries.

people who were interested in joining the community of faith. Reflections on his life in terms of the prophecies in the Jewish Bible became part of Christian worship services. And perhaps most important, Jesus' words were not only recalled but applied to the experiences of the early Christians as they began to share and celebrate and live out his message in their daily life.

In other words, Jesus' life and words and works were never recorded in a logical, day-by-day, biographical fashion. Not all the available information about Jesus was preserved, but only those events and works and teachings that had a particularly profound effect on the early Christians. In many cases this meant eliminating descriptive details from the accounts. For example, if we look at the Gospel stories of Jesus' miracles, we find

only the briefest descriptions, which often makes the stories seem stark and unreal. Or sometimes Jesus' words as recorded in the Gospels are so direct, so straight to the point, that they seem harsh.

For several decades this information about Jesus was shared primarily by word of mouth among the Christians, developing into what is called an **oral tradition.** On the basis of these carefully selected and highly polished recollections, and from their application to the early church's experience, the Gospels would eventually be written.

Many examples from the Gospels will be used throughout this course. In pursuing an understanding of Jesus and his message, it is important to not lose sight of this "oral tradition" stage in the development of the Gospels.

■

Illustration: **While sharing meals, the early Christians passed on stories about Jesus and his teachings, and reflected on the meaning of his message for their own daily life.**

Like a Many-Layered Drawing

One scholar describes the Gospels' development in this way:

> When we have a complicated diagram to reproduce (an industrial design, for example, or the anatomy of the human body), we may sometimes build up a series of sheets of tracing paper. The first will contain a basic framework (perhaps the human skeleton), and on top of that we may put other drawings made to the same scale on tracing paper, representing the muscles, the various organs, and so on. In this way we can look at each drawing separately or, if we wish, we can put them together and see one superimposed on top of another.
>
> We can understand the Gospels in the same way. On top of the portrait of Jesus of Nazareth that they had kept in their memories, the Evangelists superimposed their understanding of the risen Jesus as they had only begun to understand him after Easter. When we read the Gospels in a rather naive if not incorrect way, everything about Jesus as the Christ of Faith proclaimed by believers might seem very clear. It seems in reading the Gospels, for example, that Jesus often directly presents himself as the Son of God, and that many people immediately recognize him as such. In fact, the modern reader might be amazed that anyone in Jesus' time could have failed to recognize the Jesus of History as the Christ of Faith or as the Son of God.
>
> Everything seems so clear to us, however, because we are looking at all the "drawings" together. This was not the case of the people

> of Jesus' time, those who witnessed his life and ministry. The Gospels, therefore, can only be fully understood in light of faith in Jesus of Nazareth as the Risen One, the Messiah, the Christ, the Son of God. (Based on Charpentier, *How to Read the New Testament,* page 19)

■

Each Gospel offers its own portrait of Jesus, emphasizing different aspects or dimensions of him. Together, the Gospels form a more complete portrait of Jesus.

Photo: **A modern African wood sculpture,** *Christ with the Crown of Thorns,* **offers a distinctive outlook on Jesus.**

Stage 3: The Early Community of Faith and the Evangelists

Jesus died around the year 30 C.E., but it was approximately forty more years before the first Gospel was written. Only after proclaiming the Good News and developing an oral tradition did the early Christians decide that the free-floating stories and words and teachings of Jesus should be collected into permanent records by the editors we call the Evangelists.

It is generally held that the first Gospel written was Mark's, around the year 70 C.E. Luke's and Matthew's Gospels were perhaps written during the middle to late eighties; and John's Gospel, not until as late as 90 to 100. More will be said about the Evangelists and their unique Gospels in a moment, but first there is a more basic subject to address: What brought about this third stage in the Gospels' development, the actual writing of them? There seem to have been at least two major factors: the passage of time and the need for continued instruction.

The Passage of Time

By the latter half of the first century, the followers of Christ had begun to be recognized as a "church," that is, something more than just a radical Jewish fringe group. As Christians slowly realized that Jesus was not going to return in glory as quickly as they had hoped, it became clear that the community of faith would probably be around for a long time.

With the realization that the church did indeed have a future, it became necessary to find a means for preserving its teachings and passing them on to future generations. This was certainly one of the motives for developing the Gospels as we now have them.

The Need for Continued Instruction

The preservation of Jesus' message for future generations was not the only reason for collecting the available material about Jesus into the Gospels. There was also a continuing need to instruct and inspire the already existing communities of faith that had been formed throughout the Roman Empire during the previous decades of missionary activity.

Each of the Gospel writers gathered pieces from among all the stories about Jesus that had emerged since his death and Resurrection. Then the writer assembled these pieces into a coherent story that would respond to the needs of a particular audience in a particular location at a particular time. This accounts for the fact that each of the Gospels is unique and that certain activities and words of Jesus recorded in one of the Gospels appear to be described or expressed differently in another. **4**

4
Fold a piece of paper in half to create two vertical columns. Title the left column "Oral Storytelling" and the right column "Written Storytelling." List at least five benefits and five shortcomings of each type of storytelling. For example, what can be done with an oral story that cannot be done with a written one, and vice versa?

■
Illustration: Each Gospel writer gathered pieces from the stories told about Jesus and assembled them into a coherent story—a complete Gospel.

Common Threads

No single Gospel provides a completely accurate understanding of Jesus. And, again, we cannot look at the Gospels as detailed biographies of Jesus. Rather, we must seek an understanding of the common threads of meaning that run through the Gospels and try to understand their significance for today. We can do this in part by studying their roots and implications in the historical, religious, and cultural times in which they were written.

For Review

- Briefly describe the three major stages in the development of the Gospels.
- *Christ* is not Jesus' last name. Explain.
- What two major factors explain the transition from an initial oral telling of the Good News to the written form of the Gospels?

The Gospels: Four Portraits of Jesus

The Gospels were not simply the result of four individuals named Matthew, Mark, Luke, and John sitting down independently and writing about Jesus based on their own personal recollections of him. Rather, each Evangelist had a wealth of material available to him:
- stories about Jesus that were told over and over again in community worship
- the words of Jesus, recalled day after day in prayer and then applied to life experiences
- insights that were drawn by preachers about the relationship between the life and message of Jesus and the history of the Jewish people

Each Evangelist also had a particular audience in mind when he began to collect this material into a coherent and understandable whole.

F • O • C • U • S
The Development of the Gospels

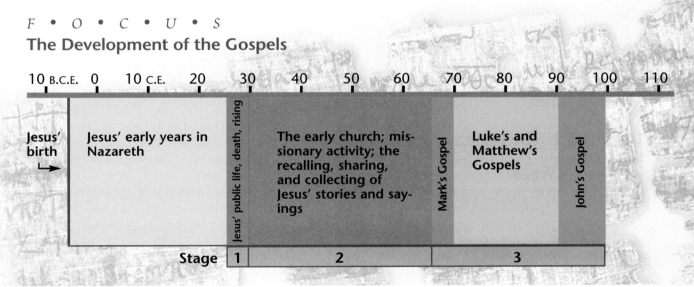

It is doubtful that any one person was responsible for the total development of any of the Gospels. It seems instead that the work was done by at least several people including friends or followers of the Evangelists who honored these men by attributing the work totally to them as individuals.

Even today, scholars are constantly studying and arriving at new speculations about the identities of the Gospel authors, their purposes in writing, and the dates when they wrote their accounts of the Good News. When reading the following very brief summaries of the most commonly held judgments about these issues, recognize that for each point mentioned here, scholars could be found who disagree. This fact can make the study and discussion of the Gospels a bit confusing, perhaps, but also as fascinating and challenging as trying to grasp the plot of a well-written mystery story.

Also note that while the following discussion identifies each Gospel as a separate and unique "portrait" of Jesus, no one Gospel tells us everything we need to know about Jesus. Rather, we need to view the Gospels as different portraits, each one offering different insights, each adding to our understanding of the truth about Jesus and his message. **5**

Mark's Portrait: The Human Jesus

By Whom and When?

Mark was a common name during the time of Jesus, and the Mark credited with writing the first Gospel could have been almost anyone. None of the Gospels actually identify their author directly, and the name we attach to each one represents the early church's traditional opinion on who the

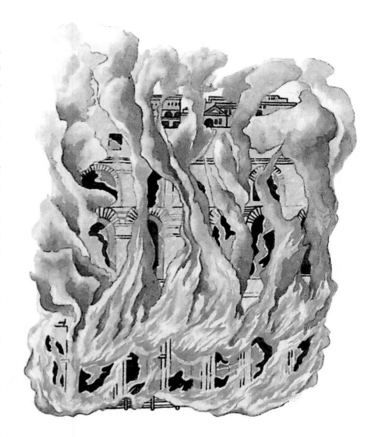

author was. Some modern-day scholars believe the author of Mark's Gospel to have been a certain John Mark who lived in Jerusalem and who might have learned about Jesus from the Apostle Peter. In the Acts of the Apostles (12:25) and elsewhere, John Mark is mentioned as a companion of Saint Paul. In addition, a group of Christians regularly met at John Mark's mother's house for prayer (Acts 12:12).

Scholars generally agree that the Gospel of Mark was written sometime between 65 and 70 C.E., that is, thirty-five to forty years after the death of Jesus. For the purposes of this course, the year 70 will be used. Some suggest that an earlier version of the Gospel, one written before the year 65, was

5
Write a paragraph describing the differences between a *painting* and a *photo* of someone. How do these differences relate to the notion of the Gospels as four "portraits" of Jesus?

■
Mark's Gospel was written against a backdrop of persecution.
Illustration: Some historical sources claim that the Emperor Nero blamed the Christians for

the burning of Rome in 64 C.E., leading to his persecution of them.

lost and that the one we now have is a revised version of the earlier one.

A heavy sense of suffering dominates the Gospel of Mark, with many references to trials and persecutions. This may reflect the persecution of the Christians by the Roman emperor Nero, who, some historians claim, blamed the Christians for the burning of Rome in the year 64 C.E. Also, we know that the Jews revolted against the Romans in a violent conflict between the years 66 and 70, and many scholars feel that Mark's account reflects an awareness of the suffering of that period as well.

For Whom and Why?

Mark's Gospel seems to have been written in Rome for the church there and for **Gentile** (non-Jewish) readers. Jewish customs that would have been readily understood by Jews themselves, for instance, are explained in Mark's Gospel in a way that indicates the customs were not familiar to the intended readers.

Mark's Gospel stresses the human suffering of Jesus in his Passion and death, perhaps to encourage the Christians who were being persecuted at the time this Gospel was proclaimed. In fact, Jesus' death is such a central point of Mark's

■
The persecution experienced by the Christians of Mark's time would continue sporadically for more than two centuries to come.

Photo: During times of intense persecution, Christians in and around Rome often celebrated the Eucharist in underground cemeteries called catacombs.

Gospel that everything else that precedes it seems to be offered almost solely by way of introduction. It seems certain, then, that one of Mark's intentions was to explain to the members of the early church how suffering is an essential part of Christian life and to give them the courage to endure it as Jesus had.

An emphasis on the humanity of Jesus comes through in Mark's Gospel. For example, it portrays Jesus expressing strong emotions. Mark may have been trying to counter the claim of some Christians during his day that Jesus was not truly human but only divine and had simply pretended to be a man. Mark's account makes it clear that Jesus was truly a human being, or as the church would much later express this reality, that Jesus truly possessed both human and divine natures.

In summary, Mark's Gospel provides us with perhaps the most intimate portrait of Jesus. It is also the shortest of the four Gospels. For these and other reasons, many suggest that anyone just beginning to study the Gospels will find it helpful to read Mark first, preferably in one sitting. In this way the reader can gain a basic sense of how a Gospel proclaims the Good News of Jesus.

Luke's Portrait:
Jesus as the Compassionate Savior

The Gospel of Luke is actually the first part of a two-volume history of early Christianity. The second part is another book of the New Testament—the Acts of the Apostles. The Gospel of Luke is often referred to as the Gospel of Jesus, and the Acts of the Apostles as the Gospel of the Holy Spirit. Acts recounts the workings of the Holy Spirit in the life of the early church. The two books are best read together.

By Whom and When?

A notion has persisted that the author of the Gospel of Luke and the Acts of the Apostles was a physician, a well-educated Gentile who had converted to Christianity. In the Letter to the Colossians (4:14), a certain Luke is identified by Saint Paul as a doctor, and some scholars have pointed out parts of Luke's Gospel that seem to indicate medical knowledge. This conclusion has probably been exaggerated, though, given the limited evidence.

Luke is mentioned three times in the New Testament, as a companion of Saint Paul. At one

■
Luke's Gospel emphasizes that God accepts persons cast out by society—persons least expected to receive God's favor.
Photo: **A homeless man sleeps near the Washington Monument.**

point Paul says that Luke is not a Jew. If what Paul says is true, then the author of Luke and Acts is probably the only non-Jewish writer of the New Testament. Luke did not know Jesus but had to rely on information received from those who were eyewitnesses to Jesus' life and ministry. Luke probably wrote his Gospel in Antioch, Syria, which was one of the largest cities in the Roman Empire.

It is difficult to date the writing of Luke's Gospel. Much evidence suggests that Luke had Mark's Gospel available to him when he was writing—especially the fact that some of Luke's material comes directly from Mark's Gospel. Based on this, we know that Luke wrote after Mark's Gospel was in circulation, which means sometime after the year 70 C.E. Most scholars say that the Gospel of Luke was written sometime during the eighties. The rough date of 85 will be used in this course.

For Whom and Why?

In the opening lines of his Gospel, Luke mentions a certain Theophilus, to whom he is addressing his Gospel. Luke tells Theophilus that he is writing "so that you may know the truth concerning the things about which you have been instructed" (1:4). Luke claims that he has studied all the available accounts of the life and ministry of Jesus and wants, "after investigating everything carefully from the very first, to write an orderly account for you" (1:3). So it seems that Luke was writing to offer those who were already Christians help in better understanding their faith and its roots.

Evidence in this Gospel indicates that Luke himself was unfamiliar with the land of Palestine and was writing to an audience made up mostly of Gentiles and perhaps well-to-do Christians. He sets out early in his writing to demonstrate the continuity of Christianity with the Judaism of the Hebrew Scriptures. And throughout his Gospel, Luke emphasizes the central role of the Holy Spirit in Jesus' life. He even closes his Gospel by stressing the continuing presence of Jesus through the Spirit after Jesus' death and Resurrection. Perhaps Luke was trying to support those readers who were discouraged that Jesus had not yet returned as they expected.

Luke, more than any other Gospel writer, stresses Jesus' mercy and compassion. Accompanying this emphasis is the idea that the Christian message is for everyone—Jews and Gentiles, men and women, rich and poor. Luke illustrates that God—through Jesus—accepts the persons who are least expected to receive God's favor. (Examples of such persons at the time of Luke were those with diseases and social outcasts of one kind or another—including women.) Also, Luke continually reminds the reader of the joy that is shared by those who experience God's forgiving love in Jesus. The Gospel of Luke, therefore, clearly depicts a Jesus who deeply loves all men and women. Because of this Gospel's beautiful writing and its portrait of the compassionate Jesus, many Christians consider it to be their favorite of the four Gospels.

Matthew's Portrait: Jesus as the Messiah of the Jews

By Whom and When?

There is no clear agreement on either the author or the date for Matthew's Gospel. Early in the history of the church, tradition held that the author was Matthew, an Apostle and therefore an eyewitness to Jesus' life and work. However, the author

Matthew's insights into the meaning of Jesus seem more developed than those of Mark or Luke.

For Whom and Why?

The Gospel of Matthew is very different in structure from the Gospels of Mark and Luke. Some scholars suggest that its organizational pattern copies that of the first five books of the Old Testament, indicating a particular desire by the author to show the Jews that Jesus was clearly the Messiah they had awaited.

The Gospel contains five great discourses, or speeches, by Jesus, demonstrating his role as a powerful teacher. The Gospel also emphasizes that all of Jesus' life was a fulfillment of the promises made by God to Israel. Jesus, for example, is presented as a true teacher of the Jewish Law, or as "the new Moses." More than 130 passages in the Gospel of Matthew refer either directly or indirectly to the Old Testament.

The author shows interest in the church itself, which may provide a clue to his intent in writing. In fact, Matthew's Gospel is sometimes referred to as the church's Gospel. It is the only Gospel to use the word *church* (see 16:18 and 18:17), and it seems concerned with the church's organization and with the communal life and teaching among the believers.

Because the Gospel of Matthew contains Jesus' teaching in such a thorough, well-organized, and understandable manner, it quickly became the most popular and widely used of all the Gospels in the early church, especially when educating new Christians. Its sensitivity to the continuity between Christianity and Judaism also made the Gospel valuable for Jews who were inquiring about the faith. These qualities explain in part why the Gospel of Matthew appears first in the New Testament today.

seems to have used almost all of Mark's Gospel and relied on Luke's account as well. It would have been strange for an eyewitness of Jesus' life to rely so heavily on other sources. Perhaps the unknown author relied heavily on the stories used by the Apostle Matthew to teach about Jesus.

Regarding the date of Matthew's writing, the majority of scholars would opt for a date anywhere between 80 and 100 C.E. This course will settle on an approximate date of 90 because

■

Photo: A Jewish scholar studies the Torah. The organization of Matthew's Gospel seems to follow the pattern of the Torah, which is the first five books of the Old Testament.

John's Portrait:
Jesus as the Divine Son of God

Different from the Synoptic Gospels

The Gospels of Matthew, Mark, and Luke are similar in so many respects that they are often referred to as the **synoptic Gospels.** (The word *synoptic* means "to see together.") It was noted earlier that the authors of the first three Gospels often seem to have used the same sources (stories told and insights drawn about Jesus) or one another's work in writing their accounts. Because of this overlapping, the synoptic Gospels can be fully understood only when seen or looked at side by side.

John's Gospel, on the other hand, is unique. Even just a quick reading of sections of it reveals this fact. Filled with symbolic language and images, this Gospel offers profound insights into the meaning of Jesus and his message. Some of its language is beautiful, and it is often used as a basis for both communal and personal prayer.

By Whom and When?

Wide disagreement persists over who authored the fourth Gospel, and we may never resolve the issue. At least some of the confusion is based on the fact that the name *John* was quite common, and it can be difficult to distinguish one John from another in the Scriptures. For years the church suggested that the author was the Apostle John. It was believed that the Apostle John wrote the Gospel at the end of a very long life, after much prayer, reflection, and personal experience of actually living out his faith in Jesus. This would account for the reflective, prayerful, and thoughtful style of the Gospel. The church has traditionally also held that the same John wrote the Book of Revelation.

■

Written for Jews, the Gospel of Matthew emphasizes that all of Jesus' life was a fulfillment of God's promise to Israel.
Photo: A Jewish man, wearing a prayer shawl, prays at the

Western Wall, in Jerusalem. The Western Wall is the only portion of the Temple that survived destruction by the Romans in 70 C.E.

However, much current discussion regarding the authorship of the fourth Gospel centers on the rather mysterious person identified in several places in the Gospel as "the disciple whom Jesus loved" (see John 13:23, 19:26, 20:2, and 21:7). Most scholars now refer to this person as the Beloved Disciple. In the past, some thought that this person and John the Apostle were one and the same. Few now accept that thinking.

Currently, the most common position on the authorship of the fourth Gospel is that it was written by members of the community or "school" founded by the Beloved Disciple. These disciples or students meditated on their leader's understanding of Jesus and gained even more profound insights into the risen Lord and his meaning. The three Epistles of John, also in the New Testament, seem to have come out of the same group, but some scholars suggest that a Christian prophet, also named John but otherwise unknown, wrote the Book of Revelation.

Regarding when the Gospel of John was written, scholars suggest that the earliest possible date would be around 90 C.E. and that it could have been as late as 100. In this course a date of 95 will be used. This late date alone would make it highly unlikely, if not impossible, for an Apostle of Jesus to have written the Gospel of John.

For Whom and Why?

The late date of the writing of the Gospel of John helps us gain an understanding of its unique style and the purposes for which it was written. Many years had passed since Jesus of Nazareth had walked among the people of Palestine, years during which the church continually deepened its understanding of his true identity. As noted earlier, it was only after the Resurrection that Jesus was fully recognized as the Christ, the Messiah, and the Son of God. The more time people had to reflect on these realities and their implications, the more central to their teaching and preaching these realities became.

Therefore, in John's Gospel—more so than in the synoptic Gospels—we see a strong attempt to present an understanding of Jesus as the divine Son of God. For this reason, many scholars feel that if we are to attempt an accurate historical portrait of Jesus as he lived and taught in Palestine, we should rely more heavily on the synoptics than on John. This does not mean that John's Gospel is not truthful, but rather that the truths it attempts to share are more deeply theological and reflective than the truths in the other Gospels.

On the other hand, the almost poetically prayerful nature of John's Gospel and its familiar and treasured imagery of Jesus as "the bread of life," "the light of the world," and "the good shepherd" have made this Gospel a favorite source for meditation on the divine significance of Jesus' life.

The synoptic Gospels are the primary sources for the information in chapters 5 through 10 of this course. However, brief excerpts from or comments on John's Gospel will be included. These will often be presented as short commentaries set off from the rest of the text and identified with the title "Focus on John."

For Review

- For each of the four Gospels, summarize the following information: *author, approximate date when written, primary audience, central themes.*

Continuing the Search

Many people today live with the illusion that it would be much easier to believe in Jesus if only they could see him, touch him, hear his voice, walk with him. They seem to think that the people who actually experienced Jesus during his earthly life in Palestine had a much easier time understanding and accepting him than people do today. The facts, however, do not support this notion.

If it was, in fact, so easy to recognize and accept Jesus in his own day, why did so many people have such a hard time doing this? If the message of Jesus was so understandable for those who heard it first-hand, why did so many of them reject it? In some ways, it is probably easier for people to accept Jesus today than it was when he lived. We today have the benefit of nearly two thousand years of historical experience with the person and message of Jesus. So much is known today that was not known in his day. History has recorded the profound impact of his vision on the world. Despite the shortcomings of Christian people throughout the years who have failed to live Jesus' message fully, it is still considered one of the most powerful and life-changing visions ever offered to humanity.

The next two chapters explore Jesus' social, cultural, and religious background as a Jew, and consider the historical setting in which he presented his vision. This can help us a great deal in understanding the meaning, impact, and significance of the one called Jesus the Christ, and the message he proclaimed.

■
Photo: John's Gospel offers a prayerful, reflective understanding of Jesus as the Son of God, "the light of the world."

3
The World of Jesus:
History and Politics

Jesus the Jew

In This Chapter . . .

- Jesus the Jew
- A Brief History of the Jewish People
- The Political World of Jesus
- An Oppressed People Dream of a Liberator

WHEN he came to Nazareth, where he had been brought up, he went to the synagogue on the sabbath day, as was his custom. He stood up to read, and the scroll of the prophet Isaiah was given to him. He unrolled the scroll and found the place where it was written:

"The Spirit of the Lord is upon me,
because he has anointed me
to bring good news to the poor.
He has sent me to proclaim release to the captives
and recovery of sight to the blind,
to let the oppressed go free,
to proclaim the year of the Lord's favor."

And he rolled up the scroll, gave it back to the attendant, and sat down. The eyes of all in the synagogue were fixed on him. Then he began to say to them, "Today this scripture has been fulfilled in your hearing." All spoke well of him and were amazed at the gracious words that came from his mouth. (Luke 4:16–22)

Understanding the Life and Times of Jesus

An essential piece of information we need to know about Jesus in order to understand him and the message he proclaimed is this: he was a deeply faith-filled and profoundly committed Jew of his day. In a startling and highly disturbing TV interview, a talk-show host one day confronted a major leader of the Ku Klux Klan with this fact. With an icy stare and hate-filled conviction, the man strongly denied that Jesus could have ever been a Jew, claiming with an almost incredible lack of understanding that Jesus was instead "the first Christian."

For most people, of course, a lack of sensitivity to the Jewish roots and religious experience of Jesus is not motivated by such bigotry. But unfortunately, many Christians over the centuries have not grasped the importance of having a solid background in Jewish religious, social, and political history in order to fully understand Jesus Christ.

Jesus in the Synagogue

Take another look at the scriptural passage that introduces this chapter. It is perhaps one of the most frequently quoted of all passages from the New Testament, one often used in prayer services because of its dramatic presentation of the mission of Jesus. But note the number of details in it that can be comprehended only within the context of the history of Israel:

To understand Jesus, we must understand his Jewish roots. *Photo, facing page:* The Sinai Range at sunrise. The Covenant that God made with the Israelites at Mount Sinai is central to the history of the Jews. *Background:* The Star of David at the ruins of an ancient synagogue in Capernaum. Jesus taught and worked a miracle in a synagogue there.

- Jesus went into the synagogue (what is a synagogue?)
- on the sabbath day (what is so special about that day?)
- as was his custom (why was it his custom?)
- he stood up to read (what gave him the right to do that?)
- from a scroll of the prophet Isaiah (who was Isaiah, what is a prophet, and what is a scroll?) **1**

What Jesus read was a very old and sacred passage from the Hebrew Scriptures, what we now call the Old Testament. It was one that Jesus felt identified both who he was and what he was all about, because, as he said, it was being fulfilled that very day in him.

History, Politics, and Religion

The main point of the above questions is that we simply cannot understand Jesus and his message outside the context of his Jewish heritage. This chapter offers some insights into the history of the Jews and then briefly discusses the political situation in which the Jewish people found themselves at the time of Jesus. The next chapter will look in more detail at the land, daily life, and religious practices of Jesus' time.

■

Photo: **An old synagogue in Nazareth. In a setting perhaps like this one, Jesus read from the prophet Isaiah and proclaimed, "Today this scripture has been fulfilled in your hearing."**

1

In writing, answer the questions in parentheses concerning the story of Jesus in the synagogue. Do the best you can without using a source other than the story itself.

With an Open Mind

Without question, the rough sketch of Jewish history that follows will greatly oversimplify the profound history of the people of faith we now call the Jews. Nevertheless, it serves as a starting point for understanding Jesus' heritage as a Jew. The many names, events, and religious places and celebrations surveyed in this chapter and the next were realities that touched Jesus deeply. Every moment of Jesus' earthly life grew out of, was touched by, and spoke directly to the Jewish community of his day.

And just as when we are listening to a new friend tell us the story of his or her life—his or her "history"—we need to keep our sometimes less-than-enthusiastic feelings about studying history from getting in the way of our learning more about Jesus. Exploring Jesus' roots can help us understand, for example, why Jesus would weep over Jerusalem, or why his cleansing of the Temple was such a striking event both for those who witnessed his powerful religious convictions and for himself as well. This is the only way we can hope to comprehend the drama of a scene like the one that introduces this chapter, where Jesus stands up before a hushed assembly, his heart pounding as he unrolls that very sacred scroll and proclaims for himself a role that will eventually lead him to the cross. Getting in touch with Jesus' roots is a way of getting in touch with him.

For Review

- Explain why studying Jewish history is important to understanding Jesus and his message.

A Brief History of the Jewish People

By this time in your religious education, you may already have acquired a sense of the basic history of the Jewish people. What follows, therefore, are only the highlights of that history, as a kind of quick review. Your teacher will be able to explain particular events in greater detail if necessary. **2**

The Story Begins: 1900 B.C.E.

Abraham

Sometime between 1900 and 1750 B.C.E.—nearly two thousand years before the time of Jesus—Jewish history began. At that time, the Jews were simply part of a number of tribes collectively known as **Hebrews.** Only later would they take on the name *Jews.* Their history as a special people started with the religious experience of a man named Abram. Abram followed one loving God in an age when people believed in countless gods, few of whom entered into any kind of friendly relationship with people. The God of Abram called him into a very special kind of personal relationship. As one sign of their unique relationship, God gave Abram a new name: **Abraham.**

This type of special relationship between God and people—either as individuals or as communities—is a covenant. The covenant with Abraham was just the first in a series that God would establish with the Hebrew people. In the covenant, God promised to take care of Abraham's people and give them a land of safety and well-being in which to live. Abraham and his people, in turn, were called to follow God loyally and lovingly.

2
As you read this history of the Jewish people, record and briefly identify the major characters, in the order in which they appear. Use the information as a study guide.

Isaac and Jacob

Though Abraham and his wife Sarah were very old, Sarah gave birth to a son named Isaac. Some years later it was revealed to Abraham that he had to sacrifice Isaac as a sign of his loyalty to God. But God withdrew that command at the last minute, recognizing that Abraham's willingness to sacrifice his son was testimony enough to the strength of the covenant.

Later, Isaac and his wife Rebekah gave birth to a son named Jacob. The covenant was renewed with Jacob when, in a dream, God told him, "Know that I am with you and will keep [protect] you wherever you go, and will bring you back to this land; for I will not leave you until I have done what I have promised you" (Genesis 28:15).

Jacob eventually fathered twelve sons and later, like Abraham before him, was given a new name —*Israel*—as a sign of his special relationship with God.

Settlement in Egypt

One of Jacob's twelve sons was named Joseph, and because he was Jacob's favorite, all of Jacob's other sons were jealous of him. The depth of their jealousy became apparent when they sold Joseph as a slave to some merchants who were on their way to Egypt. But Joseph ended up serving as a steward in a rich Egyptian's house and eventually worked his way up to the position of prime minister of the country. From that position of authority, Joseph invited his father, Jacob, and all his brothers, whom he had long since forgiven, to join him and live in Egypt. After Jacob died, the Hebrews became prosperous in Egypt.

The End of the Patriarchal Period

The settlement in Egypt ended the patriarchal period of Jewish history. That period was dominated by the three **patriarchs**—Abraham, Isaac, and Jacob. (The word *patriarch* means "father and leader of a family or a people.") References to "the God of Abraham, Isaac, and Jacob" and "the God of our fathers," which appear throughout the Scriptures, point to the patriarchal period.

Unfortunately, the recorders of Jewish history—like those who have recorded much of the world's history—often ignored or minimized the important role of women. Certainly women—some of them mothers, or **matriarchs**—played key roles throughout Jewish history. As will be seen later, in his time Jesus uniquely recognized and affirmed the dignity of women.

Because Jacob had been given the name *Israel* by God, his people became known as the **Israelites** during the period of history that centered around him and his sons. The prosperity of the Israelites in Egypt did not last. After about 150 years of living under kind pharaohs who came from a people related to their own, the Israelites came to be dominated by Egyptian pharaohs who enslaved them. The Israelites were given the backbreaking jobs of brickmaking and constructing public buildings. For a people who had always been free, this enslavement was miserable, and the Israelites dreamed of being liberated. The one who would lead them to freedom would be born several generations later.

■

Abraham probably belonged to a tribe of nomads—people who wandered from place to place, supporting themselves chiefly by raising herds of sheep and goats.

Photo: **The nomadic lifestyle of the Bedouin tribes in the Middle East today resembles that of Abraham and his family.**

The Story of Moses: 1290 B.C.E.

The man called to free the Israelites from slavery in Egypt was the powerful figure Moses. Moses sensed God's call to this mission during a profound religious experience. In the biblical account of this experience, God tells Moses, "The cry of the Israelites has now come to me; I have seen how the Egyptians oppress them. So come, I will send you to Pharaoh to bring my people, the Israelites, out of Egypt" (Exodus 3:9–10). It is at this point that God does something truly startling, something that we can understand only if we have a firm sense of the Israelite mentality: God reveals the name of God to Moses.

A Special Revelation

God's revelation to Moses on Mount Sinai (also known as Mount Horeb) is expressed through the biblical imagery of the Book of Exodus:

But Moses said to God, "If I come to the Israelites and say to them, 'The God of your ancestors has sent me to you,' and they ask me, 'What is his name?' what shall I say to them?" God said to Moses, "I AM WHO I AM." He said further, "Thus you shall say to the Israelites, 'I AM has sent me to you.'" God also said to Moses, "Thus you shall say to the Israelites, 'The LORD, the God of your ancestors, the God of Abraham, the God of Isaac, and the God of Jacob, has sent me to you':

"This is my name forever,
and this my title for all generations."

(Exodus 3:13–15)

Many versions of the Old Testament translate the word **Lord** (see the word in the biblical passage above) as **Yahweh**, the most important name for God in the Old Testament. The name **Yahweh** is thought to come from the Hebrew word for the

F • O • C • U • S

A Clarifying Word About God's Name

The name *Yahweh* continues to be treated with great reverence by Jews today. In an effort to demonstrate sensitivity to Jewish religious beliefs, some writers and Bible translations use the word LORD rather than *Yahweh* when referring to the Hebrew name for God. (The all-capital letters in LORD are meant to reflect the Hebrew symbol YHWH.) This is the case with the New Revised Standard Version of the Bible quoted in this course.

Further confusing this treatment of the name for God, however, is that Jesus frequently is referred to as Lord in the New Testament. In the Gospels, the title is often intended simply as a respectful form of address meaning "Master" or "Sir." But at times in the Gospels and especially in the epistles of Paul, the title is meant to show Jesus' total unity with God (a concept that will be discussed later in this course).

The Exodus

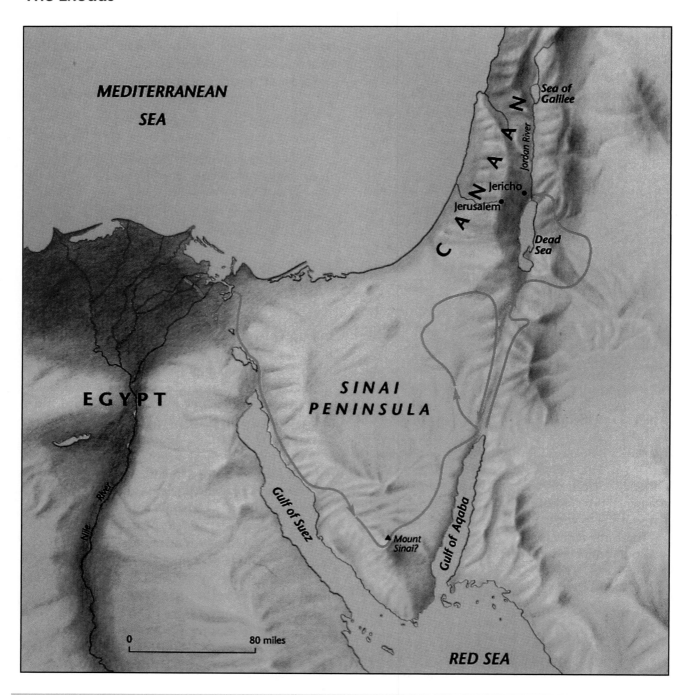

MEDITERRANEAN SEA

EGYPT

SINAI PENINSULA

CANAAN

Sea of Galilee

Jordan River

Jericho

Jerusalem

Dead Sea

Gulf of Suez

Gulf of Aqaba

▲ Mount Sinai?

Nile River

RED SEA

0   80 miles

■ *Map:* The red line indicates the traditional but much-debated route of the Israelites as Moses led them out of Egypt to the Promised Land of Canaan. Later the Greeks would rename the Promised Land *Palestine,* which is what it was called in Jesus' time. The "sea of reeds," believed to have been crossed by Moses and the Israelites, was most likely one of the lakes to the north of what is now known as the Gulf of Suez.

verb "to be," and it signifies that God is the Creator, the Ruler of nature and history, and the One who is always present.

The significance of God's name being revealed to the Israelite people (rather than the people coming up with their own name for God) lies in the fact that for the Israelites, the act of naming anything indicated the power of the namer over the named. By revealing God's name first, God claimed sovereignty over the people. It is also significant that at a time when many gods were believed in, the Israelite people were told who the one true God was.

Over the years, the Israelite people would come to regard as very sacred the name that God had revealed to them, and they would not even pronounce this name for fear of misusing it. In their Scriptures, the Israelites actually used only the symbol YHWH and accompanied it with the word *Adonai* (meaning "my great Lord") to remind the reader to say "Lord" rather than "Yahweh." To call God by name would have been the greatest sacrilege, implying that people had control over God.

As will be seen later, Jesus himself would grapple with this understanding of his God—the God of Abraham, Isaac, and Jacob—and he would offer his own startling and deep insights into God's nature. Jesus would even offer a new name for God, which would not only astound but deeply anger many of the faithful Jews who heard him speak.

The First Passover

Moses was sent by God to convince Pharaoh to free the Israelite people from bondage. But Pharaoh was not easily persuaded, and God had to provide a great deal of help so that Moses could accomplish the mission. Pharaoh's hand was forced when a series of ten plagues revealed God's power over the lives of people. The tenth plague—the one that ultimately freed the Israelites from Pharaoh's grip—also resulted in key religious rituals that to this very day highlight the spiritual life of the Jewish people.

The tenth plague was to cause the death of all the firstborn children in Egypt. But God gave the Israelites a sign that would protect them—and them alone—from this disaster. They were to slaughter either sheep or goats from their flocks and then take some of the blood from the slaughter and put it on the doorposts and above the doors of their homes. The flesh of the slaughtered animals was to be eaten along with unleavened bread and bitter herbs. Later, as the firstborn children in all of Egypt were killed, God *passed over* the homes on which the blood had been poured, saving the Israelites and convincing the Egyptians to let them go. And God said to the Israelites, "This day [Passover] shall be a day of remembrance for you. You shall celebrate it as a festival to the LORD; throughout your generations you shall observe it as a perpetual ordinance" (Exodus 12:14). A discussion of key Jewish feasts, including Passover, will come later.

The Covenant of Sinai

Following the Exodus from Egypt, the Israelites wandered in the desert. After fifty days, God ratified the Covenant with them in one of the most important events recorded in all the Scriptures. In a dramatic encounter (see Exodus, chapters 19 to 20), Yahweh called Moses to the top of Mount Sinai and there said to him:

Thus you shall say to the house of Jacob, and tell the Israelites: You have seen what I did to the Egyptians, and how I bore you on eagles' wings and brought you to myself. Now therefore, if you obey my voice and keep my covenant, you shall be my treasured

possession out of all the peoples. Indeed, the whole earth is mine, but you shall be for me a priestly kingdom and a holy nation. These are the words that you shall speak to the Israelites. (Exodus 19:3–6)

So God had now extended the offer of the Covenant to an entire people—the implications of which will become clear in a moment.

A covenant is a two-way relationship, and because God chose the Israelites as God's people, something was expected of them by God. Their end of the bargain was to follow the elaborate sys-

tem of the Jewish Law, of which the cornerstone was the **Ten Commandments**. The Law would one day be misused and would be a stumbling block between Jesus and his own people. But at this point in Jewish history, it was recognized for what it truly was—a wonderful gift that uniquely established a relationship of love between God and God's people.

As was said earlier, the Covenant of Sinai is one of the central events in the Scriptures and in the history of the Jews. God transformed a crowd of poor slaves into a nation—God's own special peo-

■

Illustration: At the time of Jesus, as today, the annual feast of Passover helped the Jews celebrate God's freeing their people from slavery in Egypt. They recalled that God had brought the Israelites unharmed through the "sea of reeds."

56

ple. Until this point God had spoken only to individuals (Abraham and Jacob, for example), and these individuals were, at most, only leaders of small clans of people. At Sinai the *People of God* were born, with the special name *Israel*. So the people became a covenant community, and it is only in terms of that community that we can come to understand the Jews and, for that matter, the real meaning of today's church.

Following the marvelous events at Sinai, the Israelites roamed the desert for forty difficult years. Even though the faith of the Israelites wavered at times, God remained firm in the commitment to this covenant community. The Lord was indeed their God, and they were God's people—though, as will be seen later, they were not always a faithful people.

Life in the Promised Land

Following the death of Moses, the Israelites in about 1250 B.C.E. crossed the Jordan River into the land that had been promised to them by God: the Promised Land of Canaan. The next few hundred years were brutal, however, with many wars and seemingly endless turmoil for the Israelites as they sought to settle in a land already occupied by other peoples. During this time, **judges**—great warriors rather than judges in our usual sense of the term— were periodically appointed to fight and defeat Israel's enemies. As land was gradually conquered, it was divided among the twelve tribes of Israel, one tribe descending from each of the twelve sons of Jacob.

In about 1050 B.C.E., around two hundred years after beginning the conquest of the land of Canaan, Israel confronted a new enemy: the Phil-

istines. With new weapons, and fighting a now-divided Israel, the Philistines proved to be too strong for the Israelites. The Philistines captured the treasured ark of the Covenant, in which Moses' written version of the Ten Commandments was stored and honored. If the Israelites were to defeat their enemies and survive as a people, they needed a strong leader. In desperation they appointed their first king, a man named Saul, in about 1020 B.C.E.

■

Photo: **In the Covenant of Sinai, God told Moses that Israel "shall be for me a priestly kingdom and a holy nation."**

The Kingdom of Israel: 1000 B.C.E.

Saul: A Warrior-King

Saul, the first king of Israel, was actually more of a warrior than a king in today's sense, and though he was a brave man in battle, he was a weak man personally. He was very jealous of a young man named David, one of the leaders in his army, who had gained public acclaim for leading the people in some of their victories over the Philistines.

When Saul became king, the twelve tribes of Israel were divided into two main groups. The ten tribes who lived mostly north of Jerusalem kept the name *Israel,* and the two tribes living to the south of Jerusalem went by the collective name *Judah.* Although all twelve tribes recognized Saul as their first king, the two groups disagreed about who should be Saul's successor. While the ten northern tribes recognized one of Saul's sons as their new king, the two southern tribes recognized David. Saul's son was a weak leader and was murdered after just a short time on the throne.

David: Uniting the People of Israel

Upon the death of Saul's son, the people turned to David as their only king. He was thirty-seven years old when he united all twelve tribes of Israel into one nation, around the year 1000 B.C.E., and he led Israel in defeating the Philistines and conquering much of the surrounding territory. Jerusalem became known as the city of David, where he built a palace and desired to build a great temple in which the reclaimed ark of the Covenant could be kept and honored. Jerusalem therefore became the center of not only the political life of the people of Israel but also their religious life. David is still recognized as the greatest of all the kings of Israel.

Solomon: Son of David

Before David died, he made sure his son Solomon was publicly crowned successor to the throne. Solomon served as king for some forty years. It was a period of great building, increased trade, and prosperity, during which Solomon built the magnificent **Temple** that David had dreamed of. But to build the Temple, King Solomon had to resort to heavily taxing the people and drafting thousands of workers a month. Though the

■
The Israelites crossed the Jordan River to enter the Promised Land. The first Canaanite town they conquered was Jericho.
Photo: **The oasis of Jericho.**

F • O • C • U • S

The Kingdoms of Israel and Judah

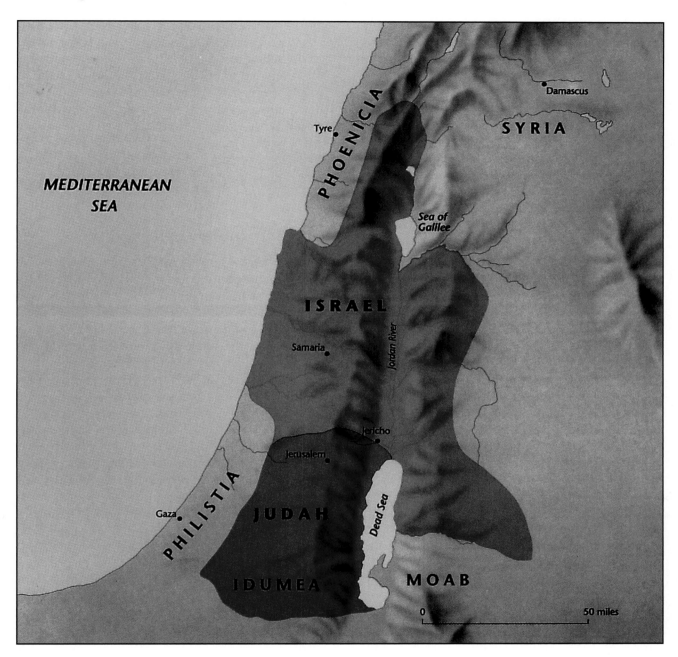

■
Map: After Solomon died, the kingdom of the Israelites split into the northern kingdom of Israel and the southern kingdom of Judah. By 721 B.C.E., the northern kingdom had fallen to the Assyrians. The kingdom of Judah was conquered by the Babylonians in 587 B.C.E., and many of its citizens were exiled.

Temple was beautiful and attracted the people to worship God, Solomon himself turned to idolatry, building pagan shrines and worshiping pagan idols. **3**

The Kingdom Divided: Israel and Judah

After Solomon died, one of his sons was immediately proclaimed king of the two tribes of Judah, in the south. Solomon's son could have been accepted as king of all the northern tribes as well, if he had been willing to listen to the demands of the people there. The people of the north wanted relief from their taxes and the labor draft. Solomon's son refused to grant them their wishes, however, and alienated them. The ten tribes in the north refused to accept him as their king and instead formed themselves into a new kingdom of Israel, thereby destroying the unified kingdom of David.

The Time of the Prophets

What followed for both Israel and Judah was a history of weak kings and religious disgrace. Great **prophets** arose, trying to call the people back to the Covenant, but the people continued to weaken. Eventually, in 721 B.C.E., the northern kingdom of Israel was destroyed by the Assyrians.

The southern kingdom of Judah was able to last about a century longer than the northern kingdom because Judah's leaders, successors of David, were somewhat more loyal to the Covenant with God than were the kings of the north.

The great prophet Isaiah, however, recognized that one day the southern kingdom also would be destroyed. He made a prediction: Comparing the royal family of David to a tree that had been cut down, Isaiah said that only a stump would be

left to represent the family that had started with David's father, Jesse (this family tree is the origin of the religious symbol of the Jesse tree, which is often referred to at Christmastime). However, said Isaiah, from this stump would come a shoot, a new branch—and this future king of David's line would be someone powerful and good, someone who would bring peace (see Isaiah 11:1–9). Christians, of course, would much later recognize that someone in the person of Jesus, one born from the line of David.

The Babylonian Exile: 597 B.C.E.

In 597 B.C.E. Jerusalem was overrun by the Babylonians, and the leading citizens of the kingdom of Judah were carried off as captives into Babylon—the southern kingdom had been destroyed just as Isaiah had predicted. Another prophet, by the name of Jeremiah, wrote to the captives in Babylon and urged them to settle as residents there, promising that someday God would return them to their home.

Back in Jerusalem everything worsened, and in 587 B.C.E. the city itself, including the Temple, was destroyed and thousands more captives were led off into the **Babylonian Exile.** Many of the people who were not captured left the country for places along the Mediterranean Sea, where small colonies of the faithful began to grow. These people made up a settlement called the **Diaspora,** from a word meaning "dispersion" or "those who have been dispersed." (The people of the Diaspora would later become important in the ministry of Saint Paul, who would travel to the widespread communities to share the message about Jesus.)

Through the voice of the prophet Jeremiah, God assured the people of everlasting love and a new

3
Choosing from among all the characters of Jewish history identified up to and including Solomon, write a paragraph on the one you would most like to meet and talk with.

F • O • C • U • S
Summary of Jewish History: 1900 to 515 B.C.E.

Key persons and events are indicated by **bold** type.

1900 B.C.E.
Jewish history began sometime after 1900 B.C.E. with **Abraham** in the land of Canaan. Abraham's wife Sarah gave birth to **Isaac.** Isaac and his wife Rebekah had two sons, one of whom was **Jacob.** Jacob had twelve sons, from whom the twelve tribes of Israel were derived. One of the twelve sons was **Joseph,** who settled in Egypt, where he was later joined by his father and brothers. One hundred fifty years of prosperity followed for the people of Israel.

1500–1290 B.C.E.
From about 1500 to 1290 B.C.E. the Israelites suffered **slavery** in Egypt.

1290–1000 B.C.E.
Around 1290 B.C.E. **Moses** led the Israelites out of Egypt (the **Exodus**), and Yahweh formed the **Covenant of Sinai** with the people. The Israelites then settled in the Promised Land, Canaan. From 1200 to 1020 B.C.E. the **judges** led the Israelites against their enemies.

1000 B.C.E.
The kingdom of Israel was formed. **Saul** was the first king, followed by **David** (1000 B.C.E.), who would be the greatest of all the kings. David established Jerusalem as the central city of his people. He was succeeded by **Solomon,** who built the **Temple.** After the death of Solomon in 922 B.C.E., the kingdom split apart into the **northern kingdom** of Israel and the **southern kingdom of Judah.**

721–587 B.C.E.
The northern kingdom was destroyed by the **Assyrians** in 721 B.C.E. The southern kingdom survived until 597 B.C.E., when its leading citizens were captured by the **Babylonians.** In 587 B.C.E. Jerusalem and the Temple were destroyed, and thousands more were led into captivity (the **Exile**).

538–515 B.C.E.
In 538 B.C.E. the **Persians** defeated the Babylonians, and the exiles were allowed to return to Jerusalem. From this point on they were known as **Jews** (from the word *Judah*). The **rebuilding of the Temple** was completed by 515 B.C.E.

Covenant. It was clear that God would never abandon them:

The days are surely coming, says the LORD, when I will make a new covenant with the house of Israel and the house of Judah. . . . I will put my law within them, and write it on their hearts; and I will be their God, and they shall be my people. (Jeremiah 31:31–33)

Renewal of the Covenant Community

A Faithful Remnant
Somehow the experience of being in exile, with Jerusalem destroyed, led many of the exiled people to a renewed appreciation of their faith in God. Certainly many of those held in Babylon gave up

in hopelessness, and the time of the captivity was perhaps the saddest in all of Jewish biblical history. But a certain number of these people—called the **remnant**—began to live much more closely to God than ever before. The Exile was seen not so much as punishment by God but rather as God's way of bringing the people back to recognition of who they were as God's chosen ones.

A Prophet's Promise

In 538 B.C.E. the Persians overcame the Babylonians, and the Persian leader allowed all the exiles in the new empire to return to their native lands with freedom of worship. This had been predicted by perhaps the greatest of all the prophets, one whose name we have never even known. His writings were added to those of the prophet Isaiah, so we have come to call this prophet Second Isaiah. He wrote some of the most beautiful passages in all of the Scriptures, including the famous "suffering servant" passages, which speak of a great servant of God who will one day save his people through his own suffering and death rather than through military conquest (see especially Isaiah 53:1–12).

To Christians of the twenty-first century, who are fully aware of the life and death of Jesus, such a prophecy makes sense. However, to the exiles, who first heard it in the middle of the sixth century before Christ, it was a bewildering kind of talk. They were a people who expected victory by fighting for it. The thought of gaining victory by suffering willingly must have seemed like utter nonsense. **4**

The Return to Judah

After the Persians freed the Jews in Babylon, some began returning to their homeland, Judah, in caravans. They worked on rebuilding the Temple, a project completed in 515 B.C.E. They were no longer a political nation united under a king, but rather a religious community under a new form of leader: the **high priest.** Because these people were a remnant from the southern kingdom of Judah, it is at this point in their history that we begin to speak of **Judaism** as we know it today. And it is also from this term, *Judaism,* that we have derived the word *Jew* for those who follow that faith.

Gradually, two main classes of leaders developed among the Jews: the **priests,** who were responsible for offering sacrifices in the Temple, and those called **scribes,** who were responsible for teaching the Law of Moses. **5**

Before continuing with this look at Jewish history, you may wish to pause and review the summary chart of this material on page 61. When you feel that you adequately understand the information summarized there, you can move on to the rest of the history.

For Review

- List two major characters in ancient Jewish history who received new names. Give both their original and their new names. Briefly explain the significance of their receiving a new name from God.
- What name did God reveal to Moses, and what does the name mean? Why was God's giving of that name so significant?
- Briefly explain the origin and meaning of the term *Passover.*
- Identify Saul, David, and Solomon and briefly explain the relationships among the three.
- Define the term *Diaspora.*

4
Look up and read the passage about the suffering servant—Isaiah 53:1–12. Think of someone you know who has suffered or given generously of self for the sake of others. Write a description of that person, telling how she or he has affected you.

5
Consult a dictionary and write down the definitions of these words: *prophet, priest, scribe.*

The Political World of Jesus

The first part of this chapter reviewed Jewish history from 1900 to 515 B.C.E., when the Jerusalem Temple was rebuilt after the Exile and the religion of Judaism formally began. The second part of this chapter covers the developments in Jewish history from roughly three hundred years before Jesus' birth until about forty years after his death.

Greek Domination of Palestine

One man seemed to dominate the world about three hundred years before the time of Jesus. He was **Alexander the Great**, and he was unquestionably one of the most remarkable figures in all of history. He lived only thirty-three years, but in that time he towered over his world. Though born in Macedonia, a country north of Greece, he was a Greek in spirit, educated by the great philosopher Aristotle and convinced that the Greek vision of life offered civilization its greatest hope of fulfillment. He was just twenty when he became king of his own country, but he quickly won the hearts and minds of the Greeks as he led his armies in victories over all the enemies of Greece. By the time he died in 323 B.C.E., he had conquered much of the Mediterranean world and lands as far east as India.

Alexander's Empire Divided

After Alexander's death, the land he had conquered was divided among the leading generals of his army. Palestine, where Jesus would be born some three hundred years later, was divided between two of Alexander's generals. Though the generals were both Greek, they did not see eye to

eye. These two men and their successors dominated Palestine for 150 years. One of these lines of generals was centered in Syria, to the north of Palestine; the other, in Egypt, to the southwest. Palestine was located directly between the two centers of power, and it was inevitably caught in the struggle for control between them, a struggle that lasted for many years. Many of the factions and groups we find in the Gospels developed out of that conflict.

Greek influence. For about the first one hundred years after Alexander's death, most of the people of Israel were ruled by the power located in Egypt. Because of the distance that separated

■
Alexander the Great, a Greek ruler, conquered much of the Mediterranean world, including Palestine, three hundred years before the time of Jesus.

Photo: **A statue of Alexander the Great.**

Egypt from Palestine, that Greek power seldom interfered in the internal affairs of the Jews. Nevertheless, Greek culture in some way had an effect on all the people who inhabited Palestine. For example, the Greek language was increasingly used throughout the land.

In Galilee (the northern region of Palestine), which the Syrian Greeks controlled, Greek culture influenced all levels of Jewish life—so much so that the region is often referred to in the Bible as Galilee of the Gentiles. (Gentiles are non-Jews, and by Jesus' time, a Jew from Galilee—like Jesus himself—was looked down on by other Jews.)

The end of tolerance. The tolerant kind of Greek occupation practiced by the power in Egypt ended in the year 198 B.C.E., when all of Palestine came under control of the power to the north, in Syria. At first the people of Israel were allowed to maintain local control of their affairs, but that changed gradually as the rulers developed a need for increased finances. The Romans, from the west, had defeated the Syrian Greeks in a naval battle and then demanded an enormous amount of money as a price of defeat. To pay off Rome and to support other Greek war efforts, the rulers in Syria began a heavy taxation of the Jews. Any peace and goodwill that had existed between the Greeks and the Jews was shattered by this.

Reactions to Greek Rule

All this history is important in a study of Jesus because of the Jews' reactions to these events and the emergence of groups that became identified with those reactions.

There were two basic reactions to the Greek influences on the people of Israel, particularly by those living in the region of Palestine called Judea, where the city of Jerusalem was located:

F • O • C • U • S
A Land, a People

The names used for the region in which the Gospel story takes place can vary and, therefore, cause confusion. For example, it is common today for people to variously refer to the area as Palestine, Israel, or the Holy Land. The issue is complicated even more by the fact that the country we now know as Israel involves a smaller area of land than the region in which the Gospel story took place. Below is an explanation of how the place names are used in this course. Not only is the following the most accurate usage, but it also reflects the way in which these terms are used in the Scriptures themselves.

- *Palestine* is the name used for the geographic setting in which the Gospel story takes place. Whenever we are talking about Palestine, therefore, we are discussing the land itself. The name *Palestine* was given to the region by the Greeks and derives from the Greek word for "Philistines," the ancient rivals of Israel who at one time dominated the region and whom King David defeated.
- Throughout the Scriptures, *Israel* is the name given to the People of God themselves, that is, the political and religious group. Therefore, Israel as a people might exist regardless of what land they occupy and, in fact, even if they have no home at all, as when they roamed the desert after the Exodus out of Egypt.

- The Jewish leaders, the wealthy landowners, and the priestly class tried to get along with the Greeks, simply because they had the most to lose in any conflicts with them.
- Another group, called the **Hasidim**, meaning "the pious ones," resented the Greek rulers and felt that any compromise with them amounted to a rejection of the Jewish faith. **6**

Out of these basic philosophical and religious differences developed many of the factions that appear in the Gospels—particularly the Sadducees and the Pharisees. These groups will be defined more clearly later.

An incredible victory. The Greek domination of Israel led to one of the greatest events in the entire history of the Jews, one that eventually resulted in a religious festival that is celebrated by the Jews even today. At one point, rebels within the Jewish community tried to overthrow their Greek overlords and regain their freedom. However, the Greek leaders in Syria, already angry about a defeat by the Romans, took out their rage on the rebelling Jews. They not only crushed the

Jewish rebellion but sacked Jerusalem and desecrated the beloved Temple. They even went so far as to build an altar to the Greek god Zeus in the holy of holies, the most sacred part of the Temple.

The Greeks had clearly gone too far and had underestimated the power of a people whose religious convictions ran as deeply as those of the Jews. All of Judea erupted in outrage at what the Syrian Greeks had done. Though the odds were strongly stacked against them, the rebelling Jews won a decisive victory over their oppressors! (One of the Jewish leaders was nicknamed Maccabeus, meaning "the hammer," because of his ferocious fighting. The revolt itself came to be known as the Maccabean War, or the Maccabean Revolt, and its story is told in two books of the Old Testament—1 and 2 Maccabees.) In 164 B.C.E. the hated altar of Zeus was removed and the sacred Temple was rededicated, an event still remembered and celebrated by Jews today, with the Feast of Dedication, or Hanukkah. By 142 B.C.E. the Greeks had granted complete freedom to Israel, and about a century of national freedom followed. A period of independence for the Jews would not be experienced again until, incredibly, the founding of the modern state of Israel in 1948.

Jewish Independence

Unfortunately for the Jews, strong leaders did not emerge to guide them during the period of independence. In fact, Jewish independence was undermined even before it was fully gained. Before complete independence was granted by the Greeks, the Jewish family that eventually assumed leadership of the Jewish state acted improperly. One member of this ruling family accepted the "gift" of the high priesthood from the Greek leaders.

■
Greek culture and rule deeply influenced the lives of all who lived in Palestine.
Photo: **A Greek temple.**

6
Consider a principle, belief, or moral standard you hold that you would not be willing to compromise. Describe it in a paragraph, along with your reasons for refusing to compromise.

respect accorded to the priesthood—a fact represented by the tensions in the Gospel stories—and it planted a seed that would soon give rise to factions among the Jews.

Political Factions Within Judaism

The violation of the priesthood and the role of high priest by the ruling family evoked a number of different responses, and different political factions began to take shape:

The Sadducees. The priestly class worked out accommodations with the new Jewish political leaders, just as they had earlier with their Greek overlords. The members of this priestly class became known as the **Sadducees.**

The Essenes. Some people reacted so strongly to the weaknesses of the Jewish political leaders that they withdrew from Jewish society altogether in order to observe strict religious traditions. These people were called the **Essenes.** Though they are never mentioned in the Bible, it is likely that Jesus knew of the Essenes and may even have been influenced by their deep religious convictions.

The Pharisees. Another group, the **Pharisees,** tried at first to find some kind of middle ground between the political accommodation of the Sadducees and the withdrawal of the Essenes. In the end, however, they refused to compromise their religious beliefs and therefore lost some influence in the higher levels of religious and political power. But among the common people they gained a strong reputation for strict faithfulness to the Covenant, and they were very much respected and therefore influential among those people. The Pharisees were an extremely important Jewish group and are mentioned often in the New Testament. **7**

The leadership position of high priest was important among the Jews during the time of foreign domination, and it had traditionally been restricted to only certain families from one of the original twelve tribes of Israel. Not only did the Greeks have no authority to choose the high priest, but the family member who accepted the gift had no right to accept it. Thus the family was seen as publicly violating the traditions of their own people. The act also greatly lessened the prestige and

---

■

Photo. **Jewish children light the menorah, used to celebrate Hanukkah. This "Feast of Lights" recalls the rededication of the Temple after the Jews' victory over their Greek oppressors.**

7
Imagine yourself as a young Jewish person living during the time of Jewish independence and facing the problem of weak and untrustworthy leaders. Which political faction would you most agree with: the Sadducees, the Essenes, the Pharisees, or none of these? Explain your response in a paragraph.

■
People in Samaria were considered suspect by their Jewish "cousins" to the south in Judea.
Photo: **The modern city of Sebastiyeh is located on the site of the ancient city of Samaria.**

Palestine at the Time of Jesus

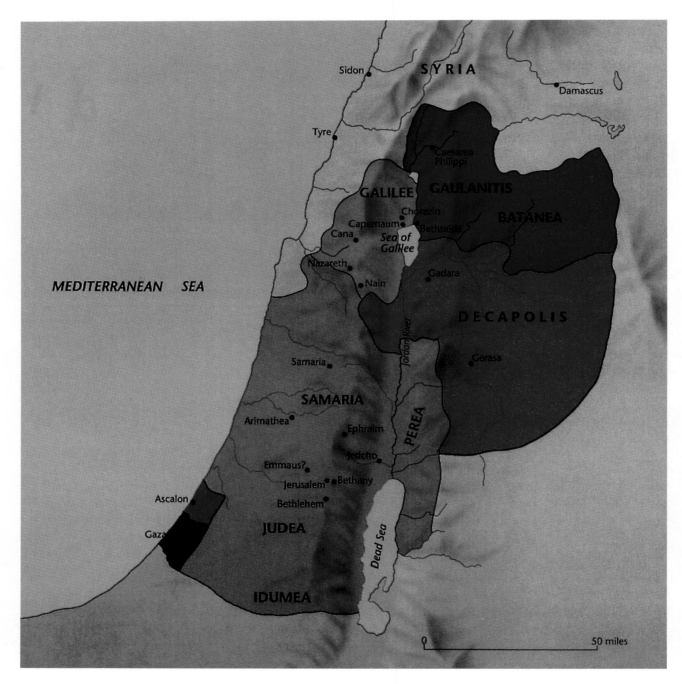

SYRIA

Sidon

Damascus

Tyre

Caesarea Philippi

GALILEE   GAULANITIS

Chorazin

BATANEA

Capernaum   Bethsaida

Cana   *Sea of Galilee*

Nazareth

Gadara

Nain

MEDITERRANEAN   SEA

DECAPOLIS

Jordan River

Samaria

Gerasa

SAMARIA

Arimathea

PEREA

Ephraim

Jericho

Emmaus?

Jerusalem   Bethany

Ascalon

Bethlehem

Gaza

JUDEA

Dead Sea

IDUMEA

0   50 miles

■ *Map:* The Gospels mention many towns and geographical regions of Palestine. The area around Capernaum is sometimes referred to as Gennesaret. Perea is also called Transjordan, or "across the Jordan," in the Gospels. Decapolis was a loose federation of ten cities and their surrounding territory.

Geographical Factions in Palestine

Much of the prejudice and bitterness between various sections of the country in Jesus' time originated during the period of Jewish independence.

The region of Judea. Judea was the region of central Palestine that had been settled by the faithful remnant, who had returned from the Exile in the sixth century B.C.E. Because Jerusalem was located there, Judea had become the religious as well as the geographic center of Judaism. During the period of Jewish independence, groups holding political power further abused their position of authority by trying to expand from their central power base in Judea out to the other regions of Palestine.

The region of Idumea. On the map on page 68 you will see that just south of Judea was the territory of Idumea. Under the leadership of the Jews holding political power, this region was quickly absorbed by Israel and forced to accept Judaism. The fact that the Idumeans' "acceptance" of the Jewish faith was brought about by force would always make the Idumean Jews suspect to the mainline Jews of Judea.

The region of Samaria. The people of Samaria, the territory just north of Judea, were also suspect. The **Samaritans** were among the descendants of the old northern tribes of the kingdom of Israel (conquered by the Assyrians in 721 B.C.E.), who had stayed in the north and lost touch with their Jewish "cousins" in the southern kingdom of Judah. They had *not* been sent into Babylon during the Exile. Many of their religious practices and traditions—including their scriptures—were different from those of the mainline Jews in the south. When the remnant returned from the Exile, they completely rejected the Samaritans and would not allow them any participation in Jewish religious or national life.

During the period of independence, the leaders of the Jews, in their effort to expand their power, went so far as to destroy the temple that the Samaritans had built in their own territory. The Jewish leaders tried to force the Samaritans to accept orthodox Judaism. The intense bitterness between the two peoples deepened, and by the time of Jesus, great hatred existed between them.

Imagine now the impact of the story Jesus would one day tell about the good Samaritan, who comes off as a hero when compared with the Jewish priest in the story (Luke 10:29–37); or Jesus' public conversation with not just a woman—which would have been scandalous enough—but a *Samaritan* woman, no less (John 4:1–30). No wonder Jesus caused problems and controversy wherever he went!

The region of Galilee. Galilee, too, was annexed by the Jewish leaders, and the non-Jews there were forced either to accept Judaism or leave the region. Many accepted, and by Jesus' time most of Galilee was Jewish. Nevertheless, the mainline Jews held a haughty attitude about Galileans. The Galileans' late acceptance of the Jewish faith added to their reputation as second-class citizens.

As mentioned earlier, and as you can see from the map on page 68, Nazareth—where Jesus was raised—was located in Galilee. This explains a comment that the mainline Jews make about him in the Gospels: "Can anything good come out of Nazareth?" (John 1:46).

An Appeal to Rome

The century of independence under inept Jewish leaders therefore quickly deteriorated— nearly to the point of civil war—because of bitter

F • O • C • U •. S

The Roman World in the Time of Jesus

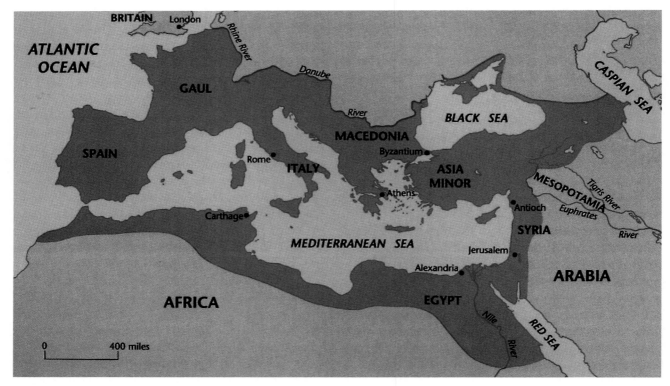

factions. Finally, both the Pharisees and the Sadducees appealed to Rome for help in settling their conflicts. But the Romans were ready to offer more "help" than the people had bargained for. In 63 B.C.E., some sixty years before the birth of Jesus, the Romans occupied Palestine and took complete control.

Israel Under Roman Domination

One of the reasons the Romans were able to build such a powerful empire in their day was the wise way in which they governed the people they con-

quered. For example, when they defeated a country and took control of it, the Romans would carefully select leaders from among the conquered people themselves. This practice gave stability to the entire empire. By 37 B.C.E. the Romans had selected a shrewd Idumean Jew named Herod to rule Israel. (Remember, Idumean Jews were not respected by mainline Jews because the faith had been forced upon the Idumeans.) Herod would rule until his death in 4 B.C.E., and toward the end of his reign, Jesus would be born. The sons of Herod would continue his dynasty until almost the end of the first century after Jesus.

■

Map: **The green area represents the extent of Roman political domination in the time of Jesus.**

Herod "the Great"

If one were to judge Herod on purely political grounds, with no regard to his morality, he would have to be judged a success as a ruler. He combined the qualities of political cunning and brutality. He was a master builder, and he began restoring the Temple to its original splendor during Jesus' time. But he was also an incredibly cruel man. For example, in Matthew 2:13–18, we find the story of Herod's execution of all male children age two and under, in the hope of destroying the Messiah, who might assume the role of "king of the Jews." This event, called the Slaughter of the Innocents, has not been historically verified, but Herod's reputation for brutality certainly makes it seem possible. (Also, the story is told that when Herod lay dying, he ordered that all prominent men in the town be executed right at the moment of his own death, so that the grief of the townspeople would be real!)

Through his political ability, Herod managed to hold the country together during his reign. But when he died, the Romans allowed his power to be passed on to his sons, most of whom seemed to have all of his cruelty but none of his political intelligence. This political situation in Palestine became the backdrop for the events described in the Gospels.

Herod Antipas

One of Herod's three sons was given control of the northeast region of Palestine. A second son, Herod Antipas (sometimes called simply Antipas to avoid confusion with his father) was given control of Galilee and Perea, a region just east of the Jordan River. Antipas's marriage to the wife of his half brother brought about the rage of John the Baptist, which in turn led Antipas to have John beheaded (Matthew 14:3–12). Jesus referred to

Antipas as "that fox" in a discussion with the Pharisees (Luke 13:31–33). The Gospels refer to him simply as Herod or occasionally as *Herod the tetrarch,* a title based on the Greek word for "four" and referring to a person who governs one-fourth of a province.

The Roman Procurator

The third son of Herod the Great was by far the worst leader of the three, but he was given the most important area to rule: Judea, Samaria, and Idumea. He was so inept as a ruler that the Romans eventually replaced him with a Roman official variously called a procurator, a prefect, or less often, a governor. The first procurator was installed by the Romans in 6 C.E., and by the time of Jesus' public ministry, five different men had held the position. The fifth procurator began his rule in the year 26, just a year or so before Jesus began his public life. The man was Pontius Pilate, and he would play a key role in the trial and execution of Jesus.

■
Illustration: **A Roman soldier's uniform and gear.**

F • O • C • U • S

Summary of Jewish History: 323 B.C.E. to 70 C.E.

Key persons and events are indicated by **bold** type.

323–200 B.C.E.

Alexander the Great died in 323 B.C.E., and the Greek empire was divided. Greek leaders located in both Syria and Egypt were given control of Palestine.

The Greeks in **Egypt** ruled most of Israel for about one hundred years. Though Greek influence was felt throughout Palestine (especially in Galilee), generally the Jews were allowed to conduct their internal affairs without interference from Greek authorities.

198–142 B.C.E.

From 198 to 142 B.C.E. the Greeks in **Syria** controlled all of Israel. The rulers imposed heavy taxation, and political and religious factions began to develop among the Jews. After the **desecration of the Temple** by the Greeks, the outraged Jews successfully rebelled. The Temple was rededicated (**Hanukkah**) in 164 B.C.E., and Jewish independence was gained by 142 B.C.E.

142–63 B.C.E.

The Jews were independent from 142 to 63 B.C.E. Unfortunately, they had poor leaders. Factions within Judaism became defined: **Sadducees** (more concerned about politics than religion), **Essenes** (religiously very strict and withdrawn), **Pharisees** (more concerned about religion than politics). Tension grew between the mainline Jews and the Galileans and between the mainline Jews and the Samaritans.

63 B.C.E.–36 C.E.

From 63 B.C.E. until well after the time of Jesus, the **Romans** ruled Palestine. In 37 B.C.E. **Herod the Great** was appointed its ruler. He was a political "success" but extremely cruel. He ruled until 4 B.C.E., and the **birth of Jesus** was very near the end of his reign (6 or 5 B.C.E.). After Herod's death came the **division of Palestine** among his three sons. One of them, **Herod Antipas**, was ruler of Galilee. Another son was put in charge of Judea, but he was such a poor leader that he was replaced with a Roman procurator. From 26 to 36 C.E. the procurator of Judea was **Pontius Pilate**, and **Jesus was crucified** during his term (about 30 C.E.).

66–70 C.E.

In 66 C.E. the **Zealots** began a revolt against the Romans, but they were totally crushed. In the year 70 came the **destruction of Jerusalem and the Temple,** and it was only on the strength of the Pharisees that Judaism was able to survive.

The Destruction of Jerusalem

The political confusion and division within Palestine lasted throughout Jesus' lifetime and beyond. Eventually the strong anti-Roman feelings among the Jews built to the point of exploding, fueled by the memory of the Jews' successful rebellion against their Greek overlords years earlier. Under the leadership of a revolutionary group known as the Zealots, an open rebellion against the Romans began in 66 C.E. But this time the Jews took on a power far too great in strength. The Romans totally crushed the rebels and destroyed Jerusalem and its Temple by the year 70. The Jews' hopes for freedom were destroyed, and only because of the strength of the Pharisees was Judaism able to survive and become the major world religion it is today.

This survey of the religious and political history of the Jewish people has been brief but certainly not simple. As the discussion of Jesus in the Gospels unfolds in the next several chapters, you may occasionally wish to refer to the brief summaries of this material offered on pages 61 and 72.

For Review

- Briefly explain how the Greeks—in particular the Syrian Greeks—came to dominate the people of Israel.
- Identify two major Jewish reactions to Greek rule.
- Identify and define three major political factions within Judaism that developed during the period of Jewish independence.
- Explain the origins of the Jewish hatred for the Samaritans.

An Oppressed People Dream of a Liberator

Out of this complex history there emerged within the Jewish people the dream that someday God would send them a great leader—the Messiah, the anointed One, the person whose title from the Greek language is "the Christ." The Jewish people dreamed of one who would overthrow their oppressors and restore them to the glory they had known in the days of David and Solomon. By the time of Jesus, the yearning among the Jews for the one who was to set them free had grown to great intensity.

From David's Line

The hope and expectation of God's promised deliverer was strongly associated with the kingship of David, the greatest of the Israelite kings. As discussed earlier in this chapter, the Israelites had

Jews of Jesus' day remembered how, centuries before, Moses had led the Israelites out of slavery in Egypt.
Photo: The desert of Midian, where the Israelites wandered after leaving Egypt; the site thought to be Mount Sinai is in the background.

turned to a king to unify them and lead them at a time when they were in chaos as a people and their very existence was threatened by their enemies. It was under David's kingship that all the tribes of Israel were finally united, and it was David who led the armies of Israel in defeating the nation's enemies.

For generations the Jews had yearned for a "son of David," one from the line of that beloved king who would restore them to their place of prominence in the world, who would lead them to victory over new enemies, who would bring them into an age of peace and prosperity.

Great Expectations

From the time of King David—about one thousand years before Jesus—"the One who is to come" was spoken of and described in different ways by different people. Over the many years of waiting, the son of David that the people yearned for took on mythic qualities.

By the time the Jews were living under the complete domination of the Romans, the Messiah had taken on the image of a mighty warrior-king, a great military leader, one who would overthrow the Romans and make the Jews a mighty and free nation once again. This militaristic image of the Messiah would clash dramatically with the life and message of Jesus and have major implications in the Gospel story. **8**

Behind the Jewish "No" to Jesus

Although the Jewish people had a wide range of understandings about the nature and role of the Messiah, it is certain that they would not have considered the Messiah to be the "divine son of God," as Christians understand him to be.

Remember that the Jewish understanding of God was such that the Jews could not even bring themselves to utter God's holy name. The idea of a human in some way "being God" would have been nothing short of unthinkable for the devout Jew. (The Jewish understanding of God would also have great implications for the Jewish response to Jesus' message in the future.)

Christians, in light of the Gospel story, profess that the One eventually sent by God was unlike any human expectation. Jesus of Nazareth was and is the Messiah and the One True Liberator. **9**

For Review

- Briefly explain the origins of the ancient Jews' expectations of the Messiah.

8
Ask a parent, or someone else a generation older than you, to tell you about an example of a people, nation, or group in the last twenty or so years that was living under an oppressive regime but was then freed from it. Write up the example.

9
Imagine what it would be like to yearn for a messiah in today's world. List five or more qualities that such a person would have to possess in order to be recognized as a great leader by people today.

One More Stop Before Jesus

Before moving directly into the story of Jesus, one final dimension of the world he entered will be explored in chapter 4. The Gospel portraits of Jesus are filled with stories and images drawn from the daily life and religion of the Jewish people—their homes, occupations, meals, customs, and more. Along with the religious history of the Jews, this information about the basic lifestyle of the people can make the Jesus of History much more real and personal to us. Background of this kind can make the Gospels more understandable and enjoyable to read, ultimately making the message of Jesus come alive for us.

■
The typical Jew of ancient Palestine dreamed of a great leader, the Messiah, who would overthrow the Roman oppressors and liberate the Jewish people.

Photo: **A Bedouin man today in Jordan, a country bordering modern-day Israel.**

4 Daily Life in Jesus' Time:
Culture and Religion

Jesus: Born in a Particular Time and Place

In This Chapter . . .

THEN the disciples of John [the Baptist] came to [Jesus], saying, "Why do we and the Pharisees fast often, but your disciples do not fast?" And Jesus said to them, "The wedding guests cannot mourn as long as the bridegroom is with them, can they? The days will come when the bridegroom is taken away from them, and then they will fast. No one sews a piece of unshrunk cloth on an old cloak, for the patch pulls away from the cloak, and a worse tear is made. Neither is new wine put into old wineskins; otherwise, the skins burst, and the wine is spilled, and the skins are destroyed; but new wine is put into fresh wineskins, and so both are preserved." (Matthew 9:14–17)

The Gospels are filled with passages like the one quoted above, expressing images and experiences from the day-to-day lives of first-century Jewish people. Along with reading about wineskins and old cloaks, we read about festivals and parties, the lilies of the field and the birds of the air, storms at sea, planting and harvesting, bread baking, young children playing, old people dying, and more.

One message of the Gospels, then, is this: Jesus was a Jew, born in a particular place within a particular culture at a particular time in history. A true understanding of Jesus must include a basic sense of his daily world. We need an appreciation for the subtle influences of his culture that were so much a part of who he was and the message he shared.

Jesus Spoke the Language of His People

Jesus' full immersion in the world of first-century Palestine enabled him to speak to his fellow Jews using images they understood and situations they could identify with. He, like them, was steeped in all the religious and social traditions of the day. He was nourished with the food and drink of his homeland and was brought to laughter by the parties and weddings of his people. Even the sickness, disease, and death that haunted daily life touched Jesus' life and often moved him to tears. Here are just a few examples of how Jesus' life experiences were woven into his teachings:

■

The Gospels are full of references to first-century Jews' everyday experiences, such as the work of farming and fishing.

Photo: **Women harvest grain in modern Israel.** *Background:* **A fishing net similar to nets the Apostles would have used.**

• The Pharisees and the Sadducees asked Jesus to show them a sign from heaven to prove he was the Messiah. Jesus responded: "When it is evening, you say, 'It will be fair weather, for the sky is red.' And in the morning, 'It will be stormy today, for the sky is red and threatening.' You know how to interpret the appearance of the sky, but you cannot interpret the signs of the times" (Matthew 16:2–3). Jesus' reference to forecasting the weather came out of his culture, and the message he conveyed with that reference was therefore significant to his listeners.

• The scribes challenged Jesus because of his dinner companions: "Why does he eat with tax collectors and sinners?" (Mark 2:16). Jesus said to them, "Those who are well have no need of a physician, but those who are sick; I have come to call not the righteous but sinners" (Mark 2:17). Discerning the meaning of this scene requires an understanding of the importance of meals in the life of the Jewish people.

• Jesus' first disciples heard his call to follow him while they were working as fishermen by the Lake of Gennesaret. Under Jesus' direction they netted such a huge number of fish that their nets began to tear, and two boats almost sank under the weight. From this experience of an almost too successful fishing trip, Jesus drew the point he wanted to make: "Do not be afraid; from now on you will be catching people" (Luke 5:10).

• Jesus was a carpenter, and the vocabulary of his trade found its way into his teaching: "Why do you see the speck in your neighbor's eye, but do not notice the log in your own eye? . . . You hypocrite, first take the log out of your own eye, and then you will see clearly to take the speck out of your neighbor's eye" (Matthew 7:3–5). The image of a log sticking out of one's eye may illustrate Jesus' occasional use of exaggeration to make a point, but without doubt his point is clearly made. **1**

This chapter will provide some general background on the geography and daily life of Jesus' time. It will also highlight key features of Judaism as it was practiced in Jesus' day. Only short glimpses into the past will be provided here, but this information should help to illuminate the rich human texture of the Gospels. This information should also enable you to read between the lines of the New Testament, and thereby better appreciate the message it often expresses through common life experiences.

For Review

• Why is a basic sense of Jesus' daily world important to understanding Jesus and his message? Illustrate your response with an example.

■

Photo: **The sun sets on the Sea of Galilee. Jesus' contemporaries forecast the weather by looking at the sky. A red sky at sunset meant the weather would be fair the next day.**

1

Select one of the four examples of Jesus' teachings given above. Keeping in mind the point Jesus was trying to make, rewrite the scene as you imagine it might occur today. For example, what words would Jesus use? Where would the scene take place?

Palestine: Great Variety in a Small Land

Today, the homeland of Jesus is commonly known as the Holy Land. In Jesus' time it was called the land of Canaan, the Promised Land, the land of Israel, or the land of Judah. As mentioned earlier, it was called Palestine by the Greeks.

A Land the People Knew Intimately

The Palestine that Jesus knew was roughly the size of Massachusetts, stretching just 145 miles from north to south and any-where from 25 to 87 miles from its western coast at the Mediterranean Sea to its eastern border. Yet this small area was the only world that Jesus ever knew. This may be astonishing, given the fact that today Jesus' home country can be traveled from one corner to another by car in a matter of just a few hours.

Even though the people of Jesus' time most often had to walk from town to town, it was still relatively easy for them to get around. The Jews were great walkers, thinking nothing of walking distances we might hesitate to drive. An average walker could go from Nazareth to Jerusalem (approximately ninety miles by road) in about two days, for example. This accounts in part for why Jesus and his disciples seem to move continually from one place to another in the Gospels. The

■ **Palestine—in Jesus' time as well as today—displays tremendous geographical diversity.**
Photo, left: **The lush western shore of the Sea of Galilee.**

Photo, inset: **The barren desert of Judah, near the Dead Sea.**

small geographic size of Palestine also explains in part the love the people had for their land—they simply knew it very well, just as a farmer knows every acre of her or his land "by heart." **2**

A Land of Beauty and Diversity

Geographical Diversity

Though Palestine was rather small, it held tremendous geographical diversity. The Gospels speak of lakeshores and hillsides, of deserts and forests. The area surrounding the Dead Sea was desolate and forbidding, and the area surrounding the Sea of Galilee (also known as the Lake of Gennesaret or the Sea of Tiberias) was lush and inviting. As one author puts it, "A walk of a single hour [took] one from the richest of plains to the bare hills where the sheep [grazed]; and the caravans, toiling under the hot wind of the desert, took hope again from the sight of the snow shining on [the mountain]" (Daniel-Rops, *Daily Life in the Time of Jesus,* page 15). The "mountains" of Palestine were really only large hills, but they gave a majesty to the land that impresses even today's traveler.

Varied Climate

In modern-day Palestine, the average temperature for the year is 72 degrees Fahrenheit. But temperature variations can be extreme, with frigid nights and hot days. Though rare, snow does fall in the region, yet the temperature around the barren Dead Sea can reach 122 degrees. Rain is scarce. When it comes, it often takes the form of violent storms, like the one mentioned in Matthew 7:24–27, where Jesus reminds his listeners of a time when "the rain fell, the floods came, and the winds blew."

Gifts of Life from the Land

Water: A Precious Resource

The lack of water was a serious issue in Jesus' time, and it is often referred to in the Gospels. The people had to dig many wells, and strict rules governed the use of water. The scarcity of water enhanced the people's love of their land's large bodies of water. They particularly treasured the Jordan River (which the Hebrew people crossed to enter the Promised Land and in whose waters Jesus himself was baptized) and the gorgeous Sea of Galilee.

In this context of scarce water, think of the imagery used by Jesus when, in talking to a Samaritan woman by a well, he referred to himself as living water:

Everyone who drinks of this water [from the well] will be thirsty again, but those who drink of the water that I will give them will never be thirsty. The water that I will give will become in them a spring of water gushing up to eternal life. (John 4:13–14) **3**

2
Write a paragraph about a natural place you know and love "by heart." Describe what that place means to you.

■
Illustration: In the desert region of Palestine, water was an especially precious resource. Hauling water from the local well was a daily chore.

3
List at least six characteristics of water that make it a symbol or image rich with meaning.

F • O • C • U • S

Sizing Up Palestine

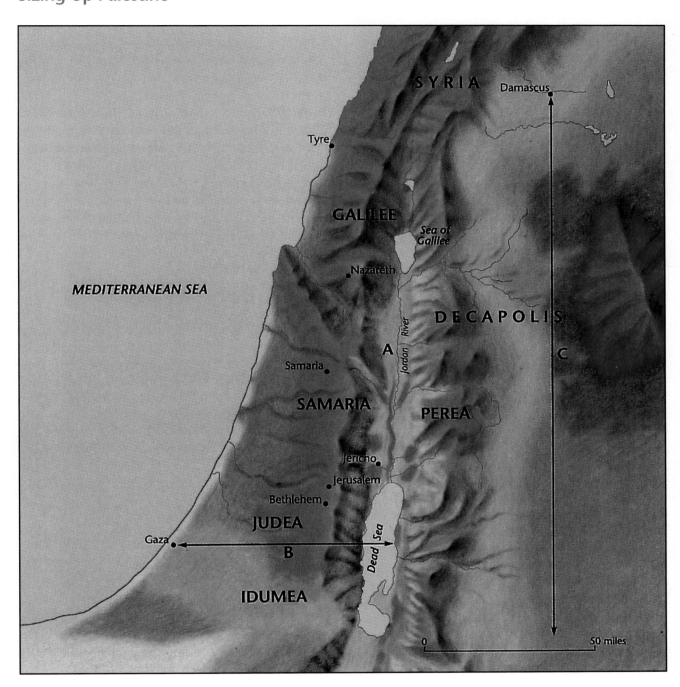

■ *A:* The Sea of Galilee and the Dead Sea are about sixty-five miles apart, but the meandering Jordan River, which connects these two bodies of water, is nearly three times that long.

B: A journey from Gaza to the eastern shore of the Dead Sea would cover about seventy miles—about the distance from San Francisco to Sacramento, or Chicago to Milwaukee.

C: A straight trip from Damascus in Syria to the southern tip of the Dead Sea covers about two hundred miles, roughly the same distance as from Boston to New York City, or Dallas to Austin.

Bread and Wine

With a great variation in climate and rainfall, it is not surprising that a wide variety of vegetation and foliage grew in Palestine. Trees and fruits were abundant, with juniper and oak the most common trees, and olive and fig trees the most valuable because of the oil and fruit they provided. And of course the people had the wonderful "fruit of the vine," the grapes from which the people made their deep, full-bodied red wines, so rich and thick that they had to be mingled with water before being served. Jesus referred to himself as the true vine (see John 15:1–17), and the Gospels refer several times to the vineyards and those who tended them.

The common grains of Jesus' time consisted of wheat—the most precious—along with oats and barley. Bread was the essential food of Jesus' day, so much so that bread alone could sometimes be a full meal. Bread was treated with great respect, and many Jewish laws governed its preparation and use. So when Jesus identified himself with the bread and wine at the Last Supper, it was clear to those gathered with him that he was revealing himself as one who could give them complete sustenance and fulfillment. He was in fact "the bread of life," who could totally satisfy the deepest hungers of people (see John 6:22–59).

The Christian celebration of the Eucharist, of "breaking bread together," has its origins in the central place that bread and wine occupied in the lives of the people of Jesus' day.

Animals

Both wild and domestic animals were abundant in Palestine. Among the common wild animals that Jesus would have known were boars, foxes, porcupines, hyenas, wolves, leopards, bears, and lions—many of which are mentioned in the Scriptures. Fish and birds of many kinds were also plentiful. The domesticated animals included sheep, oxen, donkeys, and cows. There were also pigs, which the Jews considered unclean animals, not to be eaten. Roosters, hens, and geese were common. The donkey was the most useful animal because of its strength and endurance; in fact, it was so highly valued that it could never be offered as a sacrifice. Camels were quite rare in Jesus' day. The only people on horseback were probably Roman soldiers. There were no family cats in Jesus' culture, and most of the dogs were half-wild relatives of wolves.

For Review

- What is one explanation for the sense that Jesus and his disciples continually move from place to place in the Gospels?
- Explain the importance of water to the people of Jesus' day.
- What was Jesus telling the people when he described himself as the bread of life?

■

A great variety of foods were grown in Palestine at the time of Jesus, as is true of the area today. *Photo:* **A woman sells vegetables in the Old City of Jerusalem.**

"Give Us This Day . . ."

Some of the richest imagery used in the Gospels is that of bread and all the tasks that surrounded the planting and harvesting of the grain from which bread was made. Some insight into these tasks is good to have when we come across such imagery in the Gospels.

The farmer of Jesus' day sowed the seed for cereal crops during November or December. By this time the autumn rains had softened the ground. Using plows pulled by oxen, some farmers plowed the soil before sowing, while others sowed the seed first and then plowed the seed into the ground. Rainfall during the winter and spring helped the crops grow, and the harvest took place between March and May.

The farmer reaped the crop with a sickle. The crop was then carried to a hard, flat piece of the ground used as a *threshing floor.* There the grain was separated from the straw by oxen either treading on it or pulling a wooden device, similar to a sled, over it.

The next task was *winnowing.* The farmer threw the threshed crop into the air with a pitchfork, and the breeze (either natural or created by a winnowing fan) carried away the light husks, or *chaff,* and the heavier grain fell back on the floor. The chaff was collected and burned, and the grain was sifted and bagged, ready to be ground into flour for bread making.

All these steps in the harvesting process, as well as the

later process of bread making, were well known by people of Jesus' day. In light of this brief description, consider the following passage from Matthew's Gospel, a passage that might normally mean little or nothing to the contemporary reader. In this passage, John the Baptist is telling his listeners about Jesus, whom he will soon baptize in the Jordan River:

> I am not worthy to carry his sandals. He will baptize you with the Holy Spirit and fire. His winnowing fork is in his hand, and he will clear his threshing floor and will gather his wheat into the granary [barn]; but the chaff he will burn with unquenchable fire.
> (Matthew 3:11–12)

(Adapted from Hughes and Travis, *Harper's Introduction to the Bible,* page 104)

■

Illustration: **Harvesters used a sickle to reap grain.**

The People and Their Daily Life

Nearly every lesson Jesus teaches in the Gospels is expressed through the common experiences of his people and their daily life—their food and meals, their housing and occupations. Here are some glimpses into these aspects of life in Jesus' time.

The Food and Meals of the Jews

Sharing a Meal: A Sacred Act

To the ancient Jewish people, the sharing of a meal was a sacred act. To "break bread" (bread was never cut but always broken) was an outward sign of unity and friendship. Whenever a meal is shared in the Gospels, you can be sure that something very significant is happening. No wonder people of the time reacted so strongly when Jesus ate with obvious sinners. The people were shocked by what they considered a demonstration of Jesus' outright approval of both the sinners and their sins. What Jesus was trying to show, however, was that he was offering a continually forgiving love to sinners, despite his disapproval of the sins they committed. "I have come to call not the righteous but sinners" (Matthew 9:13). **4**

Meat: On Special Occasions Only

Most people in Jesus' day ate very little meat. This food was considered a luxury and was available on a regular basis only to the wealthy. When Jesus told the parable of the prodigal son, he used this fact to express effectively the profound joy that the father felt when his son returned home:

Photo: **A Jewish woman, *right*, and her Arab neighbor prepare bread in Israel.**

4
According to many religious leaders, some of the problems of modern families can be explained by the fact that family members rarely eat meals together. Explain in writing why you agree or disagree with that claim.

"And get the fatted calf and kill it, and let us eat and celebrate; for this son of mine was dead and is alive again; he was lost and is found!" (Luke 15:23–24)

The people listening to Jesus knew that one only ate meat on very special occasions or during major celebrations, such as the Passover feast, when lambs were prepared and eaten.

Common Fare
The most common food other than bread was fish, and together bread and fish formed the most typical meal of Jesus' day. The people often dried and salted fish to preserve it, and they cooked fresh fish over a charcoal fire, as we see Jesus doing during an appearance to his disciples after his Resurrection (John 21:9–10).

Fruit was also an abundant food, as were nuts like walnuts, almonds, and pistachios. The only drink more common than wine was water. The wine was stored either in large jars or in containers made of goatskin. Jesus refers to these wineskins when teaching a lesson (as in Matthew 9:17).

The Dinner Table
Meals were often eaten in the open air and at flexible times of the day, for the people of Palestine had few of the concerns about schedules that often frustrate us today. At formal meals people ate in a reclining position rather than a sitting position. They generally ate with their hands from a flattened metal cup rather than using forks, spoons, and plates. Though most of their meals were simple, the Jews loved their occasional feasts and parties because of the sense of family and community togetherness these gatherings provided. Many times in the Gospels, a feast or another celebration forms a backdrop for the message of Jesus. **5**

The Typical House: Simple but Adequate

Design and Construction
Most of the houses of Jesus' time were neither large nor impressive. The majority of people were part of what we today would call the lower class, and their houses were usually one-room, whitewashed cubes. The houses normally had only one door, and the one room was often divided in half, with the people living on one side of the room and their animals living on the other. Some houses were built into the side of a hill, so that part of them was actually a cave. Most houses were made of clay, which was sometimes baked into bricks. Only the homes of the rich were made of stone.

The roof of the common house was made of wattling, which consisted of poles bound together by reeds and grass and then covered with earth. The wattling could be lifted off easily, as can be seen in the story of the cure of a paralyzed man:

• In order to get a paralyzed man to Jesus, the people who were carrying the man "removed the roof above [Jesus]; and after having dug through it, they let down the mat on which the paralytic lay" (Mark 2:4).

The roof usually had just enough slope to carry off rainwater. The people often kept tools on the roof, spread linen there to dry after washing, and even slept there on cool evenings. It was also quite common to sit on the roof during times of prayer and meditation.

Furnishings
Only the houses of the rich contained wood-burning stoves, but every village had at least one communal oven that all could use for cooking. The people's furniture was simple, consisting perhaps

5
Choose any one of the four Gospels and page through it. Jot down the chapter and verse numbers for every instance in which eating a meal is mentioned. For each one, describe the setting and reason for the meal.

of just a chest for storage and a bushel basket or wood container used for measuring grain at the market and then turned over for use as a table in the home. Small lamps were used for light. These were placed on lampstands and fueled by rancid olive oil, giving a familiar but unpleasant odor to all the houses. Jesus referred to these items when he said that people would not hide a lamp under a bushel basket, but rather would place it on a lampstand, where it could give light: "In the same way, let your light shine before others, so that they may see your good works and give glory to your Father in heaven" (Matthew 5:15–16; see also Mark 4:21–23; Luke 8:16–18).

The people slept on mats, which they rolled out in the evening, and they used pieces of wood or even stones as pillows. For warmth at night they wrapped themselves in their cloaks. These cloaks were made of camel or goat hair and were very thick, heavy, and waterproof. They were so sturdy, in fact, that they could stand up on their own! During the daytime these cloaks could be worn over lighter woolen tunics or coats. When Jesus told his followers, "If anyone wants to sue you and take your coat, give your cloak as well," he was telling them to turn over a very valuable possession—literally the shirt off their back (Matthew 5:40).

Above all, a person's home was the center around which his or her entire life revolved, primarily because Jewish family life was considered sacred—as will be seen later in this chapter.

■
Photo: **The village of Silwân (formerly Siloam) contains residential architecture reminiscent of ancient Jerusalem.**

F • O • C • U • S
John: Images from Daily Life

A quick scan of John's Gospel reveals frequent references to the daily life of the people of Jesus' time. John always tapped into apparently simple, commonplace realities to express deep insights into the meaning of Jesus and the God whom Jesus revealed. You may want to read one or more of the following passages from John, reflecting on them in light of the content of this chapter:

- The wedding at Cana (2:1–11)
- The multiplication of the loaves (6:1–15)
- Jesus as the bread of life (6:22–59)
- Jesus as the source of "living water" (7:37–39)
- Jesus as the good shepherd (10:1–21)
- "Unless a grain of wheat dies . . ." (12:20–26)
- The vine and the branches (15:1–17)

Common Occupations

Agriculture

The Jewish people of Jesus' day had a particular love for work related to the earth.

Farmers. Many people were farmers and shepherds, and images from these occupations fill the Gospels: the sower and the seed, the fields of wheat, the picking of corn (a grain unlike the corn we raise today), the people tending their sheep or cattle, and the laborers in the vineyard. Plowing, sowing, and harvesting all enter into the teachings of Jesus.

Fishers. Given the nature of the land and the diet of the people, it should not be surprising that fishing was another common and respected occupation. Jesus called his first disciples from this work (see Matthew 4:18–22; Luke 5:1–11), and he used imagery from fishing in many of his teachings. The basic qualities that made one a successful fisher may have attracted Jesus to those whom he chose as his first disciples. They were men of courage and patience, and they had hearty spirits. (In the Gospel of Mark, Jesus calls two of them, James and John, sons of thunder.) Perhaps most important, they had a basic trust in the goodness

■

Photo: **Bread was the essential food of Jesus' day. Christians today continue to celebrate Jesus as "the bread of life" in the Eucharist.**

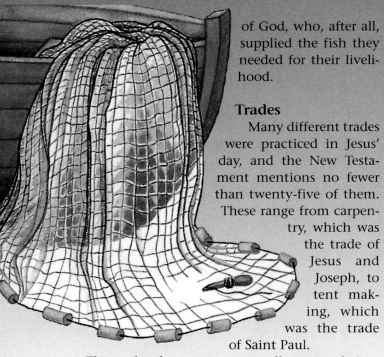

of God, who, after all, supplied the fish they needed for their livelihood.

Trades

Many different trades were practiced in Jesus' day, and the New Testament mentions no fewer than twenty-five of them. These range from carpentry, which was the trade of Jesus and Joseph, to tent making, which was the trade of Saint Paul.

The trade of carpentry was well respected. As a carpenter, Jesus may have built cabinets, made tools and other equipment for farmers, constructed small bridges, and so on. We can imagine that his years in that work gave him a sensitivity to the needs of the people he worked with. His trade would have also put him in touch with the glories of God's creation as he roamed the forests in search of good wood and then struggled to create something useful out of it.

Jewish society provided the earliest social legislation governing trade masters and their apprentices, and trade unions were even beginning among the Jewish laborers.

For Review

- What status did meals have among the Jews of Jesus' day?
- What qualities of fishers might have attracted Jesus to them when he was seeking disciples?
- What might Jesus have learned about life from his years as a carpenter?

■

Illustration, left: Jesus' first disciples were fishermen, and he used fishing imagery in many of his teachings.

■

Illustration, right: A carpenter's saw, typical of the kind Jesus would have used.

The Jewish Family: A Community of Faith

Not surprisingly, much of Jewish family life revolved around religion, including many family traditions and customs, the education of children at the synagogues, and so on. (More on Jewish religious practices will be offered later in this chapter.) The family was clearly recognized as the essential foundation of Jewish society, and the Law upheld the permanence and authority of the family. In fact, for the Jews, the family unit was a true religious community in and of itself, with the father being the chief leader, or celebrant, of many family religious feasts.

Betrothal and Marriage

People in Jesus' day married early in life. The men usually married at no later than age twenty. The women normally married as soon as they were physically able to bear children, which the Law defined as twelve and a half years of age. Mary, the mother of Jesus, was probably no older than fourteen when she bore him.

A Period of Engagement

Marriages were most commonly arranged by the parents, chiefly the father of the prospective husband. The actual marriage was preceded by a period of betrothal, or engagement, which lasted for about a year. This period gave the couple time to get to know each other. The Law, however, already recognized many of the rights and obligations of marriage during the time of betrothal. For example, a betrothed woman found guilty of adultery was stoned to death, just as she would have been if she were married; she was already considered the property of her future husband. Generally such punishment applied only to the woman. Adultery by a man was a crime only if it involved a married or betrothed woman, because in that case the act injured the stability of a family. This helps explain why Joseph wanted to quietly divorce Mary, rather than publicly accuse her of adultery, when he found out she was pregnant. If he had accused her publicly, the Law would have demanded that she be killed. (See Matthew 1:18–19.)

The Wedding Feast

The actual wedding was a great event, sometimes lasting for more than a week. There was much eating and drinking, as illustrated by the wedding at Cana. At that wedding Jesus' mother recognized that the lack of wine might ruin the party, and Jesus responded with his first miracle (John 2:1–11).

The Husband's Role

After the marriage, the husband was recognized as truly the head of the family. His wife even called him lord or master. Sons and daughters were recognized as his property, and the Law even allowed the father to sell them into slavery if they committed a crime. The commandment to "love thy father and mother" was so strong that historically the father had the right to put to death a child who disobeyed! This severe tradition was virtually gone by the time of Jesus, however.

Monogamy: The Ideal

Polygamy, or having more than one spouse at the same time, had been allowed for men early in the history of the Jews. By the time of Jesus, however, monogamy, the commitment to one spouse, was recognized as the ideal. Jesus, though he never directly condemned polygamy, elevated the role of women in his day dramatically and spoke out strongly on the sanctity of the marriage commitment.

Men and Women in Ancient Jewish Society

A Patriarchal Society

As the ancient laws governing adultery suggest, women were considered the property of men. In fact, in just about every way imaginable, women were considered inferior to men. For example, women did not eat with men but instead ate while standing and serving them. Women kept a dis-

Illustration: **For most people of Palestine in Jesus' time, daily life revolved around the activities of the village.**

tance from men on the streets and were restricted to certain areas of the Temple.

Only after learning of this male domination can one appreciate the tremendous effect of many of Jesus' words and actions on women in the Gospels. Take, for example, the apparently simple yet remarkable scene in which Jesus carries on a discussion with a woman at a public well. His disciples "were astonished that he was speaking with a woman" (John 4:27), because the practice was not tolerated. Consider also that in the Gospels, some of the first followers to learn of Jesus' Resurrection and proclaim it are women. What is so astonishing about this is that at the time, the testimony of women was not even recognized or accepted in a court of law.

A Just Society in Other Ways

Despite the inequalities just mentioned, Jewish women and children actually had a better life and were more respected and loved than those of many other cultures of the time. Women did have some recognized rights in Jewish society—for example, the right to be housed, clothed, and fed—and Jewish men took this responsibility seriously. Children were always recognized as a great blessing to Jewish families. Girls, however, were less desired than boys because girls married at such a young age and then became the property of someone else. Even so, the ancient Jews, to their credit, never resorted to the horrible pagan custom of the day in which unwanted children were simply and cruelly destroyed. In Jewish society, in fact, children were recognized as adults, with adult responsibilities and rights, at age thirteen. **6**

In Jesus' culture women did not eat with men but ate while standing and serving them. *Photo:* Women in Israel today.

For Review

- Why did Joseph want to quietly divorce Mary when he discovered she was pregnant?
- What was unusual about Jesus' actions and attitudes regarding women?
- Why were female children in Jesus' day regarded as less desirable than male children?

6

Fold a piece of paper in half to create two vertical columns. In the left column, list the major characteristics of Jewish family life in Jesus' day. In the right column, note how modern family life compares on each point listed in the left column.

Social Classes in the World of Jesus

Every society, it seems, gradually develops a series of social classes or groups: the "haves" and the "have-nots," the prestigious and the scorned, the politically powerful and the oppressed. Jesus' world was no different, except that the gap between the various classes was perhaps far greater than what most of us experience in the Western world today.

Predictably enough, in the Jewish society, part of what determined social position was religious tradition. The priestly class, for example, could claim some degree of social importance or nobility on religious grounds, though they had lost some of their historical power and influence to the scribes by the time of Jesus.

A Few Rich, Many Poor

No Middle Class

As in most cultures, social standing in Jewish society had a lot to do with money. Jesus talked often about the rich and the poor, primarily because the gap between the two was so great. A middle class in today's sense of the term simply did not exist. There were very few rich people, only those who had somehow acquired land and the power that went with it or who had accumulated wealth through trade or political influence. The vast majority of the people were part of the working class, who did not have much by our standards. Jewish society also had its very poor, who were comparable with today's homeless people.

Slavery in Jesus' Time

Slavery existed at the time of Jesus, and it enters into several of his parables (though in the New Testament, the term often used for slaves is *servants*). But slavery among the Jews was not nearly as common as it was among the Romans and the Greeks, where as much as one quarter of the population may have been slaves. Historical records show that in the Greek city of Delos, ten thousand slaves might have been traded in one day. And a wealthy Roman of the first century C.E. might have owned as many as two thousand slaves. Most Jews could not afford slaves.

The Law of Moses called for much better treatment of slaves than what was required in Roman culture, though no doubt Jewish legal principles were not always followed. The Jewish Law did demand, however, that all slaves be freed after seven years of service, and this fact made a Jewish slave worth much less money than a pagan slave. Therefore, Jewish slaves were less popular and fewer in number than pagan slaves, and this may partly explain why Jesus did not seem greatly concerned about the slavery issue directly. Certainly, however, Jesus' entire message of love and human freedom contradicted every argument people could use to justify slavery.

In-groups and Outcasts

As noted earlier, ancient Jewish society included many occupations and trades. People who worked hard were greatly respected. Some workers, however, were held in higher esteem than others. Sandal makers and woodworkers were thought to be better, for example, than tanners (who smelled bad) and perfume salesmen (who were in continual contact with prostitutes).

As discussed in chapter 3, mainline Jews felt great contempt for groups such as the Samaritans. Other social outcasts included those who were labeled unclean (lepers, for example), the extremely poor, the sick, and of course, women. Judaism excluded all of these people from the center of religious life. **7**

The Social Classes and Jesus' Ministry

Imagine the incredible impact of Jesus' ministry and message in the ancient Jewish social setting. Jesus challenged and even condemned his own society on virtually every level.

■

Photo: **Jesus freely associated with women and accepted them as central participants in his ministry.**

7
List the groups considered outsiders in the religion or the culture you are most familiar with. For each group, provide at least one example of how the members are discriminated against.

- The society rejected the poor and the weak, yet Jesus made these people the very center of his message and those to be most honored.
- The Jewish people deeply hated the Samaritans, yet in Jesus' preaching the Samaritan is seen as good, while the selfishness of the Jewish priest is condemned (Luke 10:29–37).
- The society, at best, tolerated women, but Jesus freely associated with them and accepted them as central participants in his ministry.
- Jesus embraced with love and compassion the sick and the "unclean," who were rejected by his people. He scolded those with wealth and power who refused to share with those in need.

Jesus was more than a social revolutionary, more than someone committed to changing the social conditions of the people. He proclaimed a freedom deeper than freedom from social, economic, or political oppression. But it can never be ignored or minimized that his message included the condemnation of all social oppression—hunger, racial and sexual discrimination, political domination, and all the things that kept people from experiencing the fullness of life that was due them as sons and daughters of a loving God.

For Review

- Why did Jesus often speak about the rich and the poor?
- Give two reasons that slavery was not practiced as much among the Jews as among the Greeks and the Romans.
- Give three examples of how Jesus challenged his society's social structure.

Major Features of Judaism

For the Jewish people, political history and religious history were heavily intertwined. Political events were understood as religious events, and political and religious leaders were often the same. Although much of the material in chapter 3 and thus far in chapter 4 has touched on aspects of Jewish faith, the following section will highlight some of the significant places, practices, and people of Judaism in Jesus' day. It will especially focus on those features that play a part in the Gospel stories. **8**

Special Places

Jerusalem: The Holy City

Jerusalem was clearly a unique and central city for the Jews of Jesus' time. Its geographical position, in central Palestine, made it ideal as a capital, a fortress, and a center of marketing. But more important, it was recognized as a holy city, and had been so for ten centuries before Jesus. The Jews of the Diaspora, who lived outside Palestine, dreamed of one day seeing Jerusalem's beautiful gates, walking its bustling streets, and setting their eyes on the Temple, the building that symbolized and celebrated the Jews' entire history as a people of faith. At the time of Jesus, Jerusalem was a major city of some 150,000 people, but that number could swell to 500,000 during the great religious feasts. For a person of Jewish faith, to take steps on the soil of the city of Jerusalem was to walk on holy ground.

To this central and holy Jewish city, Jesus would cry out:

8

As you read the following section on the major features of Judaism in Jesus' day, make a list of those features. For each one, try to identify a parallel feature in modern Roman Catholicism.

Jerusalem, Jerusalem, the city that kills the prophets and stones those who are sent to it! How often have I desired to gather your children together as a hen gathers her brood under her wings, and you were not willing! (Matthew 23:37)

The Temple

Rebuilt by Herod. Just before Jesus' time, Herod the Great began adding the last beautiful touches to Jerusalem, which the remnant had begun to rebuild five hundred years earlier. The crowning achievement of his building efforts would be to rebuild the Temple as it was in Solomon's time. Herod's work on the Temple began about fifteen years before Jesus' birth. It was not completed until nearly thirty-five years after Jesus' death, only to be totally destroyed by the Romans a short time after its completion. The present Western Wall, in Jerusalem, is all that remains of Herod's efforts.

It is hard for us to gain a sense of the Temple's splendor. Thirteen gates opened into the Temple proper, and one of them, the Nicanor Gate, was made entirely of bronze and was so large that it took twenty men just to open it! The sound of this gate opening signaled the beginning of the day for the people of Jerusalem.

A place of offerings, prayer, and governing. The Temple was at the center of the lives of the People of God. Sacrifices were offered there. Particularly important sacrifices accompanied all major feasts, and lesser sacrifices were offered as signs of thanksgiving or by those seeking forgiveness for their sins. Such rituals were officially recognized by the Jews as outward signs of an honest interior religious attitude. Still, many of the people actually viewed these sacrifices as having almost magical power.

The Temple was for prayer as well as sacrifice. (The story of the Pharisee and the tax collector, in Luke 18:9–14, illustrates this fact.) It was also the seat of the religious, political, and judicial body of the Jews, which was called the Great Sanhedrin. The Temple was so large that it could hold literally thousands of priests and tens of thousands of believers at once.

A den of robbers? By recognizing the centrality of the Temple to the religious life of the Jews, we can begin to appreciate why at one point Jesus stormed into the Temple. He was enraged by the way the money changers had been desecrating it and cheating the people. Turning over tables and scattering chairs and pigeons alike, he shouted words of the Scriptures of Judaism: "'My house shall be a house of prayer'; / but you have made it a den of robbers" (Luke 19:46).

■
The Temple in Jerusalem was the center of Jewish life.
Photo: **A model of Herod's Temple, part of the scale model of Jerusalem displayed at the Holyland Hotel, Jerusalem.**

F • O • C • U • S

The Scriptures of Judaism

The Scriptures of Judaism (known to most Christians as the Old Testament) were originally sacred stories and teachings that the people of Israel passed on by word of mouth from generation to generation. Some of these stories and teachings—the Psalms, for example—were actually songs before they were committed to writing.

The Jews became known as the People of the Book because of their total commitment to their Scriptures. So thoroughly did these writings dominate their lives that not a single written work from ancient Israel has been found that is not directly related to their Bible.

The works of the prophets held particular importance for the Jews. Two of these prophets—Isaiah and Jeremiah—were referred to in chapter 3's brief overview of the history of the Jews. Other prophets, like Elijah, Amos, Hosea, and Ezekiel, were also cherished by the Jews. This accounts for the recurring phrase, in the Gospels and elsewhere, about the Jewish commitment to "the Law and the prophets."

The Hebrew Bible developed over a very long period. Even the individual books of the Hebrew Bible took a long time to develop, with the Book of Psalms, for example, taking as long as eight hundred years to be compiled.

Jesus was deeply and prayerfully aware of the Scriptures of Judaism, and many of his sayings and teachings reflect this fact. Anytime we hear Jesus say, "You have heard it said . . ." or "It is written that . . . ," he is referring to the Bible of the Jews or, less often, to the teachings of the rabbis regarding those sacred Scriptures.

About two hundred years before Jesus' time, a Greek version of the Jewish Scriptures was developed, and the early church used this version in its worship. When Jewish leaders set the canon of their Scriptures in about 90 C.E., however, they did not include a few of the books from the Greek version. The Catholic canon of the Old Testament consists of all forty-six books from the Greek version.

■
The Hebrew Bible is as central to worship at Jewish synagogues today as it was in Jesus' time. After the Romans destroyed the Temple in 70 C.E., synagogues became the places of worship.

Photo: **A synagogue today.**

Synagogues

After the Temple's destruction by the Romans in 70 C.E., the synagogues became the central places of worship. Some traditions say that these houses of prayer originated during the Babylonian Exile as a substitute for the Temple.

Each village had at least one synagogue, and any adult male Jew had the right to erect one or even turn his house into one. Sacrifices were never offered in the synagogues, but precious scrolls containing the Scriptures of Judaism were kept there.

A synagogue was open three times a day for prayer and occasionally for other gatherings, but weekly Sabbath worship was the chief gathering held there. It is hard to overestimate the importance of the synagogue in the lives of the believers of Israel. In John's Gospel, for example, it is mentioned that the Jews who followed Jesus were threatened with the denial of their synagogue privileges as a severe punishment.

The synagogue remains to this day the center of Jewish communal life. It assured the Jews' survival as a people over the last two thousand years, as Judaism became strictly a "religion of the word," based on the sacred Scriptures.

Central Religious Practices

Daily Life: Consecrated to God in Prayer

The faithful Jew was expected to live a life of personal prayer in the home. At dawn and at nightfall, the Jew recited the familiar **Shema** prayer:

Hear, O Israel: The Lord is our God, the Lord alone. You shall love the Lord your God with all your heart, and with all your soul, and with all your might. (Deuteronomy 6:4–5)

This was the minimum of religious observance.

The truly faithful Jew also set aside three other times for prayer each day: morning, afternoon, and evening. These were primarily times for prayers of praise and prayers asking for God's blessing. Thus Jesus grew up in a religious tradition based heavily on personal and communal prayer as well as on the sacred Scriptures.

The Week: Consecrated to God on the Sabbath

A sign of the covenant. The **Sabbath** is a weekly day of rest and prayer for the Jews. It is such a significant religious observance that it is mentioned nearly seventy times in the Gospels alone. The Sabbath day is based on the Creation story from the Book of Genesis, in which God rests after creating the world. The day is also linked historically to the Exodus. In the early history of the Jews, people who violated the Sabbath laws were put to death, but this severe practice was no longer the case in Jesus' time. Still, the Sabbath was recognized as a sacred sign of God's covenant and presence with the people.

Unlike our days, which begin at midnight, a day for the Jew begins at sunset. Therefore, the Jewish Sabbath actually lasts from what we know as Friday evening through the daylight hours of Saturday. In ancient times, the Sabbath was the only day of the week that had a name of its own. All other days were either numbered or identified in relation to it. For example, a Jew might have referred to "the day before Sabbath."

Prohibitions and regulations. Strict prohibitions and regulations governed observance of the Sabbath: No housework or cooking could be done by the women; no labor of any kind could be

The Impact of Religion: Greater than We Think

Jesus was a devout Jew, immersed in the history, religious traditions, and rich prayer life of the Jewish people. To gain a sense of the importance of Jesus' religion to him, consider for a moment the ways religious heritage touches all dimensions of the lives of Roman Catholics. Try to imagine, for example, how Catholics would be affected by the following:

• if all Catholic churches in every part of the world locked their doors for one year so that Catholics and their families could not celebrate communal worship
• if Christmas and everything surrounding it—the worship, the carols, the gift giving, the manger scenes, the family traditions—were dropped for one year
• if Easter and all the joyous events that surround it were not allowed for one year
• if every religious symbol and expression in a Catholic's home—from a religious picture on the wall to family prayer before meals—were taken away for a year

• if a practicing Catholic could be controlled in such a way that she or he were unable to pray even privately for one year, never able to turn to God in moments of need
• if every Bible in every home, church, and school were confiscated and locked away for a year

Granted, this is hard to imagine, but that is precisely the point. The purpose of this exercise is to illustrate that religious traditions are part of a person's identity, not simply realities that are artificially attached and therefore easily discarded. Many religious impulses arise from within—as in the need to reach out to God in prayer at certain moments in life, or in yearning to celebrate great and joyous events with other people. As individuals become more deeply involved in communal religious experiences, these communal experiences become a deeper part of life—personally valuable and life-giving.

performed. It was unlawful to light a fire, so the people had "Sabbath lamps," which were fueled and tended by the woman of the house during the Sabbath observance. It was even against the law to walk using a wooden leg on this day! After the Friday evening meal, the people could not eat again until after the Saturday morning synagogue service, and special prayers then accompanied each meal during the remainder of the Sabbath. **9**

The rabbis constantly argued with others and among themselves about how closely the Sabbath laws were to be followed. Jesus spoke for many of the rabbis when he proclaimed, "The sabbath was made for humankind, and not humankind for the sabbath." But he added, "the Son of Man is lord even of the sabbath," a claim that could not help but offend and greatly anger many people (Mark 2:27–28).

9
Give your opinion in writing about this statement: *In today's world, it is a good idea to set aside one day every week for rest and reflection.*

The Jewish Year: Consecrated to God Through Religious Feasts

The Gospels indicate the central role of several key religious festivals and feasts in Jewish religious life. These were occasions to glorify, thank, and petition Yahweh. Some of the feasts were celebrated in the people's homes or in small groups with a master and his disciples. But even these feasts had a strong communal character, with the individual Jews sensing their unity as one nation turned to its God. Each feast had public ceremonies as well, and for the Jews of the Diaspora, many feasts were occasions for pilgrimages to Jerusalem.

Initially some of the Jewish feasts were probably nature feasts borrowed from other traditions—for example, feasts of spring and the harvest—which gradually took on religious dimensions through the Jews' long history. Many of the feasts were serious and penitential in nature, reminding the Jews of their failures to follow the will of God. Other feasts were highly festive and had a cheerful, carnival atmosphere.

We must be conscious of three major Jewish feasts if we are to fully understand the Gospel accounts of Jesus' life. These religious feasts are still celebrated by Jews around the world.

Pentecost. Also known as the Feast of Weeks, **Pentecost** is a celebration of Yahweh's giving the Law to Moses. The word *Pentecost* itself is based on the Greek word for "fiftieth" and reflects the fact that it was fifty days after leaving Egypt before Moses received the Law on Mount Sinai. Historically, this feast also celebrated the Jews' harvesttime, a time for experiencing and expressing deep gratitude for the wonderful gifts of Yahweh. (The Christian feast of Pentecost celebrates the coming of the Holy Spirit to the Apostles, which occurred during the Jewish feast of Pentecost.)

The Day of Atonement. In autumn, a series of three feasts follow in quick succession—all within twenty-two days of each other: the Feast of the Jewish New Year (Rosh Hashanah), the **Day of Atonement** (Yom Kippur), and the Feast of Tabernacles. The Day of Atonement is of such central importance to the Jews that if a person simply mentions "the Day," everyone knows that he or she is referring to this special feast. It is a time for the Jews to solemnly repent of all their sins.

In Jesus' time—as today—the Day of Atonement involved moving ceremonies, fasting, prayer, and ritual bathings. Also on this day, the high priest would enter the sacred Holy of Holies in the Temple to purify it with the mingled blood of a goat and a bull.

Passover. Of all the feasts of the year, the holiest and most celebrated is **Passover,** commemorating the miraculous liberation of the Israelites

Photo: A Jewish family gathers for Friday evening Sabbath prayer.

from Egypt. Lasting a week, this marks the beginning of the Jewish religious year. It traditionally included the Temple sacrifice of lambs (known as **paschal lambs**, from the word *pasch,* meaning "to pass over") and the ritual of a special meal recalling the one eaten by Moses and the Israelites before the Exodus. Obviously, Passover is a very cheerful feast for the Jews. It played a central role in the Gospel events surrounding the final days of Jesus' life. **10**

Key Religious-Political Groups and Persons

The Gospels repeatedly refer to various factions within Judaism. The following groups or classes of people are particularly significant. (The Sadducees and the Pharisees were discussed briefly in chapter 3; see page 66.)

The Priestly Caste

Priests were known in Jewish history as far back as the time of Moses, but they took on special importance during the time of the kings, when the Temple became a national institution. The priests served as go-betweens, or intermediaries, between God and the people, offering sacrifices in the Temple. They were considered the guardians of worship.

Originally a man could be recognized as a priest simply because he was a member of a certain tribe. By the time of Jesus, however, the powerful officials of the Temple—the Great Sanhedrin (described below)—chose priests from among the many members of that particular tribe. The priests were supposedly selected on the basis of "respectability," but that often meant wealth or social prestige. The priesthood, therefore, became a very exclusive class and was often hated by the common people.

The high priest. The high priest was the head of the priestly caste. He held a special kind of authority that went beyond his role as a spiritual leader. He was anointed in much the same way that the kings of his day were anointed, he lived in a lavish palace, and he dressed in colorful and highly recognizable clothing. The appointment of the high priest was made by political masters of the country, and a lot of intrigue—and sometimes money—entered into the selection. As the spiritual leader of his people, the high priest had so much influence that politicians always wanted to stay on his good side.

■

Photo: **Olive trees were prized for the oil their fruit produced. Olive oil was used extensively both in religious rituals and in daily life.**

10
Find out from someone who is Jewish how the feast of Passover is celebrated, or research this feast if you cannot speak to anyone personally. Write a description of the feast.

All of this helps explain the role of the high priest in the Gospels, particularly in the trial of Jesus. During the trial, the high priest is a man named Caiaphas. Pontius Pilate treats Caiaphas with real caution and consideration because of his position of importance and influence among the Jewish people.

Sadducees

The Sadducees were mainly the aristocracy of the priestly caste. Though not all Sadducees were priests, all were part of the Jewish upper class— meaning that they had a lot of political power. The power base of the Sadducees was Jerusalem because of their great commitment to the Temple and its sacrificial worship. They were liberal in politics (in that they were willing to compromise with the people in power), but they were very conservative in religion. For example, they accepted only the first five books of the Hebrew Scriptures (called the Pentateuch, the **Torah,** or simply the Law), and they rejected all attempts to add to or interpret the basic Law contained there. They also rejected any belief in a resurrection after death, which at Jesus' time was a rather recent religious belief among some Jews. An example of the Sadducees' conflicts with Jesus on this point can be found in Mark 12:18–27, in which they pose a problem for him.

With the destruction of the Temple by the Romans in 70 C.E., this group eventually lost power and died out.

Pharisees

The Pharisees were the chief political and religious rivals of the Sadducees, so there was often tension between the two groups. The Pharisees originated from the Hasidim, the group known as the pious ones because of their strict adherence to the Law. By the time of Jesus, however, the Pharisees were far more liberal in religious matters than were the Sadducees. For example, the Pharisees were open to new developments in Jewish thought, such as accepting other books of the Scriptures besides the first five when judging matters of the Law. This openness led them to create an extensive oral commentary on the Law to help people live it more fully. Their commitment to the Law rather than the Temple, as in the case of the Sadducees, enabled the Pharisees to survive beyond the destruction of the Temple in 70 C.E. The Judaism of today is derived from Pharisaism.

Unlike the Sadducees, the Pharisees were conservative politically; that is, they rejected any attempts to compromise with their political rulers. Because of this attitude they were greatly respected by the common people.

A caution on stereotyping. Perhaps no single group receives a more negative treatment in the Gospels than the Pharisees. Jesus' comments about this group (and about the scribes) in Matthew 23:13–36 can make the reader wince, nearly embarrassed by the rage of Jesus against these people. The strongly negative image of the Pharisees presented in the Gospels may well reflect some of the early church's conflicts with this group; this is particularly the case in John's Gospel. We should be careful, however, about stereotyping the Pharisees according to this limited impression of them.

No doubt, Jesus did have serious conflicts with the Pharisees over their interpretation of the Law and their tendency to be overly legalistic. But certainly Jesus must have greatly admired some of the Pharisees for their religious fervor. Note, too, that the Pharisees had no official part in the trial and execution of Jesus.

An exaggerated negative understanding of the Pharisees, especially when used as a description of the Jewish people in general, has led in part to bitter **anti-Semitism**, or social rejection of the Jews, throughout the Jews' long history. Christians have an obligation to help change this false perception of the Jews, and nothing will accomplish that more than a clear presentation of the facts.

Zealots

The beginnings of the **Zealots**—at least the beginnings of the attitudes they represented— may have gone back to the time of the Jewish revolt against the Greek overlords from Syria, almost two hundred years before Jesus' time. The Zealots maintained that Jewish independence could be attained only through a military overthrow of the Romans. It is possible that some of them may have been attracted to Jesus at first because of his strong leadership, but his obvious commitment to nonviolence likely led them to reject him eventually.

Tax Collectors

As mentioned in chapter 3, the Syrian Greeks began taxing the Jews to help pay off debts to the Romans. The Jews were also expected to pay a Temple tax to their own leaders, and this double taxation became nearly unbearable, amounting to some 40 percent of a family's total income. In order to collect the taxes from the Jews, the Romans hired Jewish agents who were expected to attain a certain quota of taxes, after which they could keep whatever "extra" money they managed to collect. These agents were the notorious **tax collectors** we read about in the Gospels, and they were clearly a despised group of men. The tax collectors were also called **publicans.**

The Great Sanhedrin

The word *sanhedrin* literally means "assembly" or "senate." The **Great Sanhedrin** was the official governing body of the Jews, and it was recognized as such by the Romans. It consisted of seventy members plus a president. The position of president was often filled by the high priest, and the members of the Great Sanhedrin were representatives of the priestly families, the scribes and doctors of the Law, and the elders (*elders* was the title given to outstanding Jewish laymen). Both the Pharisees and the Sadducees were represented, but the Sadducees had much greater influence because of their strong relationship with the political powers. The Great Sanhedrin voted on the laws, had its own police force, and controlled everything to do with religion—which, as has been noted, meant virtually all of Jewish life. In the trial of Jesus, the Great Sanhedrin acted like a kind of supreme court.

Scribes

The scribes had their origins during the Exile in Babylon. They were both writers (as the term *scribe* indicates) and jurists, or interpreters of the Law. They had the task of carefully studying the Law and passing judgment on those who broke it. This group organized the Hebrew Scriptures much as we know them in the Old Testament today. The most respected of the scribes were given the title *doctor of the Law,* and when scribes were in a position of teaching, they were given the title **rabbi,** meaning "master" or "teacher." They taught in the synagogues. The scribes, as previously noted, are often mentioned in the Gospels along with the Pharisees, but the two groups were not identical. Though many of the scribes no doubt belonged to the Pharisaic party, not all of them did. **11**

For Review

- Why did the synagogues become more important for the Jews after the time of Jesus?
- What was the origin of the Sabbath day, and what was it a sign of?
- Identify and briefly describe the three major religious feasts of the Jews.
- Identify the major characteristics of both the Sadducees and the Pharisees. Why did the Sadducees have greater political power than the Pharisees?

On to the Story of Jesus

Chapters 3 and 4 have sketched out the social, political, and religious world that Jesus entered, preached to, and was largely rejected by. As you have learned, it was a complex setting of deep religious convictions and great political tensions. The oppression and near despair of the People of God was profoundly real, and their hunger for salvation and a savior was intense. Chapter 5 will turn to the story of Jesus and the message he proclaimed to that desperate world.

11
Using an encyclopedia or other sources, write a one-page essay that expands on any feature of ancient Judaism discussed in this chapter.

■
Jesus entered a world whose people suffered oppression and despair, and who longed for a savior.
Photo: **The sun breaks through a storm on the Sea of Galilee.**

5
The Mission Begins:
Preparing the Way of the Lord

In This Chapter . . .

- The Infancy Narratives
- The Hidden Years of Jesus' Life
- The Beginnings of Jesus' Public Life
- Wandering Preacher, Unique Teacher

THE beginning of the good news of Jesus Christ, the Son of God.

As it is written in the prophet Isaiah,

"See, I am sending my messenger ahead of you, who will prepare your way."

. . . .

John the baptizer appeared in the wilderness, proclaiming a baptism of repentance for the forgiveness of sins. And people from the whole Judean countryside and all the people of Jerusalem were going out to him, and were baptized by him in the river Jordan, confessing their sins. . . . [John] proclaimed, "The one who is more powerful than I is coming after me; I am not worthy to stoop down and untie the thongs of his sandals. I have baptized you with water; but he will baptize you with the Holy Spirit."

In those days Jesus came from Nazareth of Galilee and was baptized by John in the Jordan. And just as he was coming up out of the water, he saw the heavens torn apart and the Spirit descending like a dove on him. And a voice came from heaven, "You are my Son, the Beloved; with you I am well pleased."

And the Spirit immediately drove him out into the wilderness. He was in the wilderness forty days, tempted by Satan. (Mark 1:1–13)

And so the mission of Jesus began—at least as it is described by the Evangelist Mark. After this brief introduction to his Gospel, Mark begins a discussion of the public ministry of Jesus.

But pause for a moment and ask yourself: Isn't there something missing here? Is this where the story of Jesus begins—with John the Baptist and the baptism of Jesus? What about the birth of Jesus, the event that Christians throughout the world celebrate to this day with elaborate and joyous traditions? What about his childhood?

These questions surrounding Jesus' birth and early years were precisely the ones raised by the early Christians as the Gospels began to develop. Many people could recall from personal experience the early days of Jesus' public ministry. Many had listened to his words and seen his works. But where did he come from, what was his childhood like, and what did he do *before* he came among them as a thirty-year-old man?

The Infancy Narratives

Familiar Scenes and Stories

In an effort to provide a faith-filled response to the natural questions of the early faith community, Matthew and Luke began their Gospels with writings that have come to be known as the infancy narratives—stories about the birth of Jesus and his early life. The Gospel of John, like that of Mark, does not describe the birth or childhood of Jesus. Instead, John's Gospel begins with a magnificent and poetic statement of what it meant for the

Jesus began his mission by being baptized in the Jordan River by John the Baptist.
Photo, facing page: The Jordan River. *Background:* The waters of baptism are a source of purification and new life.

John: "In the Beginning . . ."

"And the Word Became Flesh"

While Matthew and Luke describe the origins of Jesus through their infancy stories, John speaks of the origins of Jesus and the nature of his ministry in a complex, poetic, highly philosophical prelude to his Gospel, called the

prologue (John 1:1–18). As is true of the prologues in most works, this one was likely written after the rest of the book had been completed. Here is just a part of what John has to say about Jesus' origins and his ministry:

> In the beginning was the Word, and the Word was with God, and the Word was God. . . .
> He was in the world, and the world came into being through him; yet the world did not know him. He came to what was his own, and his own people did not accept him. . . .
> And the Word became flesh and lived among us, and we have seen his glory, the glory as of a father's only son, full of grace and truth. (1:1,10–14)

Revealing the Very Essence of God

The Gospel of John was the last Gospel to be written, and it reflects many years of prayerful reflection about the nature of Jesus and his message. To decipher the full meaning of Jesus, John goes

back in time further than Jesus' human birth in Bethlehem. John explores the origins of Jesus in the heart of God before the beginning of time. To do this, John speaks of Jesus as "the Word." What does John mean by this? Words, whether spoken or written, communicate to us the reality or meaning they represent. So as the divine Word, Jesus reveals to us the reality of God. John tells us that in Jesus we encounter the fullest expression, the very essence, of God.

The other Gospels, for the most part, slowly and gradually reveal Jesus' true identity as the Son of God. John's Gospel proclaims Jesus as the Son of God at its starting point.

■
"And the Word became flesh and lived among us."
Photo: **A view of earth from the Apollo 11 spacecraft; most of Africa and portions of Europe and Asia can be seen.**

"Word of God" to become human in the person of Jesus. (See "John: 'In the Beginning . . .'" on page 106.) **1**

In the Gospel of Matthew

In the Gospel of Matthew we do not read about the public preaching of John the Baptist or the baptism of Jesus until the third chapter. That material is preceded by an introduction.

- The introduction begins with the genealogy, or family tree, of Jesus, tracing his roots back to Abraham (1:1–17).
- The genealogy is followed by the story of Mary and Joseph (including the statement that the child she has conceived is "from the Holy Spirit") and then a simple description of Jesus' birth and the giving of his name (1:18–25).
- We then learn of the visit of the Magi, or Wise Men, who follow a star to the place of Jesus' birth and present gifts of gold, frankincense, and myrrh (2:1–12).
- The story of the Magi is followed by that of the flight of Joseph, Mary, and Jesus into Egypt as Herod begins to slaughter innocent children, in the hope of eliminating a possible rival to his throne (2:13–18).
- Last, we read of the return of Jesus' family to Palestine and the town of Nazareth in Galilee, where Jesus is to be raised (2:19–23).

These are very familiar scenes to most Christians. The touching images are recalled by families and parish communities each Christmas season.

In the Gospel of Luke

If we look at Luke's treatment of the early life of Jesus, we discover information not contained in Matthew's account.

Luke's preface to the stories about Jesus' birth. Luke begins his infancy narrative with events that happened before Jesus was born, mainly dealing with Jesus' announcer, John the Baptist.

1
Make a list of words, phrases, objects, places, and names associated with Christmas—as many as you can think of. While reading about the infancy narratives, put a check mark by the items on your list that seem to have a basis in the Gospels.

■
Photo: A depiction of the adoration of Jesus by the Magi, a fifteenth-century painting by Fra Angelico and Fra Filippo Lippi.

- In Luke's preface we find a rather detailed description of how John the Baptist came to be born to a priest named Zechariah and his elderly wife, Elizabeth (1:5–25).
- The preface is followed by the angel Gabriel's announcement to Mary that she is to bear a son named Jesus, who will be called the "Son of the Most High" (1:26–38). (Catholics celebrate this event even today with the Feast of the Annunciation, on March 25.)
- We then learn of Mary's visit to Elizabeth, who is her relative (1:39–45). Upon discovering that Mary is pregnant, Elizabeth exclaims, "Blessed is the fruit of your womb." Elizabeth's exclamation, together with the angel Gabriel's greeting to Mary, form the first part of the prayer we now know as the Hail Mary.
- In a prayer now called the **Magnificat**, we read Mary's beautiful response to the realization that she is to bear a special son (1:46–55). Mary's prayer is actually a collection of many verses from the Old Testament.
- Last, we find several scenes centering on John the Baptist: his birth, his circumcision and naming, and a prophetic prayer by his father, Zechariah (1:57–80).

Luke's stories about Jesus' birth and early life. It is only after all of the above information has been shared that Luke begins to describe the birth of Jesus and the events that follow it. Much in Luke's version of these events has found its way into Christmas traditions and therefore into the minds and hearts of most Christians. Some of these ideas are found only in Luke's Gospel.

- Luke offers this familiar description of the birth of Jesus: "[Mary] wrapped him in bands of cloth, and laid him in a manger, because there was no place for them in the inn" (2:7).

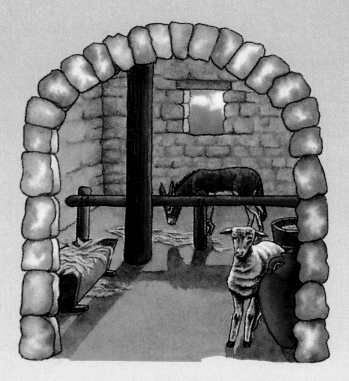

- As noted earlier, in Matthew's Gospel the Magi are led by a star to the place where they find Jesus. But in Luke's Gospel, poor shepherds hear of the marvelous birth from an angel who announces, "to you is born this day in the city of David a Savior, who is the Messiah, the Lord" (2:11). Luke does not mention the Wise Men, nor does Matthew mention the shepherds.
- After telling us of the poor shepherds, Luke tells of the circumcision of Jesus, his presentation in the Temple in accordance with the Law, and prophecies about Jesus by a man named Simeon and a woman named Anna (2:21–38).
- Finally, Luke is the only Evangelist to offer the familiar story of Jesus at age twelve when his parents lose track of him during a trip to Jerusalem (2:41–50). They eventually find him

■

Illustration: Luke's Gospel emphasizes the humble, poor circumstances of Jesus' birth.

in the Temple, "sitting among the teachers, listening to them and asking them questions. And all who heard him were amazed at his understanding and his answers."

Luke's closing statement. Luke closes his description of the early life of Jesus with this important statement:

[Jesus] went down with [his parents] and came to Nazareth, and was obedient to them. His mother treasured all these things in her heart.

And Jesus increased in wisdom and in years, and in divine and human favor. (2:51–52)

The Infancy Narratives in Light of the Gospels

Most Christians learn about the birth of Jesus through a lifetime of experiences with Christmas traditions. Manger scenes, Christmas carols, and other religious customs retelling the story have developed throughout the history of the church. Sorting out all these traditions in terms of the Gospels can be difficult at times. Yet we must do this because the Gospels are the documents that ultimately serve as the foundation and source of the Christian understanding of Jesus. And, as was said early in this book, the intention of this course is not to provide simple answers but sound ones, answers that will help you move toward a more mature and meaningful understanding of Christianity, particularly Catholic Christianity. **2**

The differing stories of Jesus' birth and early years as they are presented in the Gospels of Matthew and Luke can be explained when seen in light of the nature, purpose, and development of the Gospels. A brief refresher on the major points raised in chapter 2 will provide the framework

needed for understanding the stories of Jesus' early life. Recall these important points made about the Gospels:

1. The Gospels are testimonies of faith. The Gospels are not biographies of Jesus. Rather, they are testimonies of faith, proclamations of the Good News written by people after they had experienced Jesus as the risen Lord.

2. The Gospels present different portraits of Jesus. Each Gospel was written by a different person, at a different time, to a different group of people, and for a different purpose.

- Mark's was the first Gospel to be written. It was directed to non-Jewish Christians, and it stressed the humanity and suffering of Jesus.
- Luke's Gospel was written approximately fifteen years after Mark's. It was directed to Gentiles, and it emphasized that the Good News of Jesus is offered to all people—rich and poor, men and women, Jews and Gentiles.
- Matthew's Gospel was written not long after Luke's, and it was directed to devout Jews. It stressed the conviction that Jesus fulfilled the Law of Moses and was the Messiah the Jews had been awaiting.
- John's Gospel is very different from the other three. It offers a profound portrait of Jesus as the Messiah and divine Son of God, often expressing that conviction through poetic and symbolic language and stories.

As noted earlier, this course's portrait of Jesus will rely primarily on the three synoptic Gospels, because of the unique nature and purposes of John's Gospel.

3. The Gospels are stories about meaning. The intention of the Gospel writers as believing Christians was not merely to provide historical

2
Write a brief essay describing the Christmas when you felt most in touch with the true meaning of the season. Explain what made that celebration of Christmas so special.

F • O • C • U • S

The Visit of the Magi

Adding to the Story

Matthew's Gospel includes the familiar story of the Magi, a story frequently recalled at Christmas (though not always with biblical accuracy) in manger scenes and Christmas carols. A careful reading of the original Bible story will reveal that some of the details often associated with the story have been added over time. Popular belief during medieval times, for example, added the notion that there were three men (probably based on the three gifts of gold, frankincense, and myrrh); that the men were kings; and that their names were Gaspar, Melchior, and Balthasar. None of this information can be found in the Gospel account.

Looking for Historical Accuracy

Over the years people have tried to demonstrate the historical accuracy of the story of the Magi. Some, for example, have tried to explain through astronomy the presence of the star that guided the Magi. (The Magi are commonly understood to have been astrologers who observed and tried to interpret the movement of the stars.) Some suggest that the "star" they saw may have been the planets Jupiter and Saturn coming close together. In ancient thought, Jupiter was a star associated with royalty and Saturn was the star of Israel. Modern-day astronomers tell us that Jupiter and Saturn come together this way only every 794 years; they calculate that this would have occurred in 7 B.C.E., around the time of Jesus' birth.

Others offer another suggestion: Chinese records state that a *nova*, a super-bright explosion of a star, appeared in the eastern sky in 5 B.C.E. Perhaps this was the star that the Magi witnessed.

Making the Point in a Memorable Way

All attempts to explain the historical accuracy of the story of the Magi seem to miss the larger and more central question that is constantly being asked in this course: What does this story mean? The story of the Magi illustrates a major point that Matthew wished to make: Jesus as the Messiah was accepted by many Gentiles and rejected by many Jews. The story of the Magi makes that point in a memorable way.

■

Photo: A bright star over Bethlehem.

facts about Jesus. Their chief aim was to describe the meaning, significance, and impact of Jesus' life and teaching on the people and events of his time.

The Infancy Narratives and the Christ of Faith

Biblical scholars agree that a great deal of symbolism is involved in the Gospel stories of Jesus' birth and early life. After all, very few people besides Jesus' parents were there to witness the events themselves. In other words, Matthew's and Luke's infancy narratives tell us as much, if not more, about Jesus as the Christ of Faith as they do about the historical aspects of Jesus' birth. Matthew and Luke wanted to teach the following main points about Jesus as the Christ of Faith through their infancy narratives.

Matthew's Intentions: Three Themes

Jesus is the Messiah. Matthew wanted to show his Jewish readers as clearly as possible that Jesus was the Messiah they had been waiting for. In the genealogy of Jesus at the beginning of his Gospel, for example, Matthew refers to Jesus as "the son of David, the son of Abraham" (1:1). Then he starts with Abraham and works his way up to Jesus. He carefully notes that Joseph was born in the town of Bethlehem from the line of David. Throughout Jewish history, the people had expected the Messiah to descend from David, and David's hometown was Bethlehem.

Jesus was accepted by Gentiles, rejected by Jews. Matthew included the story of the Magi, non-Jewish men who were members of the priest-

ly caste of the Persians and who served as chaplains to and representatives of the Persian royalty. The Magi were known for their understanding of astrology and the occult, the mysterious dimension of life. (Our words *magic* and *magician* come from the same root word.) By way of the story of the Magi, Matthew was showing his Jewish readers that Gentiles often accepted Jesus as the Messiah even though many Jews rejected him. This theme is repeated throughout Matthew's Gospel.

Jesus is "the new Moses." Matthew filled his entire infancy account with quotes and images from the Scriptures, all of which would have held

■
Luke included the shepherds in his story of the Nativity, indicating that the poor and downtrodden would be the first to recognize and respond to Jesus.

Photo: A shepherd and his flock, near Bethlehem.

■ Every age and culture imagines the birth of Jesus in its own way. *Illustration:* In his woodcut *Christmas (1954),* artist Fritz Eichenberg depicts Jesus coming for the modern urban poor. What might the dragons under the stable symbolize?

a deeper meaning for his Jewish readers. For example, in Matthew's Gospel, the Holy Family flees to Egypt, and then an angel calls them out of Egypt to Israel after the death of Herod. Who else was called out of Egypt by God? The Israelites, of course, who were led out of their bondage in Egypt by Moses. So Matthew recognized Jesus as "the new Moses," one who totally fulfilled the Law, the Messiah, who would lead the people to salvation.

Luke's Intentions:
The Good News Is for Everyone

Luke had a different audience and a different message in mind as he wrote his story of the birth and early years of Jesus. Though Luke made it clear that Jesus was the Messiah, he did not use a lot of quotes from the Old Testament. Luke's readers, who were Gentiles, would not have been as concerned about this as Matthew's Jewish readers. As mentioned earlier, Luke's Gospel stresses that the Good News is for everyone, especially those who are poor and downtrodden. That was Luke's reason for including the shepherds in his story, indicating that the poor would be the first to recognize and respond to Jesus.

Luke's emphasis on the fact that Jesus offers the Good News to everyone is also illustrated later in a genealogy he offers for Jesus (3:23–38). Luke's version of Jesus' genealogy differs dramatically from Matthew's. Matthew, as noted, starts with Abraham and works his way up to Jesus. Luke, on the other hand, begins with Jesus and works all the way back to Adam. As the "first man," Adam is the father of all people, not just the Jews, and with this clever point Luke again affirms the universality of the message of Jesus. **3**

Focusing on the Meaning

When we look at the meaning the Gospel writers were trying to convey, the reasons for the differences in the infancy narratives become clearer. The writers were trying not so much to provide historical facts but to explain the significance of historical events. In fact, in their infancy narratives, Matthew and Luke may have moved beyond historical concerns altogether, focusing instead on insights into the origins of Jesus that only people of faith would be concerned about.

This course does not seek to explain the meaning of every line of the Gospels. But certainly we cannot understand any of the events described in the Gospels without asking questions about the meaning of Jesus and his message as understood by writers of the Gospels. From this point on—whether in discussing specific events in the life of Jesus, his miracles, or the parables he shared—the emphasis will be on the following questions:

- What do these things mean?
- What point were the Gospel writers trying to make?
- What can we understand about Jesus from this?

These questions are at the core of trying to understand the Jesus of History as the Christ of Faith.

For Review

- Define *infancy narrative* and name the Gospels that contain an infancy narrative.
- List the major intentions of each writer of the infancy narratives. Give an example of how each intention is reflected in the writer's narrative.

3
Read or recall Charles Dickens's *A Christmas Carol,* then write a reflection on this question: *Dickens's emphasis in his story is most similar to the emphasis in which infancy narrative— Matthew's or Luke's?*

The Hidden Years of Jesus' Life

Beyond what Matthew and Luke tell us about Jesus' birth and early years, much of his life prior to his public ministry is unknown to us. The entire period before the start of Jesus' public life is often referred to as Jesus' hidden years. In addition to the infancy narratives, information about the history of the Jewish people, their beliefs, their religious practices, their family and social life, and so on, can help answer the question, What were the hidden years of Jesus' life like?

It can probably be said that Jesus of History experienced life as a typical Jew of his day—but this claim is made with some reservation. Jesus was a special person even as a young boy. He must have been particularly gifted, intelligent, and sensitive. This much can be surmised just by studying him as an adult. **4**

Jesus:
One with Us in All Things but Sin

Jesus was obviously special, but we must be careful not to think of him as strange, weird, or so different from us as to seem almost inhuman.

In the early church, there were writings and stories about Jesus that did not find their way into our Gospels. One of the stories describes Jesus as a young boy who, in order to entertain and impress his friends, would take clay models of birds and magically make them come alive and fly away! Many of us have impressions of Jesus that are not far from this kind of fanciful image. For instance, we might think of the baby Jesus lying in the

4
Based on what you know of the adult Jesus, write a description of what Jesus might have been like when he was fifteen years old. For example, how would he have related to his parents? Would he have been popular among his peers or a loner?

■
Jesus likely experienced his childhood in Nazareth as a typical Jewish boy of his day.
Photo: An old street in Nazareth today.

manger with the power to know all things, to read people's minds, or to go without food and drink. Such images can make Jesus seem like a freak of sorts, rather than what the church has continually claimed him to be—the Son of God, certainly, but also a human who was one with us in all things but sin.

In one of his epistles, Saint Paul says this about Jesus:

Who, though he was in the form of God,
did not regard equality with God
as something to be exploited,
but emptied himself,
taking the form of a slave,
being born in human likeness.
And being found in human form,
he humbled himself
and became obedient to the point of death—
even death on a cross.

(Philippians 2:6–8)

Saint Paul is saying that Jesus became as other humans are, with all the physical, emotional, intellectual, and spiritual needs each of us experiences.

Jesus' Birthday

Based on our understanding of the Jewish people and their history, we can say a number of things about Jesus' early life, beginning with his birthday.

Born During Herod's Reign

This course has stated that Jesus was born in or around 6 or 5 B.C.E. If, as traditionally held, our calendar begins with the year 0, marking the birth of Jesus, proposing such a date for his birth can be a bit confusing! The reasons for this discrepancy

are too complex to discuss in full here. Basically what happened is this: When our modern calendar was first developed during the sixth century C.E., a miscalculation was made in determining the year in which Jesus was born, and that mistake was never corrected.

We know from the Gospels, however, that Jesus was born during the reign of Herod the Great, and we know with certainty from other sources that Herod died in the year 4 B.C.E. So Jesus was certainly born before that year. Scholars differ on the precise year of his birth, claiming anywhere from 8 to 5 B.C.E. It is obvious that the Evangelists, like most of the people of Jesus' day, did not share our concern for precise information about such an event.

■
Photo: **The Gezer calendar, a simple aid for remembering the agricultural seasons, etched in stone in Hebrew, was probably used by schoolchildren in Jesus' culture.**

A biography today would probably mention the subject's date of birth right away, but we should not expect such information in the Gospels.

Circumcised According to the Law of Moses

Eight days after his birth in Bethlehem, Jesus was circumcised according to the Law of Moses. Circumcision was a religious practice that involved removing the foreskin of the male child's penis as a permanent sign of the child's membership in the covenant community of the Jews. This practice can be traced back to God's first covenant with Abraham (see Genesis 17:9–14), in which God said, "You shall circumcise the flesh of your foreskins, and it shall be a sign of the covenant between me and you. Throughout your generations every male among you shall be circumcised when he is eight days old."

At the time of his circumcision, Jesus was given his name. (As mentioned earlier, *Jesus* was a popular Jewish name of the day, and it meant "Yahweh saves" or "Yahweh is salvation.") Then Jesus' parents presented him in the Temple in Jerusalem, where they consecrated him to God with the offering of a pair of turtledoves, or pigeons, the common sacrifice of the poor.

Jesus' Childhood in Nazareth

A Carpenter for a Father

Jesus' hometown of Nazareth was a community of just a few thousand people. He probably lived in the kind of one-room house described earlier. His father, Joseph, was a carpenter by trade, and as was the common practice of the day, Jesus probably worked along with his father and eventually became a carpenter himself. **5**

■
Photo: **Children play in the hills near contemporary Nazareth.**

5
Talk with a carpenter or woodworker about the satisfactions and frustrations of the work. Then write up an imaginary reflection Jesus could have had about his work with wood.

A Good Education

Jesus seems to have had a good education. He knew Hebrew, which was fairly rare among the lower-class people of his day. Because of the historical setting in which he was raised, and also due to the location of Nazareth geographically, Jesus probably spoke three languages: Hebrew, Greek, and Aramaic, the common language of Palestine. From age eight to age thirteen he likely attended school in a room attached to the synagogue, where his study revolved around the Scriptures and the faith and history of his people, the Jews.

Jesus' education was also enhanced by life in Nazareth itself. Though Galilee was held in low esteem by many Jews, it was an area in which Jesus would have encountered many of the new ideas of the Greeks and the Romans.

A Faith-Filled Family Life

Jesus' strong Jewish faith had its source in the faith of his parents. Both Joseph and Mary were devout Jews, and, as we know, the Jewish family was recognized as a religious community in itself.

Most likely the family of Jesus was deeply prayerful and committed to following faithfully not only the Law but also the spirit of the Jewish religion.

From that early foundation of a strong, loving, and truly religious family, Jesus grew. He developed a great love and understanding of the Jewish Bible and became fully committed to the faith life of his people. For some thirty years he "increased in wisdom and in years, and in divine and human favor" (Luke 2:52).

Jesus was unquestionably a man of deep prayer, as is constantly reflected in the Gospels. He had an intense religious awareness, an understanding of God and God's relationship with men and women that would one day put him in direct conflict with his people, his friends, and perhaps even his family (see Matthew 12:46–50). His vision would eventually lead him to death on the cross, which would offer all people the possibility of fullness of life. **6**

For Review

- Why must we be careful about the images we have of Jesus during his early life and hidden years?
- Identify at least four influences on Jesus' life while he was growing up.

■

Photo: Jewish boys in Israel read from the Scriptures to prepare for their bar mitzvah, a ceremony that indicates they have reached the age of religious duty and responsibility.

6
Of all the things that influenced Jesus while he was growing up, which do you think had the greatest effect on him? Explain your opinion in a paragraph.

The Beginnings of Jesus' Public Life

John the Baptist was one of the many wandering prophets at the time of Jesus. He was different, however, in that he did not proclaim himself as the Messiah, Savior, or Liberator yearned for by the Jewish people. Rather, he pointed to "one who is more powerful than I" (Luke 3:16). John's task was to prepare the way for Jesus' ministry by calling people to an awareness of their sin and to repentance. He announced that a whole new order, a new society, was about to begin and that the people were to get ready for it by having a change of heart.

The sign John used to express this change of heart, this openness of mind and spirit, was a ritual bathing called baptism. The act of bathing in water as a sign of spiritual purification was a common practice for many religions of the time, including Judaism. By accepting baptism from John in the Jordan River, people acknowledged both their own sinfulness and their desire to join the new kingdom by changing the way they were living. Later Jesus would praise John, saying that "among those born of women no one is greater than John" (Luke 7:28).

Jesus' Baptism

Differences Between the Gospel Accounts

All the synoptic Gospels record the baptism of Jesus, and John's Gospel alludes to it, but there are some differences between the accounts.

Mark's account. In Mark's account (1:9–11), Jesus is baptized, and then he sees "the heavens torn apart and the Spirit descending like a dove on him." A voice comes from the heavens, saying, "You are my Son, the Beloved; with you I am well pleased."

Matthew's account. In the account of Matthew (3:13–17), Jesus is baptized only after some disagreement with John about whether John should baptize him. After the baptism, Jesus sees "the Spirit of God descending like a dove," and a voice from the heavens proclaims, "This is my Son, the Beloved, with whom I am well pleased."

Luke's account. In Luke's account (3:21–22), Jesus is seen at prayer after the baptism has taken place, and it is then that the Spirit descends upon him "in bodily form like a dove." A voice from heaven proclaims, "You are my Son, the Beloved; with you I am well pleased."

John's Gospel. Unlike the synoptic Gospels, John's Gospel does not describe the baptism of Jesus. However, it does include a passage of testimony by John the Baptist that seems to echo the baptism scenes of the synoptics (see John 1:29–34). This passage also includes some language that contemporary Catholics hear during the Mass when Jesus is referred to as "the Lamb of God who takes away the sin of the world."

Symbolism in the Baptism Accounts

Certainly some symbolism appears in all the accounts of Jesus' baptism:

- *The dove:* In ancient times, the dove was often a symbol for Israel as a whole and, less often, a symbol for the Spirit of God.

■
Illustration: Jesus' baptism in the Jordan was apparently a pivotal time of self-discovery for him, a time when he began to recognize what God was calling him to do.

- *The voice from the heavens:* At times in the Old Testament, God is depicted as speaking to the people in a voice from the heavens. Often God is concealed by a cloud.

The Evangelists likely used these images to express Jesus' interior experience of God during his baptism. That is, the dove and the voice from the heavens may not have been seen and heard by those gathered about Jesus. Note, for instance, that it is Jesus who sees the Spirit of God descending and that, in two of the accounts, the voice speaks directly to Jesus: "*You* are my Son, the Beloved . . ." rather than "*This* is my Son, the Beloved. . . ."

The Development of the Baptism Accounts

It is interesting to note the development of the accounts of Jesus' baptism from the earliest version (Mark's) to the later versions (Matthew's and Luke's). Mark is straightforward and direct in describing the scene, while Matthew introduces the disagreement with John the Baptist over whether Jesus should be baptized at all. Luke almost skips over the actual baptism and shows Jesus in prayer after the event, and John does not give a direct account of Jesus' baptism. Scholars claim that this reflects the Evangelists'—and the early church's—increasing discomfort with the whole notion of Jesus' accepting baptism.

Why Jesus Accepted Baptism— According to Matthew

As the early church reflected on the identity of Jesus and grew to recognize him as the divine Son of God, it was faced with this question: Why would Jesus, as Messiah and sinless Son of God, accept a baptism that John the Baptist himself proclaimed was one of "repentance for the for-giveness of sins" (Mark 1:4; Luke 3:3)? Matthew's statement about John's reluctance to baptize Jesus (3:14) was an attempt by the Evangelist to offer an explanation. According to Matthew, Jesus accepted baptism because "it is proper for us in this way to fulfill all righteousness" (3:15). That is, Jesus saw the act as part of God's plan, and he accepted it on that basis. Matthew wanted to show that Jesus' acceptance was not an admission of sin. Rather, it indicated his willingness to immerse himself completely in the life and concerns of his people, to live as they lived. For Matthew, Jesus' water baptism was the first step on the road to the cross. (Jesus would later refer to the cross as a baptism he could not avoid; see Mark 10:38; Luke 12:50.)

Jesus' Baptism: A Moment of Self-Discovery

The accounts of Jesus' baptism reflect some interesting concerns of the early community of faith, but they also reveal Jesus' growing understanding of himself and his mission. Jesus, like each of us, struggled to find his place in the world. His baptism was no doubt a pivotal time of self-discovery, a kind of "aha! moment" in which he came to some recognition of what he was being called to by God.

Jesus learned two chief lessons from his baptism, both symbolized by the writers of the Gospels with vivid biblical imagery:

- Jesus recognized that he was chosen in a special way to proclaim and begin a new kingdom. The words spoken from the heavens echoed those of Isaiah 42:1, which told of God's suffering servant, who would one day save the people.
- Jesus learned that he would be given the power to fulfill his role through the Spirit of God, represented by the descending dove. (That same

Spirit of God drove Jesus into the desert immediately following his baptism, and would continue to lead him throughout his ministry.) **7**

Jesus' realization of his unique relationship with God had a profound effect on his ministry, freeing him to do and say things that went well beyond what any other prophet, teacher, or religious leader could do or say. Jesus' ministry would be one that could only be accomplished by the Son of God.

Temptation in the Desert

In the scriptural quotation at the beginning of this chapter, Mark simply states that after Jesus' baptism, "the Spirit immediately drove him out into the wilderness. He was in the wilderness forty days, tempted by Satan." The Gospels of Matthew and Luke expand this scene and describe a threefold temptation that Jesus experiences while in the desert (see Matthew 4:1–11; Luke 4:1–13).

In Matthew's Gospel, the tempter, or "devil," asks Jesus first to turn stones into bread, then to throw himself down from a high point of the Temple and have God catch him (in order to prove his special relationship with God), and finally to fall at the feet of the devil and worship him, for which Jesus would then receive "all the kingdoms of the world." In Luke's Gospel, the order of the second and third temptations is reversed, but the content is essentially the same.

According to Matthew's account, Jesus responds to all three temptations by giving direct quotes from the Book of Deuteronomy, which is part of the Old Testament. In response to the three temptations, Jesus says, in turn:

1. "'One does not live by bread alone, / but by every word that comes from the mouth of God'" (see Deuteronomy 8:3).
2. "'Do not put the Lord your God to the test'" (see Deuteronomy 6:16).
3. "'Worship the Lord your God, / and serve only him'" (see Deuteronomy 6:13).

Jesus' Priorities in the Desert Experience

Again we must ask, What does this story mean? What were the Gospel writers trying to say about Jesus and his mission?

7
If you have been baptized, write a short description of the event based on recollections by your parents and others.

■
Jesus' time in the desert was an intense, prayerful preparation for his ministry.
Photo: The mountains of the desert of Judah.

"The new Israel" did not fail. Each of the synoptic Gospels refers to the forty days that Jesus spent in the desert, and every Jew of Jesus' time would immediately have been reminded of the forty years that the people of Israel spent wandering in the desert in search of the Promised Land. The Israelites were severely tempted in the desert, and they ultimately failed to stay true to God. Jesus, as "the new Israel," was tempted as well, but he did not fail.

Jesus refused the messiahship expected by his people. A major lesson from the Gospels is that Jesus flatly rejected the political and militaristic messiahship that the Jewish people had come to expect. The story of the three temptations il-lustrates this point quite well, for it deals with the kinds of power that Jesus refused to exercise throughout his ministry.

- *Economic power:* Jesus' messiahship was not to be based on his ability to provide for the material wants and needs of the people (symbolized by turning stones into bread). Rather, he came to provide for the spiritual hunger of the people by proclaiming the word of God, which offers true life.

- *Magical power:* Nor was Jesus' messiahship to be based on magic or tricks done to impress people and almost force them to believe in him (symbolized by throwing himself off the top of the Temple and surviving). Jesus responded to the devil's temptation by saying that God does not

■
Jesus resisted the temptations of economic power, magical power, and political power.
Photo: **The Mount of Temptation, popularly believed to be the place where Jesus was tempted.**

reveal divine power through trickery and magic. (Wonder-working would constantly be an expectation of the crowds throughout Jesus' ministry, as we will see in our later discussion of his miracles. Jesus, however, never works miracles simply to impress people but only to bring about good in the world.)

- *Political power:* Finally, Jesus' messiahship was not to be based on political power (symbolized by the temptation to worship the devil and control all the kingdoms of the world). Jesus said that God alone was to be worshiped and that the Reign of God in the world would take place in the hearts of the people, not in political domination of them.

All three of the temptations we see Jesus confronting—and defeating—in the desert represent the kind of temptations he would have to deal with throughout his ministry.

We must remember that the Gospels were written to guide the early church and its members. The writers, in addition to relaying information about Jesus' ministry, were warning Christians to resist the temptation to find their meaning and purpose in life through economic security or through personal or political power over others. **8**

For Review

- Describe the significance of John the Baptist in the story of Jesus.
- Why was the early church uncomfortable with Jesus' accepting baptism? How did Matthew respond to the church's concern?
- What two chief lessons did Jesus learn from his baptism?
- What does the story of the three temptations in the desert tell us about Jesus' understanding of his messiahship?

8
For each of the three temptations Jesus experienced in the desert, write a brief explanation of how a similar temptation might be experienced by a young person in today's society.

Wandering Preacher, Unique Teacher

Like the Rabbis of His Day

Following his baptism, Jesus became a wandering preacher and religious teacher. It was common for Jewish rabbis, or teachers of the Law (sometimes called scribes), to roam from place to place teaching. Often the rabbis were accompanied by a band of disciples, young men who freely chose to follow and study under them. It was common for the rabbis to teach in the synagogues and, less often, wherever people were willing to gather to listen to them—on mountainsides, in fields, or along the roadsides. So even though Jesus was probably not a rabbi in an official or legal sense, in many ways his ministry appears similar to a rabbi's.

Unlike the Rabbis of His Day

Several factors in the content of the message Jesus proclaimed, in the way he shared it, and in his relationship to his disciples clearly set him apart from the other teachers of his day.

Jesus proclaimed the Kingdom of God. Jesus proclaimed in both his words and his actions the coming of a new Kingdom of God. The notion of such a Kingdom was a central one for the Jewish people of his day, so it was not surprising in itself that Jesus would speak of it. But his sense of the Kingdom was truly different.

Jesus claimed a special role. Jesus not only proclaimed the coming of a new Kingdom, but he also claimed for himself a special role as the one who would personally establish and embody it,

F • O • C • U • S

The Apostle Peter

So Much Like Us

The Gospels' portrait of the Apostle Peter—also called Simon or Simon Peter—is one of the most thorough, intriguing, and enlightening character studies in the entire Bible. He is mentioned more than any other disciple. Among Roman Catholics, Peter is of primary significance because of the leadership role he played in the early community of faith, a role that leads Catholics to identify him as the first pope (see Matthew 16:18). But Peter's great calling is not always evident in the Gospels' portrait of him. In fact, the portrait of Peter that we have from the Gospels at times seems to be just the opposite of a leader!

Peter is a wonderfully appealing person to read about because he is so much like us—at our best and at our weakest. He makes mistakes and requires forgiveness. He is often bold, even hotheaded, and then cowardly. He can seem terribly bright, then incredibly ignorant. He, more than any other person in the Gospels, exemplifies the claim that the Apostles were ordinary people who, because of their association with Jesus, were capable of extraordinary things.

Selected Gospel Passages on Peter

The following are a number of key Gospel passages on Peter. They are organized, to the extent possible, in chronological order. You are encouraged to read some if not all of these passages to gain a rich sense of Peter's personality and an appreciation of how much he was like us.

Luke 5:1–11
Jesus recruits Peter after an almost too successful fishing trip.

Matthew 14:22–33
Peter learns a lesson about humility while taking an unexpected swim.

Mark 9:2–8
Peter sees Jesus in a new "light."

Matthew 16:13–23
Peter shows deep faith in Jesus and proves for just a moment that he is ready for more responsibility —until he questions Jesus' ability to understand what the future holds and gets reprimanded by Jesus for his limited understanding.

Luke 22:31–34
Jesus sees through Peter's cocky self-confidence.

John 13:4–9
After initially rejecting a quick foot-washing by Jesus, Peter volunteers for a total bath.

Matthew 26:36–41
A sleepy Peter keeps nodding off when Jesus most needs him.

Mark 14:66–72
Peter, as predicted by Jesus, fails a major test, not just once but three times.

John 21:1–19
After a breakfast barbecue on the beach with the risen Jesus, Peter makes up for his earlier failures by passing another test . . . again, three times.

not only announce it. We will say more about this in chapter 6.

Jesus taught with unique authority. Jesus amazed the crowds not only with the content of his message but also with the attitude he possessed while sharing it. As we read in Matthew's Gospel, "the crowds were astounded at his teaching, for he taught them as one having authority, and not as their scribes" (7:28–29).

Rabbis at the time of Jesus were called to study the Jewish Bible and the teaching of other rabbis thoroughly. Whenever they taught they were expected to back up what they were saying with direct quotes from the Scriptures or statements from other respected rabbis.

Jesus, on the other hand, claimed himself as the sole judge of the truth of what he taught. At times he would even say, for example, "You have heard that it was said to those of ancient times, . . . but I say . . ." (see Matthew 5:21–48). This was a clear break from the common practice, and it both attracted and alienated many people who listened to him preach.

Jesus used parables and performed miracles. Finally, Jesus differed dramatically from the other teachers of his time in his use of parables and in the miracles he performed.

Jesus and His Disciples: A Unique Relationship

The Meaning of Discipleship

As has been mentioned, it was typical for a rabbi to attract disciples who would study under him. The disciples would learn from the rabbi in a process of lengthy discussion, memorization through word games, and so on. The goal was for the dis-

ciples to learn perfectly the teachings of the rabbi, to the point of being able to repeat his teachings word for word. Once they had done this, the disciples would leave the rabbi and become independent rabbis themselves.

With Jesus and his disciples, however, the relationship was different.

- First of all, Jesus' disciples did not choose him; rather, he called them (see Mark 1:16–20; Luke 5:1–11).
- Second, unlike other rabbis, Jesus did not simply share with his disciples a body of teachings that they were expected to memorize word for word. According to the common practice, one who had mastered all the teachings of a rabbi would in turn be recognized as a rabbi himself and could claim some personal authority on that basis. But Jesus told his disciples that they were not to take the title *rabbi,* because their only basis of authority came from their relationship with him (see Matthew 23:8–10).
- Third, the disciples of Jesus were not only expected to watch and learn from Jesus, but they were actually called to share in his mission of proclaiming the Kingdom (see Luke 9:1–6).

The special role of the first disciples of Jesus lends insight into what it means to be a disciple of his today. Jesus calls each Christian to a personal, lasting relationship of love with God, and Jesus also sends his followers out to share in his mission of proclaiming the Kingdom. **9**

The Twelve Apostles

Many people responded to Jesus' message and followed him, and all these men and women might qualify as his disciples. But the Gospels are clear that Jesus carefully selected special men who were to play a central and significant role during his ministry and in the future. These men were

9
Reflect in writing on this question: *In what ways can teenagers today be disciples of Jesus?*

the **Apostles**, most frequently referred to in the Gospels as the Twelve. (Their names are recorded in Matthew 10:2–4; Mark 3:16–19; and Luke 6:13–16.) Curiously, the Twelve are not mentioned in John's Gospel at all, perhaps because John wished to focus more specifically on Jesus himself as the one called to manifest God's presence and power.

The Twelve echoed the twelve tribes of Israel. It is significant that the Evangelists portrayed Jesus as choosing twelve Apostles and that the early community of faith would work to maintain that number after the death of one of them (see Acts of the Apostles 1:15–26). Think back to the earlier discussion of the history of the Jews. You will recall that the Israelites at one time consisted of twelve tribes, each descending from one of the twelve sons of Jacob. It seems certain that the early Christian community recognized twelve Apostles to suggest that they would be the foundation of a new community of faith, a new Israel, what we today recognize as the Christian church.

What was so special about the Apostles? The Apostles were, of course, disciples of Jesus. But they were selected by him to be his constant companions, traveling with him from place to place and becoming thoroughly instructed in the truths he shared. The word *apostle* comes from a Greek word meaning "to send forth." Jesus commissioned these men to go out and carry on his Good News about the Kingdom of God. In a special way, the Twelve shared Jesus' power, and after his death and Resurrection they continued, in his name, to preach, to heal, and to make disciples through baptism (Matthew 28:16–20).

Ordinary People with an Extraordinary Calling

What sort of people did Jesus seek for this mission as Apostles? Some were simple fishermen. One was a hated tax collector. Two were such hotheads that Jesus called them sons of thunder. One would eventually betray him. One was a leader who could show signs of great insight but could also demonstrate outright cowardice. The Gospels often portray these men as dull, baffled, unable to understand what Jesus is telling them. At times they seem to hunger for great power. Eventually they desert Jesus out of fear. In the end, though, all of them but Judas reconcile with Jesus after his Resurrection, and most if not all of them go on to die as heroes in the early church. In short, the Apostles were ordinary people, but because of their association with Jesus, they were capable of extraordinary things. **10**

■
Photo: Jesus calls Peter and Andrew to be his Apostles.

10
According to the Gospels, the Apostles came from ordinary walks of life. Write a brief description of twelve people Jesus might choose as Apostles today. Consider questions such as these: *Would the twelve people all be men? What occupations would they come from? In terms of personality traits, would they be similar to one another or a mix?*

For Review

- In what ways was Jesus the teacher both similar to and different from the rabbis of his day?
- Briefly describe Jesus' relationship with his disciples.
- What connection can be made between the twelve Apostles and the early history of the Jews?

The Proclamation of the Kingdom

Central to Jesus' identity, mission, and message is the notion of the Kingdom of God. Jesus' history as a Jew inspired the notion of the Kingdom. His prayer and life experiences led him to identify himself as the proclaimer and possessor of the Kingdom. His parables pointed to and described the Kingdom, and his miracles were signs of its presence in the people's midst. Therefore, to understand Jesus, we must understand what he meant by the Kingdom of God.

■
Photo: **A view of olive trees on a hillside in Bethlehem against a glorious sunset.**

6

The Kingdom of God:
Proclaiming the Dream of Jesus

The Dream of Jesus: The Kingdom of God

ONE of the scribes . . . asked [Jesus], "Which commandment is the first of all?" Jesus answered, "The first is, 'Hear, O Israel: The Lord our God, the Lord is one; you shall love the Lord your God with all your heart, and with all your soul, and with all your mind, and with all your strength.' The second is this, 'You shall love your neighbor as yourself.' There is no other commandment greater than these." Then the scribe said to him, "You are right, Teacher; you have truly said that 'he is one, and besides him there is no other'; and 'to love him with all the heart, and with all the understanding, and with all the strength,' and 'to love one's neighbor as oneself,'—this is much more important than all whole burnt offerings and sacrifices." When Jesus saw that [the scribe] answered wisely, he said to [the scribe], "You are not far from the kingdom of God." (Mark 12:28–34)

The Human Need to Hope

All religions—indeed, all people—reflect a human need to hope for a future that is in some way better than the present. Sometimes such hoping is expressed in a vision of a future society in which all the idealistic dreams of the particular religion are fulfilled. We might call such an idealized picture of the future a religion's *Dream,* with a capital *D.*

A particular religion's Dream will vary depending on what the believers ground their hopes in. For example, a given religion might focus on the military defeat of its enemies. Its Dream would be of a future in which the members of the religion dominate their world with political and military power.

Another religion might be based on the conviction that all its members can experience a deep personal sense of peace. This religion might offer as its Dream a picture of what society would look like if all people attained such inner tranquility.

Jesus, too, had a strong vision of an ideal future, and he dedicated his life to making that future a reality. Jesus referred to his vision as the **Kingdom of God.** Many of his teachings and stories revealed his understanding of the Kingdom. His miracles were expressions of the fact that God was inaugurating the Kingdom through Jesus himself. Jesus' vision came to serve as the driving force for all who would follow him. A complete understanding of Jesus—and, therefore, of all Christianity—requires

"The kingdom of God is as if someone would scatter seed on the ground, and would sleep and rise night and day, and the seed would sprout and grow, he does not know how. . . . But when the grain is ripe . . . the harvest has come" (Mark 4:26–29).
Photo, facing page: The full beauty of this hillside in Galilee . . .
Background: . . . started out as no more than a handful of seeds.

an understanding of the Dream that Jesus proclaimed. The purpose of this chapter is to help you understand that Dream. **1**

The Kingdom of God Proclaimed

The word *kingdom* can sometimes get in the way of our understanding what Jesus meant when he preached about the *Kingdom* of God. For us, the Kingdom of God can imply a place or a region. When discussing Jesus' teachings, a better reference might be the *Reign* of God or the *Rule* of God over all the created world. With this qualification in mind, let's explore what God's Reign or Rule over the world meant to Jesus and, therefore, what it should mean to all Christians.

The Focus of the Synoptic Gospels

We must look primarily to the synoptic Gospels for an understanding of the Kingdom of God. Significantly, John's Gospel never explicitly mentions the theme of the Kingdom. John seems to suggest that Jesus himself already embodied the Dream that the synoptic authors describe as primarily a future kingdom. Matthew, Mark, and Luke, then, tell us most directly about Jesus' understanding of the Kingdom of God, and a key part of their message concerns what Jesus did *not* see as the Kingdom.

What Jesus Did Not See as the Kingdom

The Jewish Notion of the Kingdom of God

The basic notion of the Kingdom of God was part of the Jewish worldview with which Jesus was

---

■
The people of Hiroshima dream of a world in which no more children will be killed by nuclear bombs and other weapons of war.

Photo: **The Children's Peace Monument in Hiroshima is dedicated with wreaths of flowers. Thousands of children died when the first atomic bomb was dropped on Hiroshima in 1945.**

1
Think about a personal Dream — a highly motivating goal for which you have sacrificed. Depict your Dream through some form of art: a drawing or painting, a collage, a song, a poem, or an essay.

raised. The Jews accepted, for example, that God was the king over all creation. Many of the Hebrew religious hymns, which we call psalms, celebrated the kingship of God. For example:

The LORD is king, he is robed in majesty;
    the LORD is robed, he is [encircled] with strength.
He has established the world; it shall never be moved;
    your throne is established from of old;
    you are from everlasting.

(Psalm 93:1–2)

So God's kingship was recognized first in the wonders of creation. Some rabbis taught as well that the Kingdom of God was present in the Law, in the Torah. They felt that the Law was God's instrument for ruling people.

It was also clear to the Jews that the Kingdom of God had not yet been fully established because so much evil obviously still existed in the world. They recognized that this was due in large part to their own failure to cooperate with God, to follow God's will completely.

New Insights into Old Ideas

Jesus certainly accepted much of the Jewish understanding of the Kingdom of God, but he also went beyond it and brought new insights into the older ideas. In some cases he actually contradicted expectations about the Kingdom that were held by the Jews of his day.

As discussed earlier, the Jews believed that the Kingdom of God would be established through a savior. In the centuries following King David's military conquests, the people's expectation of a savior became bound up with the notion of a new national, political kingship. And by the time of Jesus' ministry, after nearly a hundred years of Roman domination, many Jews expected the Kingdom to begin with a military takeover of the country and the expulsion of the Romans. This overthrow was to be led by the Messiah, who was by then expected to be a military leader, a warrior. Jesus' understanding of the Kingdom and of his messiahship proved to be far different from what his people commonly understood.

Ideas That Jesus Rejected

From the story about Jesus' temptation in the desert—and from all his teachings and actions— it is clear that Jesus rejected specific ideas in the Jewish understanding of the Kingdom. He was certainly not trying to begin a new political reign over his people. In the Gospels, people try to make Jesus a king or political ruler, and he firmly rejects the notion.

Jesus' opposition to any violence eliminated the possibility of a military takeover of any kind. It is also clear from the Gospels that he did not have in mind a geographical state or nation when he spoke of the Kingdom. Jesus' Kingdom would have no

■

For the Jews, God was the ruler over creation, and they praised God for the beauty of the natural world.
Photo: **The Tel Dan Reserve in upper Galilee.**

Celebrating the Kingdom of God

Jesus frequently used stories and figures of speech to describe the Kingdom of God, probably because he realized that what he was trying to describe was far beyond what anyone might imagine. How might we today get an idea of what the Kingdom of God is like? Any attempt to describe the Kingdom is sure to fall short of its wonderful reality, but as an example we might look to the experience of the pilgrims to World Youth Day, a biannual event in which young people gather with the pope and bishops.

In 1997, more than 500,000 Catholic youth from about 150 countries around the world celebrated their faith with one another in Paris. The event's theme, taken from John 1:38–39, was about searching for Jesus: "[The disciples] said to [Jesus], 'Rabbi,' . . . 'where are you staying?' He said to them: 'Come and see.'" As one journalist covering World Youth Day described it, the young people transformed the city—and one another—with their presence:

Everywhere they went in Paris, the World Youth Day pilgrims raised a rainbow of color and a song of joy. They laughed, chanted, waved flags and banners, and sang—and sang and sang, everywhere, for any reason, in every language and style. There were Hungarians singing and playing pipes on the train, Lebanese and Egyptians dancing to strange Arabian instruments, Africans drumming and singing under the Eiffel Tower, Italians singing the Hallelujah chorus to work commuters on the subway. . . .

That atmosphere allowed people—pilgrims and Parisians alike—to make friends with whomever happened to be handy, striking up conversations with each other on the subway and exchanging e-mail addresses and t-shirts. Some Americans even adopted the European custom of kissing cheeks during the sign of peace at Mass. "Paris smiled," read the headlines in several French newspapers, as if this were a rare event.

Throughout the week, the pilgrims prayed together, served the poor with fasting and service work, learned about social justice issues,

At World Youth Day, hundreds of thousands of young Catholics responded to the call to "come and see" Jesus.

Photo: World Youth Day participants fill the streets of Paris with song and dance.

and shared stories of their faith. They celebrated their diversity by filling the air with the songs and the colorful flags of their countries. But they also celebrated their unity in Christ. At meals, people from different countries sat in small circles to literally break bread together; at the same time they broke down language barriers with hand signs and smiles. During the opening Mass, they prayed the Our Father out loud in their native languages, filling the air with a "holy noise." And before they left, the pilgrims circled Paris in a human "chain of fellowship" twenty-three miles long, wearing t-shirts decorated with signs of peace, and facing outward into the world.

At the end of the event, the youth published a statement expressing their own Dream of "changing the world" and the church through prayer, faith, and actions that would serve as "signs of peace."

"We simply want a renewed church, a church which embodies the Kingdom of God," said Michael Zimmerman, a participant from the United States. "We want a church which has the ability to change the world for the better by . . . the strength of [its] faith and commitment and enthusiasm." (Jerry Daoust)

At World Youth Day, young people came together to follow Jesus and work toward a better world. In doing so, they broke down the barriers that normally separated them—and so experienced a taste of the Kingdom.

■

Photo: **Young people break down barriers of nationality, race, and language as they express their desire to be a church that "embodies the Kingdom of God."**

Jesus' Understanding of God

Jesus' vision of the Kingdom of God was closely tied to his understanding of God, which differed dramatically from the understanding of God commonly held by the Jewish people.

God as Father

The Traditional Jewish Understanding

Jesus was thoroughly Jewish, so his understanding of the Kingdom of God necessarily flowed out of Jewish history, the Jewish people's Scriptures, Jewish worship, and, of course, his own personal prayer and reflection on all of these. That personal prayer and reflection led him to a unique and remarkable recognition of God as his "Father." The notion of God as Father was not entirely new to Jesus. The Scriptures of his Jewish heritage occasionally used this term for God. But as noted earlier, the Jews held God in such awe and reverence that they would not even consider using the name of God, Yahweh, in prayer and worship. Instead they said "the Lord," "the Most High," or "the Holy One." Calling God "Father" was definitely out of the question.

Jesus' Teachings

Jesus shattered Jewish belief and practice by taking the incredible position of referring to God as "Abba, Father" (Mark 14:36). *Abba* is an Aramaic word that means something far more intimate than just "father." It was the word used by young Jewish children for their fathers; it had the sense of "da-da," which is uttered so easily by infants. The term *abba* was also used by adults as an affectionate term for their father, much as adults of

boundaries, no borders separating one nation from another. **2**

Nor was Jesus' concept of the Kingdom of God simply a new philosophy or a new plan for social reform. But if the Kingdom was none of these things, what was it?

For Review

- Briefly explain the Jewish notion of God as a king.
- Why did the ancient Jews believe the Messiah would be a great warrior who would establish the Kingdom through military conquest?
- What ideas about the Kingdom of God did Jesus clearly reject?

■
Illustration: Jesus rejected specific ideas common to the ancient Jews regarding the Kingdom, such as the notion that the Messiah would be a political ruler or a member of royalty.

2
Suppose that Jesus had chosen to meet the Jewish expectations of a military messiah whose goal was to create a political Kingdom of God. Imagine a scene in which Jesus tries to motivate his followers, and write it like a scene in a movie.

F • O • C • U • S

Images of God

As we discussed in chapter 4, the Jewish culture of Jesus' time was *patriarchal*—that is, dominated almost exclusively by men. That cultural standard extended to the Jewish understanding of God, to whom the Scriptures usually refer in masculine terms, using pronouns such as *he, him,* and *his*. This can pose a challenge for modern readers accustomed to cultural standards that attempt to treat all people equally, regardless of gender.

Sometimes, however, the Scriptures use female imagery to describe God. Consider the following passage, in which God's love is compared to the love a mother has for her child: "For thus says the LORD: / . . . As a mother comforts her child, / so I will comfort you" (Isaiah 66:13). This passage and others like it remind us that thinking of God in terms of just one gender fails to capture the fullness of who God is. God is neither masculine nor feminine in the common sense of those terms. God is spirit and does not have a sexual identity in the same way that people or other creatures do. Christians believe that we are all, male and female, made in the image of God.

Throughout his public ministry, Jesus made it clear that he came for all people, regardless of their social position. That stance often surprised the leadership of his time, and it is worth remembering in order to keep the male-centered language of the Scriptures in perspective.

■

Photo: **We can think of God as Mother as well as Father.**

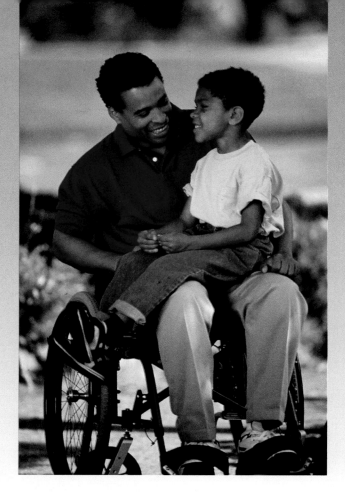

today may continue to call their father "Dad" or "Daddy." No Jew would have ever dared such intimacy, and it must have shocked many to hear Jesus speak of God with such a sense of childlike affection. **3**

A God Who Loves Without Condition

The Traditional Jewish Understanding

Some Christians unfairly stereotype the God of Judaism as "a God of fear and justice" and Jesus' God as "a God of love." Actually, the Jewish notion of a loving God was very strong. But because the Jewish reverence for God was so great that the people could not even utter the divine name, they often experienced God as distant and removed.

One way the Jews expressed their feeling of distance from God was by referring to God as the heavens. This explains an interesting expression that Matthew uses in his discussion of the Kingdom of God. Remember, Matthew was writing to a Jewish audience, and he was sensitive to their feelings and religious practices and convictions. Therefore, instead of writing "the kingdom of God," Matthew wrote "the kingdom of heaven." The God of the ancient Jewish people was full of mystery, as demonstrated by the holy of holies in the Temple, that sacred place reserved for God alone.

Jesus' Teachings

Out of his own experience of an intimate relationship with God, Jesus taught about God's relationship with all people—and indeed with all of creation. That conviction of God's intimate union with people was a primary part of Jesus' vision of the Kingdom of God. Jesus experienced the nourishing love of God in a deeply personal sense. In the Gospels, Jesus refers often to "my Father," indicating a special relationship that he alone had with God. But he also teaches people to pray to "our Father." Jesus saw God as a passionately caring parent whose love is tireless, healing, unlimited, and unreserved. God offers that love to sinners as well as to the just, to rich and poor people alike, to women and men, to slaves and free people. To the people of Jesus' time, this was a radically new vision, a vision of a God in whom they could place their complete trust. This trust is beautifully expressed in a passage from Matthew that has been treasured by Christians throughout the ages:

■

Photo: **Jesus taught people that they could refer to God not only by name but even with the word** *Abba*—**an equivalent of our word** *Dad* **or** *Daddy.*

3
Slowly say the Lord's Prayer to yourself. Then repeat the prayer, substituting the words "My Daddy" for "Our Father." In a paragraph, describe any feelings or insight you had from this exercise.

Look at the birds of the air; they neither sow nor reap nor gather into barns, and yet your heavenly Father feeds them. Are you not of more value than they? And can any of you by worrying add a single hour to your span of life? And why do you worry about clothing? Consider the lilies of the field, how they grow; they neither toil nor spin, yet I tell you, even Solomon in all his glory was not clothed like one of these. . . .

So do not worry about tomorrow, for tomorrow will bring worries of its own. Today's trouble is enough for today. (Matthew 6:26–34) **4**

The Kingdom that Jesus announced, therefore, was in fact a new understanding of a relationship that God had always offered. In his teachings about the Kingdom of God, Jesus was sharing new insights into the nature of God.

For Review

- With what Aramaic word did Jesus address God? Why did this shock the people of Jesus' time?

Jesus' Understanding of the Command to Love

According to Jesus, the ability to recognize and fully participate in the Reign of God requires a **conversion**, a change of heart, a turning from selfishness to openness to God and the call to love. When this conversion happens, the Kingdom of God takes root in the heart of the believer. Jesus' initial call, therefore, is to repentance, to a change in the way we live. Jesus said, "The time is fulfilled, and the kingdom of God has come near; repent, and believe in the good news" (Mark 1:15).

Not Just "Me and God"

The Reign of God proclaimed by Jesus was not simply a "me and God" situation, a one-to-one relationship between God and an individual person. Rather, Jesus clearly understood the Kingdom as being communal in nature, implying a new relationship not only between God and individuals but *among* individuals. That is, Jesus saw the Kingdom as the rule of God's love over the very hearts of people and, consequently, as a new social order based on people's unconditional love for one another. This meant that an entirely new era in history had begun, a time characterized by peace, joy, freedom, and love.

The Jewish Roots of the Command to Love

Jesus' concept of love for others—like his concepts of the Kingdom and of God as Father—was not so

---

■

Illustration: **Referring to the beautiful wildflowers growing in the fields of Galilee, Jesus said, "Consider the lilies . . . even Solomon in all his glory was not clothed like one of these."**

4

Referring to Matthew 6:26–34, as quoted above, select one line that you think is particularly significant for young people today. Write a short explanation of your choice.

much an entirely new notion as an expansion of a notion already held by the Jews. The Jews had such a deep sense of communal love, of concern for the poor, and of generosity that these attitudes had become their identifying traits to the other cultures that surrounded them.

The Ten Commandments, the cornerstone of the Jewish Law, included seven commandments directly related to relationships between people. The giving of alms, or contributions, to the poor was required, not merely suggested, by the Jewish Law. And in a touching example of Jewish generosity, the Law forbade the harvesting of corn on the outer edges of the fields, so that poor people would have easy access to it. The rabbis even went

beyond the basic Law and insisted on attitudes of kindness and gentleness. Over time, however, there developed among the Jews two main problems that conflicted with the command to love others. These were the problems of nationalism and legalism.

Nationalism

The first problem that developed among the Jews was an excessive sense of nationalism. The Jewish sense of separation from all other cultures led some Jews to believe that "love your neighbor" referred to Jewish neighbors only. Some Jews—though certainly not all—even believed that they were called to love their neighbor but hate their

Illustration: **In Jesus' Dream of the Kingdom of God, barriers of prejudice and nationalism would no longer divide people. All people—poor and rich, male and female, Jew and Gentile, slave** and free, oppressed and oppressor, young and old, prestigious and outcast—would be able to sit down together in peace and joy at the banquet of God's love.

enemy. (Jesus refers to this belief in Matthew 5:43: "You have heard that it was said, 'You shall love your neighbor and hate your enemy.'" But Jesus knew that such a command to hate is never actually stated in the Scriptures or in the writings of the rabbis.) **5**

Legalism

Another problem among the Jews was legalism. This was particularly true among the Pharisees.

The Jews looked upon the Law as a great gift from God, a sign of God's love for them. And certainly, some laws are necessary if a society is to maintain any reasonable kind of order. However, over time, minute rules and regulations had developed in Jewish society, not only guiding but dominating virtually every aspect of life. The combination of the Torah (the written version of the Law contained in the Scriptures of the Jews) and the oral teachings of the rabbis, which grew up over the years, led to an extensive system of religious laws. The Torah alone listed over six hundred such laws, governing everything from the Sabbath rest to ritual cleanliness, food and meal preparation, circumcision, and so on. In other words, a basic and decent moral foundation had become overly legalistic and was no longer just guiding the people but actually oppressing them. As we will discuss later in this course, Saint Paul would have much to say about legalism and the Law in light of Jesus' life and message. **6**

Love Without Limits

Jesus went beyond the limitations of the Law, shattering any sense of narrow nationalism as well as breaking down the barriers of legalism. A particularly marvelous Gospel passage captures this well: In Luke 10:25–37, Jesus asks a lawyer to explain what the Law requires for eternal life. The lawyer responds, as every good Jew would, with the dual commandment to love God and neighbor, and Jesus approves. But then the lawyer presses the issue by asking, "And who is my neighbor?" Jesus responds with the thought-provoking story of the good Samaritan. Remember how deeply the mainline Jews despised the Samaritans. By telling the story of the good Samaritan in the context of the command to love, Jesus is clearly telling his listeners that they are called beyond the limits of their own Judaism to love all people, even their enemies. **7**

Jesus teaches the same lesson in the Gospel of Matthew:

> But I say to you, Love your enemies and pray for those who persecute you, so that you may be children of your Father in heaven; for he makes his sun rise on the evil and on the good, and sends rain on the righteous and on the unrighteous. For if you love those who love you, what reward do you have? Do not even the tax collectors do the same? And if you greet only your brothers and sisters, what more are you doing than others? Do not even the Gentiles do the same? Be perfect, therefore, as your heavenly Father is perfect. (5:44–48)

Jesus' call to love one's enemies was unique to him, with no parallel in either the Old Testament or the writings of the rabbis.

Jesus did not believe that the Law, in itself, was bad. Rather, he recognized that the many spin-offs and additions to it had actually crippled the believers' ability to respond to one another with compassion and love. Jesus' challenge to certain dimensions of the Law—for example, the Sabbath laws (Mark 2:23–28) and the laws on ritual cleanliness (Mark 7:14–23)—could not help but alienate many who based their lives on the Law.

5
Find an example of national or ethnic conflict in the news that exemplifies "loving your neighbor but hating your enemy." Briefly describe how Jesus' teaching could change the situation.

6
In writing, respond to the following question and support your response with an example. *Do Christians have the same tendency toward legalism that the Jews of Jesus' time had?*

7
Rewrite the story of the good Samaritan (Luke 10:25–37) as you believe Jesus would tell it today if he were addressing your class or school.

Love Expressed in Deeds

Jesus did not actually use the word *love* all that much. He spoke more often of the results or expressions of love: service to others, compassion, forgiveness, and reconciliation. For a powerful summary of Jesus' teaching on the law of love, we need only read his familiar story of the last judgment in the Gospel of Matthew: Jesus says that at the end of time, "the Son of Man" will offer "the kingdom prepared . . . [since] the foundation of the world" to all those who responded to his needs when he was hungry, thirsty, lonely, naked, ill, imprisoned (25:31–36). The story continues:

> Then the righteous will answer him, "Lord, when was it that we saw you hungry and gave you food, or thirsty and gave you something to drink? And when was it that we saw you a stranger and welcomed you, or naked and gave you clothing? And when was it that we saw you sick or in prison and visited you?" And the king [Son of Man] will answer them, "Truly I tell you, just as you did it to one of the least of these who are members of my family, you did it to me." (25:37–40)

According to Jesus, faith in God cannot be lived out apart from service to people in need.

Jesus also claimed that the call to love is a call to unlimited forgiveness, and that God's willingness to forgive people is very much related to their willingness to forgive one another (Matthew 6:14–15). In the Lord's Prayer, Christians pray, "Forgive us our trespasses, *as we forgive those who trespass against us.*" Perhaps if people were more conscious of what they were saying, those words would not come out so easily!

F • O • C • U • S

The Roman Catholic Church and the Kingdom of God

At times in its long history, Roman Catholic church members have understood the church and the Kingdom of God to be one and the same. In recent years, however, the leaders of Catholicism have been careful to distinguish between the church itself and the Kingdom. The Kingdom of God is realized whenever and wherever the power of God's love is manifest, whenever and wherever the will of God is fulfilled. Because of that, the Kingdom is a reality much "bigger" than the church. For instance, Catholics today believe that other, non-Christian religions can also bring about the Kingdom of God to the degree that their members live in dedication to service, compassion, forgiveness, and reconciliation.

At the same time, the church cannot be understood apart from Jesus' vision of the Kingdom of God. The mission of the members of the church is to live in such a way that the Dream of Jesus is proved possible. The church is called to be a community transformed by the spirit of God into a people of faith, hope, love, freedom, and truth. When it exhibits such characteristics, the church proclaims in word and action that Jesus' vision of the Kingdom is not a pipe dream, not a "pie in the sky," but a reality within reach of people who dare to share that Dream.

Jesus' Teachings on Love: A Source of Challenge

The key to comprehending Jesus' teaching about the Kingdom of God, therefore, is in understanding his conviction about the passionate, unrestricted, unconditional love of God—and the power of that love to release and free people to love one another unconditionally, without restrictions. The Reign of God is revealed when God reigns over the hearts of people, and God reigns over the hearts of people when people are in tune with God's will. It has been said that "the will of God is the good of people." This means that when people conform their lives to God's will, there will be peace, joy, and love for all—that is, the Kingdom of God will be fully realized. **8**

For Review

- According to Jesus, what is the meaning of the word *conversion?*
- What does it mean to say that Jesus understood the Kingdom of God as being communal in nature?
- Name and briefly describe the two problems that developed among the Jews and conflicted with their following the command to love one another.
- When does Jesus' Dream of the Kingdom of God become realized?

The Reign of God and the "Reign of Sin"

Jesus' understanding of the Reign of God also touches on one of the most difficult realities of life: the presence of sin and evil in the world. In praying the Lord's Prayer, Christians ask God to "lead us not into temptation, but deliver us from evil." As the Lord's Prayer is found in the Gospel of Matthew, it reads, "And do not bring us to the time of trial, but rescue us from the evil one" (6:13). In one sense or another, all religions acknowledge the experience of sin and evil in life and offer some response to it.

Sometimes the source of evil is personified, or given almost human characteristics. In those cases, evil may be represented as a devil or as Satan. At times, Jesus uses such images in the Gospels, reflecting the common beliefs of the Jews of his day. As a faithful Jew, Jesus would have been very familiar with the Book of Genesis and its story of Adam and Eve in the garden (see Genesis, chapter 3). This story was the attempt by Jesus' people to explain the presence of evil in the world, while acknowledging that all that had come from God was good. The point of the story is that people are responsible for evil and its effects, because people choose to reject God, not the other way around. Several hundred years after the death of Jesus, the church named this historic rupture between God and people *original sin*, the effects of which have been passed down through the ages from generation to generation.

8
In a paragraph, react to the following statement: *True Christianity can never be understood as a "me and God" religion.*

The chief points to recognize here are that sin and evil do exist in the world and that the conflict between good and evil takes place both in the hearts of individual people and in their relationships with one another. **9**

Sin: Both Personal and Communal

Sin can be defined, understood, and experienced in several ways. Catholics commonly think of **sin** as personal, freely chosen actions that have negative effects on the sinners as individuals and on their relationships with others. But sin can also be understood as a social evil that affects all people simply because we live in community with one another. That is, we can say that the effects of the sinful actions of individual people accumulate over time into communal sin, which affects all who are born into it. This kind of sin is reflected in the isolation, alienation, and loneliness that

9
"Deliver us from evil." Which sin in our society do you think we most need to be delivered from? Respond in writing, giving your reasons.

■
The effects of the sinful actions of individual people accumulate over time into communal sin, which affects us all. War and poverty are examples of communal sin.

Photo: This family in Guayaquil, Ecuador, is forced by poverty to live in a dump. Hundreds of millions of people around the world live in extreme poverty.

afflict so many people today. Examples of communal sin and its effects are war, poverty, and the destruction of the environment.

Evil That Is Not Caused by Sin

Another evil—different from the moral evil associated with and brought about by sin, different from the evil that is chosen—often challenges Christians' basic conviction about the goodness of God. This kind of evil is expressed in the suffering, pain, and often untimely deaths brought about by natural destruction (such as hurricanes and earthquakes) and also by sickness and diseases such as cancer. Such occurrences are not evil in a moral sense but are nonetheless great tragedies for human beings.

There is no simple explanation for, or response to, such tragedies. The ancient Jews thought that even this kind of evil was a sign of personal sin. They believed, for example, that someone suffering from a disease was in some way being punished by God. Jesus did not accept such an explanation. Yet if the message of Jesus was to be truly heard as Good News, he clearly had to say something about both sin and evil, and especially about the power of God in him to ultimately overcome sin and evil. **10**

For Review

- Define *sin,* both personal and communal.
- In what sense are sin and evil different realities? What kind of evil is not caused by sin?

10
Write a brief essay about a time in your life when you struggled to understand an evil situation for which no single person seemed responsible.

The Kingdom Fulfilled Through Jesus

As has been noted, Jesus' proclamation of the Kingdom was rooted in the Jewish religious tradition. Prophets and teachers had been proclaiming similar messages of conversion, love, and good works to the people of Israel for at least a thousand years before Jesus. Although he presented those ideas with unique authority and a new perspective, if Jesus had simply proclaimed his message and done nothing else, he would have been merely another in a long line of great prophets.

But Jesus went beyond merely proclaiming the Kingdom; he also claimed that it would be established through him. For Jesus, bringing the Kingdom to its fullest reality meant saving the world from the effects of all evil by undoing the effects of original sin, and reconciling all people with God.

Jesus' Claim to Divine Authority

Scriptural scholars debate just how openly Jesus claimed to be the awaited Messiah of Israel, as well as exactly when he became aware that his own death would be the way of salvation. Clearly, however, Jesus claimed a unique role in God's plan to save humanity from sin. The divine authority that came with that role allowed him to proclaim the Kingdom of God in ways that no mere prophet could have:

Calling God "my Father." Jesus' ability to call God "my Father" and to refer to himself as God's Son was wholly unique. That relationship made it

possible for him to proclaim the intimacy between God and all people, an intimacy exemplified by the Our Father prayer.

Being beyond the Law. Jesus claimed an authority greater than that of the Law. In turn, he was able to call people beyond mere legalism to an interpretation of the Law in the light of unlimited love. For instance, he challenged the law governing Sabbath rest by performing healing miracles on that day (Luke 6:6–11); he amended the law governing divorce to call couples to a greater commitment to love (Matthew 19:3–9); and he pointed out the hypocrisy of following laws about keeping the body clean but ignoring the cleanliness of the heart (Mark 7:1–23).

Forgiving sins. Jesus said he had the authority to forgive sins on behalf of God—a claim that scandalized many devout Jews, but also allowed Jesus to call his followers to forgive one another without limit (Matthew 9:2–8).

Ridding the Temple of injustice. Jesus' special authority even enabled him to enter the Temple and rid it of the money changers who had been cheating the people (Matthew 21:12–14). Jesus' action embodied the justice of the Kingdom of God, but it also greatly angered the Jewish leaders, and probably was a factor leading to his Crucifixion.

God Is Ultimately Victorious

In the end, Jesus would "walk the talk," taking his proclamation of the Kingdom of God in terms of unlimited love and putting it into action by freely accepting death on the cross. Through that act, God in Jesus conquered evil in all its manifestations—including death, which was overcome

■
To bring about the Kingdom of God, we must accept the challenge to love as Jesus did—patiently and hopefully.
Photo: This mural made by young people at World Youth Day expresses, in many languages, their prayers and hopes for a world ruled by justice and peace.

F • O • C • U • S

The Kingdom of God Is Among You

Jesus' Dream of the Kingdom of God is made a reality whenever people are compassionate, concerned, and willing to extend themselves in service to others. Jesus' teaching on the last judgment in Matthew, chapter 25, shows the many ways such compassion can be lived out. If we really think about Jesus' words, we can see how the Kingdom of God is made real by the actions of young people today:

"I was hungry and you gave me food, I was thirsty and you gave me something to drink" (verse 35).
- Victor contributes the cost of one fast-food meal a week to an agency that works with poor people.

- One day each month Jackie volunteers to work at the local soup kitchen.
- Sharon makes a special effort to thank her parents for the meals they provide.

"I was a stranger and you welcomed me" (verse 35).
- Rochelle occasionally eats lunch in the cafeteria with a student who seems left out and lonely.
- Ben, an eleventh grader, volunteers to help make incoming ninth graders feel more welcome in his school.
- During a volleyball game, Mora invites Bruce to play, even though he has little ability for the game.

"I was naked and you gave me clothing" (verse 36).
- Jamisha decides to buy a less expensive pair of jeans than she would like and gives the money she saves to a special cause.
- Bret stops one of his friends who is ridiculing a student who cannot afford popular clothes.

"I was sick and you took care of me" (verse 36).
- Janelle's mother suffers from migraine headaches. Janelle avoids using her stereo and keeps the volume on the television very low at those times.
- Craig's friend is out of school with the flu for almost a week. Craig makes copies of all his own class notes and offers to tutor his friend when he feels better.
- Linda volunteers to tend her neighbor's yard while the neighbor's broken leg heals.

■
God's Kingdom exists wherever people are compassionate, concerned, and willing to help others. *Photo:* **Young people bring happiness and friendship to a woman in a nursing home.**

when Jesus was raised to life in the Resurrection. That is precisely what the Kingdom of God is all about: God is ultimately victorious; love is stronger than hate; good always wins over evil; and life, not death, has the last say.

The Kingdom of God: Right Now, but Not Yet

In reading the Gospels, we encounter repeated tension, if not complete contradiction, between various claims made about the Kingdom of God. For example, at one point it seems that the Kingdom is very close to us—right around the corner, so to speak (Mark 1:15). At another point it seems that the Kingdom is something to be achieved only at the end of time (Matthew 25:31–46). On one occasion Jesus states that "the kingdom of God is among you" (Luke 17:21), but on another occasion he tells people to pray for it to come (Matthew 6:10). Three important realizations can be gained from these apparent contradictions:

1. Jesus embodied the Kingdom of God. Jesus believed that the Kingdom was being revealed in his words, deeds, and actions. Toward the end of his mission, he became increasingly aware that his own death would be the central event in bringing about the Kingdom.

2. Jesus' followers fully recognized the Kingdom only after Jesus' Resurrection. God's Reign, as fulfilled in the life and message of Jesus, was fully recognized by the early community of faith only after Jesus' death, his Resurrection, and the sending of the Holy Spirit at Pentecost. This was when the full meaning of Jesus' words and actions became clear to his followers and they began, with the guidance of the Spirit, to understand him and his message in a different light. The entire Gospel presentation of Jesus' life and ministry was shaped by this recognition.

3. We must respond to Jesus' invitation to enter the Kingdom. How can the Kingdom be "right now," but "not yet"? The parables Jesus used to describe the Kingdom of God give us a clue. For instance, Jesus compared the Kingdom to a great dinner party (Luke 14:15–24) and to a valuable pearl (Matthew 13:34). In each case, the Kingdom is already present, symbolized by the party and the pearl. But to experience the Kingdom, people must respond to its presence. Only the people who said yes to the party invitation were able to enjoy the party. The merchant who found the beautiful pearl sold everything he had in order to own it. Likewise, God fully established the Kingdom through Jesus' death and Resurrection, and it is already present among us through the Holy Spirit. But we must say yes to God's invitation in order to fully experience the Kingdom. Jesus calls us to be like the merchant, to "sell all that we have"—not literally, but in the way Jesus always gave all of himself to God. When people love as Jesus did, they find themselves fully present in God's Reign. **11**

For Review

- What unique role did Jesus claim for himself in the Kingdom of God?
- Name two examples of how Jesus exercised his claim to divine authority.
- What does it mean to say that the Kingdom of God is "right now, but not yet"?

11
Read the material in the sidebar titled "The Kingdom of God Is Among You" (page 145). Write a paragraph explaining how the examples in the sidebar illustrate the "right now, but not yet" quality of the Kingdom of God. Add an example or two from your own experience.

Jesus' Special Stories

Ultimately we must confront the sense of mystery that accompanies the coming of the Kingdom of God. The Gospels' language about the Kingdom is so diverse that it is impossible to describe the Kingdom precisely. For example, it may come suddenly, like the unexpected return of a traveler (Mark 13:33–37), or slowly and secretly, like yeast working in bread dough (Matthew 13:33). The Gospels' variety of language is an expression of a truly wonderful reality: What God can do for people is far greater than anything we can imagine or understand. The vision of the Kingdom—that is, the Dream of Jesus—is magnificent beyond our understanding, yet somehow simple enough that all can respond to its challenge and invitation.

The complex nature of the Kingdom explains, at least to some degree, Jesus' unique use of parables—stories that allow us to catch a glimpse of something that is too big for words. Chapter 7 discusses these special stories told by Jesus.

■
We cannot fully understand the magnificence of the Dream of Jesus. Still, we can imagine a peaceful, loving world and work toward it.

Photo: The Waterton-Glacier International Peace Park in Montana and Alberta, Canada, is dedicated to the hope that the world's nations can live in peace.

7
Jesus Speaks:
Sayings and Stories of the Kingdom

In This Chapter . . .

- Unlocking Jesus' Words
- Jesus' Sayings and Stories in the Gospels
- A Closer Look at the Parables

AGAIN [Jesus] began to teach beside the sea. . . . He began to teach them many things in parables, and in his teaching he said to them: "Listen! A sower went out to sow. And as he sowed, some seed fell on the path, and the birds came and ate it up. Other seed fell on rocky ground, where it did not have much soil, and it sprang up quickly, since it had no depth of soil. And when the sun rose, it was scorched; and since it had no root, it withered away. Other seed fell among thorns, and the thorns grew up and choked it, and it yielded no grain. Other seed fell into good soil and brought forth grain, growing up and increasing and yielding thirty and sixty and a hundredfold." And he said, "Let anyone with ears to hear listen!" . . .

With many such parables he spoke the word to them, as they were able to hear it; he did not speak to them except in parables, but he explained everything in private to his disciples. (Mark 4:1–34)

Unlocking Jesus' Words

Previous chapters in this course briefly discussed Jesus' public life in terms of his role as a teacher. The title *teacher* is a common one for Jesus in the Gospels, appearing at least thirty times in direct reference to him. Other related titles used for Jesus in the Gospels are *master* and *rabbi*. Different translations of the Gospels use these three terms almost interchangeably.

Jesus' style as a teacher, which differed from the traditional style of the rabbis, has also been mentioned in this course.

- Jesus relied on himself alone as the judge of the truths he shared, rather than depending on the teachings of other rabbis to support his ideas.
- Jesus called his disciples into a lifelong relationship with him and then commissioned them to share in his ministry of spreading the Good News.
- Jesus referred to God as Abba, an intimate name that did not appear as a title for God in the Scriptures he used or in the writings of the rabbis.

This chapter pursues Jesus' role as a teacher a bit further, looking at his words and sayings and, in particular, reflecting on his special form of storytelling, the parables.

Do We Know What Jesus Really Said?

The Gospels: Not Records of Everyday Conversation

Readers of the Gospels are often struck by the fact that many of Jesus' words seem stark and blunt

---

The Gospels tell us that Jesus' teaching astounded his listeners with its unique authority and wisdom.
Photo, facing page: A view of the north end of the Sea of Galilee from the Mountain of the Beatitudes, where popular tradition says Jesus taught. *Background:* "Look at the birds of the air; they neither sow nor reap nor gather into barns, and yet your heavenly Father feeds them. Are you not of more value than they?" (Matthew 6:26).

—sometimes even cruel. When calling his first disciples, for example, he simply walks up to them and says, "Follow me and I will make you fish for people" (Mark 1:17). And at once they leave their nets and follow him. It is difficult to understand how Jesus could get such an immediate response with so little explanation of what he was calling the disciples to.

On another occasion, Jesus says:

If any of you put a stumbling block before one of these little ones who believe in me, it would be better for you if a great millstone were hung around your neck and you were thrown into the sea. If your hand causes you to stumble, cut it off; it is better for you to enter life maimed than to have two hands and to go to . . . the unquenchable fire. (Mark 9:42–43) **1**

Clearly, Jesus could talk tough when he wanted to!

To understand the words, sayings, and stories of Jesus, we must keep in mind the vehicle by which they come to us: the Gospels. The Gospels are the early faith community's reflections on and expressions of Jesus' life and message as understood in light of his Resurrection. In other words, we do not find Jesus' everyday, casual con-

versation in the Gospels. We have, rather, his most significant thoughts and ideas—expressed through the words of those who heard him. In most cases, these words were passed on orally for many years before finally being recorded in the Gospels.

Jesus' Words: Reflections of a Unique Message

So the Gospels do not record Jesus' words with the exactness of a tape recording. Scholars do agree, however, that Jesus used two words in a distinctive way:

- *Abba* was Jesus' distinctive and characteristic way of addressing God.
- Jesus also demonstrated an unusual use of the word *amen* in his teachings. In Jesus' day, the word *amen* was normally used much as it is today—as a statement of agreement or affirmation at the conclusion of a prayer. Jesus, however, *began* many of his teachings with this

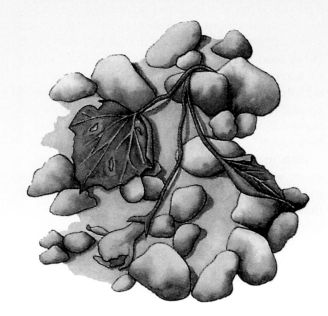

1
Give a contemporary example of exaggerated speech and explain what the phrase or sentence really means (for example, "I nearly had a heart attack when she opened the door"). Comment in a paragraph on what Jesus probably meant in the passage given here from Mark.

■
Illustrations: Jesus taught in parables: "Other seed fell on rocky ground. . . . Other seed fell among thorns. . . ."

word, saying, "Amen, amen, I say to you . . ." and then making a statement of some kind. Used in this way, the word was a confirmation of Jesus' own teaching, a manner of giving weight to what he was saying. This use of the word *amen* was unheard of in Jesus' time.

So whenever we see *amen* or *Abba* in the Gospels, we are probably reading something at least close to Jesus' original words. For other sayings, pronouncements, and stories spoken by Jesus in the Gospels, we cannot be sure exactly which words are his own and which might be interpretations of his message by the early faith community.

Jesus' Words . . . and Then Some

As stated at the beginning of this course, the omission of some factual material from the Gospels does not mean that we cannot find truth in them. Rather, what we find in the Gospels is *more* than just some words Jesus said; we also find the *meaning* his words had for his followers. And because Christians believe that the Gospels were written with the guidance of the Holy Spirit, they also believe that the words of Jesus as recorded in the Gospels convey the truths Jesus taught to his original followers.

A Jew Speaking to Fellow Jews

Another key to understanding Jesus' words is to remember that Jesus was thoroughly Jewish, as were most of his followers. He naturally spoke to them with their imagery and speech patterns, and within the context of how they experienced and understood the world.

Engaging the Whole Person

Our own culture has been heavily influenced by the Greek way of thinking. That is, we expect

ideas and arguments to be arranged in an orderly manner, and we expect logical proofs for things. But this way of thinking and talking was not common among the Jews of Jesus' day.

For the ancient Jews, the art of speaking was not so much a matter of convincing people through logical formulas, but rather one of establishing contact with the *total* person—with the listener's emotions and feelings as well as her or his intellect. Thus, the Jewish manner of speaking was far more poetic than our own, filled with a heavy use of symbolism, figures of speech, exaggeration, and so on. For example, Jesus said, "If your hand causes you to stumble, cut it off" (Mark 9:43). Surely

■

Illustration: "Other seed fell into good soil . . . yielding . . . a hundredfold." In Jesus' day, a harvest that yielded several times more grain than was sowed would have been considered very good. A harvest that yielded one hundred times the grain sowed would have been miraculous indeed.

Jesus did not mean this literally but was using exaggeration to make a point as strongly as possible. **2**

Supporting Statements with the Scriptures

In the Jewish tradition, a master of public speaking also filled his presentations with imagery from the Scriptures. Virtually every statement had to be supported with the word of God as preserved in the Hebrew Bible.

Jesus demonstrated a thorough familiarity with the sacred writings, and his teachings were filled with references to them. In fact, some of his most striking statements were actually biblical quotes. For example, most of us are familiar with his statement that we are called to "turn the other cheek" if someone strikes us. But this statement by Jesus was actually based on one already contained in

the Book of Lamentations (3:30), of the Old Testament. Jesus was following a common practice when he taught in this way, though he often gave his own special "twist" or insight when doing so.

For Review

- Do the Gospels give us Jesus' actual words? Explain your answer.
- What two words do scholars agree were used by Jesus in a distinctive way? What was distinctive about Jesus' use of these words?
- Why do Christians believe they can trust the Gospels to accurately convey the truth of Jesus' teaching?
- In what ways did Jesus follow the traditional Jewish format of public speaking? Why did he speak in these ways?

■
Jesus often taught in the synagogues, referring to the Hebrew Scriptures frequently.
Photo: **Ruins of a second-century synagogue in Capernaum, where Jesus based his ministry.**

2
Find another example in the Gospels of Jesus' use of symbolism, a figure of speech, or exaggeration. Write it down and comment on what point you think he was trying to make.

Jesus' Sayings and Stories in the Gospels

Jesus' teaching and preaching included a variety of styles of speech, but most common were these four: direct pronouncements, short sayings, instructions for disciples, and—perhaps most significant—parables.

Pronouncement Stories

Setups for a Punch Line

The Gospel writers situated Jesus' pronouncements within stories. A story acted as a setup for a pronouncement, much like a joke is told today to get to a punch line. Jesus' "punch lines" contained the main lessons he wanted to get across. Some scholars think that although the pronouncements themselves probably originated with Jesus, the stories preceding them might have been composed by the Evangelists to meet the needs of their audiences. This would be one explanation of why a pronouncement by Jesus sometimes appears with different stories in different Gospels.

Examples of Pronouncement Stories

Pronouncement stories were popular in ancient cultures and were often told about famous teachers. The stories commonly described a scene of tension—for example, the opponents of the teacher posing a difficult question. The teacher, in heroic fashion, would respond with an insightful proverb or statement, demonstrating wisdom superior to that of the opponents. Here are two examples of pronouncement stories used by the Gospel writers:

Picking corn on the Sabbath. In Mark 2:23–28, Jesus and his disciples are seen walking through cornfields, or grain fields, on the Sabbath. As they walk along, the disciples begin picking the corn—a direct violation of the laws restricting work on the Sabbath. The Pharisees confront Jesus about this, and he responds with a story about David and his followers. The scene closes with Jesus saying, "The sabbath was made for humankind, and not humankind for the sabbath." The point of the entire episode is to get to that "clincher," a direct and powerfully simple statement about the relationship of the Law to the needs of people. (This pronouncement story has parallels in Matthew 12:1–8 and Luke 6:1–5.) **3**

Responding to a scribe. Another pronouncement story (Mark 12:28–34) can be found at the opening of chapter 6 of this course. In that story, a scribe asks Jesus which of the commandments is

3
Create a modern pronouncement story that leads to this "punch line": *People were not made for Sunday Mass; Sunday Mass was made for people.*

■
"The sabbath was made for humankind, and not humankind for the sabbath."
Photo: In the Christian vision, Sundays are for celebrating God's

gifts to us with worship, renewal, and relaxation.

most important, and then the scribe affirms Jesus' answer. The central point of the entire story is Jesus' closing statement—that the scribe demonstrates by his understanding that he is "not far from the kingdom of God."

Short Sayings

"Words to the Wise"

The Jews were very fond of proverbs, short statements that were "words to the wise." These were offered without any story leading up to them. For example, in the Gospel of Mark, Jesus offers this series of short but highly thought-provoking statements:

If any want to become my followers, let them deny themselves and take up their cross and follow me. For those who want to save their life will lose it, and those who lose their life for my sake, and for the sake of the gospel, will save it. For what will it profit them to gain the whole world and forfeit their life? Indeed, what can they give in return for their life? Those who are ashamed of me and of my words in this adulterous and sinful generation, of them the Son of Man will also be ashamed when he comes in the glory of his Father with the holy angels. (8:34–38)

■
The Beatitudes are one part of the Sermon on the Mount, found in Matthew's Gospel.
Illustration: "Blessed are the poor in spirit, for theirs is the Kingdom of heaven" (Matthew 5:3).

F • O • C • U • S
The Beatitudes

The **Beatitudes**, which are part of Jesus' Sermon on the Mount (Matthew 5:3–12), are among the most familiar passages of the New Testament. Luke's Gospel has a shorter and somewhat different version of the Beatitudes, offered as part of "the Sermon on the Plain" (see Luke 6:20–23).

Lessons to Live By

Both Matthew's and Luke's versions of the Beatitudes convey three main lessons:

1. The Kingdom's fulfillment is yet to come. The Beatitudes point to the future, when God's Reign over the hearts of all people will fulfill their deepest desires and needs.

2. The Kingdom is in our midst. While the Beatitudes point to the future, they also teach that God's Kingdom is even now being proclaimed and inaugurated by Jesus. That is, Jesus himself embodies the Kingdom, and he wants his followers to live in response to an already-present reality.

3. Participation in the Kingdom requires a life of love. The Beatitudes paint a portrait of a life of loving service to others. In doing so, they call Jesus' followers to live out certain values and attitudes now, knowing that only later will they be rewarded ("Blessed are those . . . for they will . . ."). Christians are called to hunger and thirst for justice, to be merciful, to be peacemakers, and to suffer persecution for others, especially the poor.

Revealing the Reign of God

The Beatitudes can be challenging because they call Christians to a life of service and persecution, even if such a life is not rewarding right now. Christians choose to live the Beatitudes because they have faith that God's Reign—the triumph of love over evil—was accomplished in Jesus' death and Resurrection, and is already present among us through the Holy Spirit. By living in God's Reign, Christians reveal its presence to the world. Jesus, of course, is the model of one who fully lived the Beatitudes.

Hardly any scene is set, no story introduces the statements—the stark and challenging words of Jesus stand alone. We can imagine the effect his words would have had on his hearers.

An example of the use of short sayings in our day would be the posters of meaningful sayings that have become popular. These posters usually combine beautiful photography with short, insightful statements that catch our attention and cause us to think. **4**

A Classic Example: The Sermon on the Mount in Matthew

Matthew, in writing his Gospel, used an interesting method for presenting the short sayings of Jesus. That is, he put them together in a sort of

---

4
Looking at the Book of Proverbs (in the Old Testament), pick a chapter from 10 to 20 and then any proverb that catches your attention within that chapter. Copy the proverb onto a sheet of paper and write down its chapter and verse numbers. Then briefly explain why the proverb caught your attention.

The Lord's Prayer

The prayer that Jesus taught us, the Lord's Prayer, may be the most fundamental statement of faith a Christian can utter. Certainly, no prayer is more familiar to Christians. Taking a closer look at the prayer as given in the Gospels can offer some new insights into its meaning.

A formula for prayer. The Lord's Prayer appears in two Gospels—Matthew's (6:9–13) and Luke's (11:2–4)—and it is the only "formula" for prayer attributed to Jesus himself. Most scholars agree, however, that the prayer consists of statements or concepts taught by Jesus that were later gathered into a formalized prayer by the early faith community.

Different settings, different purposes. Luke shows Jesus teaching the Lord's Prayer in response to a request from his disciples, who have been watching him pray. Matthew places the prayer as part of a comparison between the prayer of Christians and the prayer of pagans. Because Luke's Gospel is considered to have been

written before Matthew's, Luke's setting is considered the original one. As frequently happened in the writing of the Gospels, Matthew most likely adapted Luke's version to address his purposes.

Different communities, different concerns. Each Gospel version of the Lord's Prayer reflects characteristics of the community in which the version was used. Matthew's version is longer than

Luke's, perhaps because Matthew added phrases to make his version more useful for communal prayer. And Matthew's Jewish audience would have been uncomfortable with Luke's addressing God as "Father"; therefore Matthew says "Our Father" and stresses God's existence "in heaven."

Themes about the Kingdom. Though the two Gospel versions of the Lord's

■
"Give us this day our daily bread . . ."
Photo: **In the Lord's Prayer, Christians ask God as their Father to take care of their human needs.**

Prayer differ slightly, they share several basic themes. These shared themes are best understood in light of Jesus' teachings about the Kingdom of God.

- The phrase "hallowed be your name" emphasizes the power and significance of God's name. The phrase means, "may all people recognize your name as holy and above all other names."
- The sentence "Your Kingdom come" asks for the reality of God's love to come into the hearts of all people. The Kingdom, or Reign, of God is already established "in heaven" through God's outpouring of love in the death and Resurrection of Jesus. It will be revealed on earth when the will of God is recognized and followed by people. Therefore, when Christians follow the will of God, they reveal the Reign of God's love by sharing that love with all people.
- The second half of the Lord's Prayer (beginning with "Give us this day") reflects the desire of the early Christians to live in such a way that God's holiness would be reflected in their behavior. The Kingdom demands that Christians express their love for God in their actions toward their sisters and brothers.
- The early church often interpreted "daily bread" as referring to the Eucharist. Today, "daily bread" is most often seen as referring to the fulfillment of the ongoing needs of Christians. The prayer is a petition for God to take care of all human needs—personal and communal, physical and spiritual.
- Both Matthew's and Luke's versions of the Lord's Prayer make a strong connection between God's forgiveness of people and people's willingness to forgive one another. When taken seriously, this can be a difficult prayer for Christians to utter. The hope is that God is far more willing and able to forgive us than we are to forgive one another! In any case, the Lord's Prayer makes it painfully clear that a believer's relationship with God cannot be understood or lived out apart from the believer's relationships with other people.

Just as we can fully understand Jesus and his proclamation of the Kingdom only in light of his Jewish roots, Christians can fully appreciate the Lord's Prayer only when they see it and pray it with the mind-set and conviction of the early Christians.

Photo: "Hallowed be your name" means "may all people recognize your name as holy."

collection. He wrote a scene in which Jesus instructs his disciples on a hill, offering them a series of proverbs (see Matthew, chapters 5 through 7). We have come to call this scene the Sermon on the Mount. It is one of the most popular sections of the Gospels, and one of the most frequently quoted.

Instructions for Disciples

Some of Jesus' teachings are recorded in the Gospels as instructions for those who would be his followers, his disciples. At times these passages incorporate other forms of teaching, such as the short sayings and the pronouncement stories.

The Lord's Prayer

One example of Jesus' instructions for disciples would be his words on prayer. Both Matthew and Luke include a section on Jesus' teaching about prayer, each section containing a version of the Lord's Prayer, or Our Father (see Matthew 6:9–15 and Luke 11:1–13). A comparison of the two versions of the prayer reveals some interesting points: For example, in Matthew's version, it appears that words and phrases have been added to Luke's original version in order to make the prayer more useful for communal worship. Some scholars suggest that the Lord's Prayer is really a summary of the entire Gospel message of Jesus, and it may have been the early church's attempt to summarize his major teachings. **5**

Matthew, Chapter 10

Matthew, chapter 10, presents another example of Jesus' telling his followers what they can expect of discipleship. This Gospel chapter includes a number of statements that some Christians might rather not hear:

- "You will be hated by all because of my name" (verse 22).
- "Whoever denies me before others, I also will deny before my Father in heaven" (verse 33).
- "I have not come to bring peace, but a sword" (verse 34).

Not easy reading! Fortunately, doom and foreboding is not all that Jesus offers. He also says:

- "Cure the sick, raise the dead, cleanse the lepers, cast out demons. You received without payment; give without payment" (verse 8).
- "Whatever town or village you enter, find out who in it is worthy, and stay there until you leave. As you enter the house, greet it" (verses 11–12).
- "Are not two sparrows sold for a penny? Yet not one of them will fall to the ground apart from your Father. And even the hairs of your head are all counted. So do not be afraid; you are of more value than many sparrows" (verses 29–31).

The Jewish affection for short, thought-provoking statements is evident throughout chapter 10 of Matthew. **6**

Parables

The parables form a central part of the synoptic Gospels. The word **parable** comes from a Greek word meaning "comparison." The term has been used to refer to a variety of Jesus' sayings, stories, riddles, and so on, but it is probably most precise to reserve it for his special stories about the Kingdom of God.

A parable usually builds from a literary device called a *simile*. In a simile, two different things are

---

5
Slowly read Matthew's version of the Lord's Prayer (6:9–13). Choose one verse and reflect on it with this question in mind: *What do these words mean for my life now?* Write your reflections.

6
Select one of the statements quoted from chapter 10 of Matthew that you have questions about. Pair up with another student and talk over the questions you both have.

compared to one another in order to illustrate a point. The word *like* often—though not always—joins the two parts of the comparison. For example, Jesus would say, "The kingdom of heaven is like . . ." and then compare it to a sower in a field, a mustard seed, or the yeast in bread (see Matthew 13:24–33). In concluding the Sermon on the Mount, Matthew offers a parable that sums up the purpose of the entire sermon:

Everyone then who hears these words of mine and acts on them will be *like* a wise man who built his house on rock. The rain fell, the floods came, and the winds blew and beat on that house, but it did not fall, because it had been founded on rock. (7:24–25, italics added)

Let's take a closer look at the use of parables in the Gospels.

For Review

- Identify and briefly define the four main styles of speech that Jesus used in his teaching.
- Explain Matthew's organization of the Sermon on the Mount.

■
Photo: "Are not two sparrows sold for a penny? Yet not one of them will fall to the ground apart from your Father. . . . So do not be afraid; you are of more value than many sparrows."

F • O • C • U • S

John: In a Different Voice

The Gospel of John uses different styles of speech than those found in the synoptic Gospels. One example that has already been noted in this course is John's use of highly symbolic, poetic language. Here are some other literary devices that characterize John's Gospel:

Long discourses. John's Gospel does not contain the rapid-fire, one-after-another miracle stories, the lists of short sayings, and so on, that characterize much of the synoptics. Rather, John offers long, unified stories and discourses, which are extended presentations by Jesus. For examples of discourses, see the "bread of life" discourse (John 6:22–59) and the Last Supper discourse (John 14:1–31).

Allegories. John does not use similes like those found in the parables in the synoptic Gospels. Instead, he uses the literary form called *allegory.* A simile is a relatively simple literary device comparing one thing to another, and the meaning of a simile should not be overanalyzed. An allegory, on the other hand, is complex, and virtually everything in it has significance. Examples of the use of allegory by John are the "good shepherd" passage (10:1–18) and the passage about the vine and the branches (15:1–11).

"I am" sayings. A distinctive feature of John's Gospel is the use of what are called "I am" sayings. These sayings are somewhat like similes in that they compare Jesus to another reality.

Recall that the name for God revered by the Jews was *Yahweh* and that the translation of the name is "I am who am." In John's Gospel, Jesus often begins his teachings with the words "I am." Scholars tell us that John intended for such references to show a direct relationship between Jesus and Yahweh. That is, the "I am" sayings signal Jesus' divinity as the Son of God.

Seven "I am" sayings appear in the Gospel of John. They are the following:

- "I am the bread of life" (6:35–40).
- "I am the light of the world" (8:12).
- "I am the gate" (10:7–10).
- "I am the good shepherd" (10:11–18).
- "I am the resurrection and the life" (11:17–27).
- "I am the way, and the truth, and the life" (14:1–7).
- "I am the true vine" (15:1–11).

■

Photo: **"I am the good shepherd. The good shepherd lays down his life for the sheep" (John 10:11).**

A Closer Look at the Parables

The Technique Behind the Parables

The use of parables is one of the most significant characteristics of Jesus' teaching style. He had a way of connecting his points to the everyday experiences of his listeners, so that his teaching would be clear to them and easily remembered.

Based on Everyday Life

The basic story elements in Jesus' parables grew out of the land, culture, and family life of his people: farming and shepherding, children playing and adults working at their trades and crafts. Naturally, some of the settings and story elements can seem strange to the modern reader. As may be quite evident by now, knowing something about the land and daily life of the Jewish people of Jesus' time is essential to grasping the meaning of Jesus' teachings. Yet it was precisely because Jesus drew from the common experiences of his listeners that his teachings—and especially his parables—were powerful. When we read the parables today, it is often helpful to find parallels between our experiences and those of the people Jesus was directly addressing. That is, we can translate the parables into familiar language. **7**

Filled with Surprises

In developing a parable, Jesus would take a common occurrence of the day and add a surprising twist to it, such as a surprise ending. These surprises would keep his listeners alert, or catch them off-guard. The idea was to make people reflect on the lessons he was trying to teach. Here are two examples of Jesus' technique:

F • O • C • U • S
A Modern Parable: "The House"

More than anything else in the whole world, a man wanted to possess a house of his own. Not just any house, but a house that everyone would marvel at. So he worked long hours and hard days over many years until at last he acquired the house of his dreams.

Alas, once he set foot in his house, he was never seen again. He dared not leave his prize for fear that thieves would steal or vandals ruin what he had labored so hard to possess.

Moral. Whatever you possess, possesses you.

(Aurelio, *Fables for God's People,* page 7)

7
Write a parable about what God is like, using something in your life and world that is familiar to you. (For instance, "God is like your school locker—the place you return to for everything you need to get through your day.")

The parable of the lost sheep. The parable of the lost sheep is found in Matthew 18:12–14 and in Luke 15:4–7. In the story, a shepherd leaves ninety-nine sheep in search of one that is lost, and then rejoices over finding the lost one. Jesus' listeners would have been taken aback by this, because no ordinary shepherd would have considered risking the entire flock for the sake of one sheep. **8**

The parable of the prodigal son. In the popular parable of the prodigal son (Luke 15:11–32), a father's younger son leaves home to go off and spend his inheritance in a wild spree, while the older son remains loyal to the father and continues to fulfill his responsibilities. When the younger son runs out of money, he returns home begging for mercy. What does the father do? He does not start comparing the younger boy with the older one, who remained loyal. Nor does he *reluctantly* agree to take back the wayward son. Instead the father throws a magnificent party for the one who was such a big disappointment to him. (Anyone listening to this parable has to be awfully sympathetic with the older son's anger about the situation!)

With both of these parables, Jesus was teaching his followers about God's boundless and forgiving love for those who have gone astray. God's love is so profound that it literally seems to defy common sense.

Themes of the Parables

Chapter 6 of this course addressed the central significance of the Kingdom of God in Jesus' message. Not surprisingly, many of Jesus' sayings and stories either relate directly to his proclamation of God's Kingdom or flow out of his own awareness of the complex nature of the Kingdom.

Although it is hard to arrive at a clear-cut breakdown of all the parables, the following organization of the parables into four main themes or purposes is helpful.

1. Descriptions of the King

Some parables describe the King of the Kingdom, namely God. That is, these parables deal primarily with God's nature, qualities, attitudes in dealing with people, and so on.

The parable of the lost sheep. As noted earlier, the parable of the lost sheep (Matthew 18:12–14 and Luke 15:4–7) demonstrates God's gracious love. God takes the initiative and seeks out those who stray.

■

Illustration: **In the parable of the talents, one servant fearfully hides his talent, or weight of silver.**

8
Rewrite Luke's version of the parable of the lost sheep (15:4–7) to make it into a modern parable.

The parables of the lost coin and the prodigal son. The stories of the lost coin and the prodigal son (Luke 15:8–32) illustrate that God will do almost anything to find us and then will rejoice when we are finally found.

The parable of the laborers in the vineyard. In the parable of the laborers in the vineyard (Matthew 20:1–16), a landowner apparently pays some laborers more than they deserve. Jesus' point, however, is to illustrate the almost overwhelming generosity of God, the fact that God operates out of a completely different "economic system" than the one used by people.

All four of these parables reflect that wonderful image of the Father presented by Jesus—the image of a God whom people can call *Abba*.

2. "Kingdom" Responses

Some of the parables emphasize how we should act if we hope to "enter the Kingdom."

The parable of the Pharisee and the tax collector. The parable of the Pharisee and the tax collector (Luke 18:9–14) tells us that we should adopt the basic attitude of humility if we are going to participate in the Kingdom. The Pharisee is self-righteous, congratulating himself on his strict religious practices, whereas the tax collector feels deep sadness for his sinfulness. Jesus says the tax collector is the more righteous of the two because the tax collector recognizes, as all people must, that the need for repentance in life is real.

The parable of the rich fool. In the parable of the rich fool (Luke 12:16–21), we find a man who is self-satisfied because he has grown huge amounts of grain. He plans to build large barns in which to store his harvest. God, however, interrupts the man's planning and says to him, "'You

fool! This very night your life is being demanded of you. And the things you have prepared, whose will they be?'" This parable illustrates the need to rely on God's graciousness rather than solely on our own resources.

The parable of the talents. In the parable of the talents (Matthew 25:14–30), a man gives each of his three servants a different number of *talents*, or weights of silver. He then leaves the servants to their own resources as to how they will manage the silver. Two of the servants work to turn a profit with their talents, but one servant fearfully hides his, afraid that he will lose it. Upon returning, the master angrily rebukes this servant for not doing something beneficial with what he has been given. The lesson to Jesus' listeners—and to us—is to make good use of the gifts and talents we have been given, in order to reveal the Kingdom.

■
In the parable of the rich fool, a man plans to build large barns in which to store the harvest that makes him wealthy.
Photo: A grain silo in Israel.

3. Relationships with Our Neighbors

Other parables address people's relationships with one another and the world at large.

The parable of the unforgiving servant. In the parable of the unforgiving servant (Matthew 18:21–35), a servant begs his master to relieve him of a debt. The master, moved with pity, completely cancels the debt, only to find later that the servant went out and had a fellow servant thrown into prison for not paying a debt owed to him. In great anger, the master has the unforgiving ser-

vant tortured. The lesson of the parable is that we must truly forgive one another from our heart if we expect to be forgiven.

The parable of the good Samaritan. The parable of the good Samaritan (Luke 10:25–37) has already been mentioned a few times in this course. Though the lesson of the parable may be clear enough to us today, it was shockingly clear to Jesus' listeners: If people want to be part of the Kingdom of God, they must open their heart to everyone, even the outcasts of society. **9**

■
Photo: Jericho Road, from Jerusalem to Jericho, was a barren place to be attacked by robbers and left to die. One of the most familiar Gospel parables is that of the good Samaritan.

9
Select one of the parables under the category of either "'Kingdom' Responses" or "Relationships with Our Neighbors." With a small group, act out the parable as a skit for your class. Use humor, music, or props if you like.

4. The Fulfillment of the Kingdom

Finally, some of the parables refer to the future coming of God's Kingdom in its fullness.

The parable of the great feast. In the parable of the great feast (Luke 14:15–24), an owner of a house gives a great dinner and invites many people. But those invited give all kinds of excuses for why they cannot come. The host, now angry at their rejection of the great feast, decides to bring in people from the streets—the poor and crippled, the blind and lame. In this parable, Jesus was trying to say that God's invitation of love—to the "heavenly banquet" of the Kingdom—will be extended to those considered undeserving, while the "deserving," those who think themselves worthy of God's favor, will refuse God's offer of love.

The parable of the weeds among the wheat and the parable of the ten bridesmaids. In the parable of the weeds among the wheat (Matthew 13:24–30), Jesus says that the weeds must be allowed to grow together with the wheat, and they will be separated from the wheat at the harvest. In the parable of the ten bridesmaids (Matthew 25:1–13), some foolish bridesmaids get locked out of the wedding banquet because they were unprepared for the arrival of the bridegroom. Both of these parables point to the end time, or the future day of judgment by God. **10**

Multiple Uses of the Parables

Occasionally a parable is used to teach different lessons in different Gospels, often by changing the setting in which Jesus tells the parable. Take the parable of the lost sheep, for example.

Matthew puts the parable in the context of Jesus' answer to the disciples' question, "Who is the greatest in the kingdom of heaven?" (18:1). Jesus uses the parable to illustrate his response that those who become like little children are most important in God's Kingdom. After telling the parable, Jesus says, "So it is not the will of your Father in heaven that one of these little ones should be lost" (18:14).

In the Gospel of Luke, Jesus tells the parable of the lost sheep to teach a group of tax collectors and sinners about God's mercy. Jesus concludes the parable by saying, "I tell you, there will be more joy in heaven over one sinner who repents than over ninety-nine righteous persons who need no repentance" (15:7).

These seemingly contradictory situations for telling the parable can be explained as follows:

• It is quite possible that Jesus used the same story more than once to illustrate different points and that the Gospel authors simply differed in which version of the story they selected.
• An individual Gospel author may have changed the setting of the parable to better illustrate the point he wished to make to his readers.

Of course, minor differences in how Jesus' parables are used do not deny the lessons they teach. If anything, the multiple use of the parables demonstrates how rich these stories truly are.

Understanding the Parables Today

The parables challenge us, as modern readers, to let them speak to our own life situations. And insofar as they give us a picture of the Kingdom, they also challenge us to accept it—that is, to accept the will of God. We, as individuals and as communities of faith, are called to identify with the lost sheep, with the wicked tenants, with the good Samaritan, and so on, just as Jesus' original listeners were. How can we meet these challenges? Here are a few suggestions that can make the reading of

10
Which is your favorite of Jesus' parables? Write in your own words the main point Jesus was trying to make in that parable.

■
Photo: One version of the parable
of the lost sheep teaches that
those who become like children
are treasured by God, who wills
that not one of them be lost.

the parables more enjoyable and enlightening for us:

1. Look for the central messages of the parables. The details in some of the parables can make the stories more interesting perhaps, but we should not try to read too much into them. The messages of Jesus are often far more direct and to the point than we might expect or recognize.

2. Look for the questions posed in the parables. Jesus sometimes asks his listeners to offer their own response to a parable, before he gives his intended message. For example, following the parable of the good Samaritan, Jesus asks his listeners, "Which of these three [men], do you think, was a neighbor to the man who fell into the hands of the robbers?" (Luke 10:36). Whenever such questions are posed directly or indirectly in the parables, we should pause and attempt to answer them ourselves.

3. Compare our answers with those recorded in the Gospels. Many times the sayings and interpretations that conclude the parables reflect the early faith community's answers to Jesus' questions. It is possible, in other words, that Jesus might not have actually answered some of his own questions or interpreted the parables for the people. Instead, he might have encouraged them to figure out as many insights as they could on their own. As we read the parables, then, we should compare the answers we would give with those given by the early church and recorded in the Gospels. Doing so can help to make the Gospels come alive for us today. **11**

For Review

- Why did Jesus often conclude his parables with a surprise ending?
- List and describe the four main themes by which we can categorize Jesus' parables. What is the common thread that runs through all these themes?
- Why might a parable be used, or even modified, to teach different lessons in different Gospels?
- List three suggestions that can make the parables more enjoyable and enlightening for us.

11
Browse through any one of the synoptic Gospels and note three occasions when Jesus asks a question. Write down each question (and its chapter and verse numbers) and try to answer it before reading the answer recorded in the Gospel. Write down the Gospel's answer if it is different from your own.

F • O • C • U • S

Jesus' Parables in the Synoptic Gospels

	Matthew	Mark	Luke
The house built on rock	7:24–27		
The sower	13:1–23	4:1–20	8:4–15
The weeds among the wheat	13:24–30		
The mustard seed	13:31–32	4:30–32	13:18–19
The hidden treasure and the pearls	13:44–46		
The unforgiving servant	18:23–35		
The good Samaritan			10:25–37
The rich fool			12:16–21
The great feast			14:15–24
The lost sheep	18:12–14		15:4–7
The lost coin			15:8–10
The prodigal son			15:11–32
The unjust servant			16:1–13
The rich man and Lazarus			16:19–31
The unjust judge			18:1–8
The Pharisee and the tax collector			18:9–14
The laborers in the vineyard	20:1–16		
The wicked tenants	21:33–46	12:1–12	20:9–19
The wedding banquet	22:1–14		
The faithful servant	24:45–51		
The ten bridesmaids	25:1–13		
The talents or sums of money	25:14–30		19:11–27

Putting Jesus' Words into Actions

When trapped by a contradiction between what they claim to believe and the way they actually live, some people fall back on the old saying, "Don't do what I do. Do what I say." A somewhat-related proverb states a similar point: "What you do speaks so loudly that I can't hear what you are saying."

In the case of Jesus, however, there were no contradictions between what he said and the way he acted. All that he said and did revealed his vision of the Reign of God over all creation and in the hearts of people. This chapter discussed the words and sayings of Jesus. But because Jesus spoke and acted, no study of him and his message can be complete without discussing some of his most challenging and perhaps confusing actions: his miracles.

■
Photo: **Unusual rock formations on the northwest shores of the Sea of Galilee**

8
Jesus Heals:
Signs of the Kingdom

Jesus' Marvelous Deeds: As Important as His Words

WHEN John [the Baptist] heard in prison what the Messiah was doing, he sent word by his [own] disciples and said to [Jesus], "Are you the one who is to come, or are we to wait for another?" Jesus answered them, "Go and tell John what you hear and see: the blind receive their sight, the lame walk, the lepers are cleansed, the deaf hear, the dead are raised, and the poor have good news brought to them. And blessed is anyone who takes no offense at me." (Matthew 11:2–6)

Chapter 6 explored Jesus' Dream of the Kingdom of God—his vision of the will of God, who releases the power of unlimited love over all creation and in the hearts of people. Chapter 7 looked at the words of Jesus, especially his parables, as teachings about the Kingdom of God.

When we read about Jesus in the Gospels today, how do we know that he was not suffering from delusions, that he was not insane or perhaps just plain lying when he spoke of the Kingdom? As some have stated it, Jesus was one of three things: a lunatic, the greatest con artist in history, or precisely who he claimed to be—"the One sent by God." What makes his words worthy of our trust?

One answer would be to examine Jesus' actions to see whether they support his claims. Jesus' actions—particularly his **miracles**, or signs—were as important to his ministry as his teachings, in part because they revealed the truth of his words. **1**

A Variety of Signs

The Gospels are filled with a variety of "works of wonder" by Jesus.

- *Healing miracles.* On many occasions Jesus is shown relieving the suffering of people afflicted with fever, paralysis, deafness, dumbness, blindness, or leprosy. (Leprosy was a general name for many kinds of skin disease in Jesus' day.)
- *Exorcisms.* Dramatic accounts portray Jesus as driving evil spirits or demons out of people.
- *Restorations of life.* Three stories tell of Jesus' raising people from the dead.

■
Jesus' miracles reveal him as one who frees us from sin and death to goodness and abundant life. *Photo, facing page:* A woman draws water at Jerusalem's pool of Siloam. Jesus cured a blind man by having him wash in the pool, according to the Gospel of John. *Background:* Jesus was concerned not only with healing eyes blind to light but also hearts blind to the Good News.

1
In a paragraph, react to this statement: *Jesus was one of three things: a lunatic, a con artist, or precisely who he claimed to be.*

- *Nature miracles.* Frequently the Gospels demonstrate Jesus' apparent control over the forces of nature: he walks on water, calms a storm, feeds thousands with just a few loaves and fish, and so on.

The miracles of Jesus are of special significance because they demonstrate that the power of God was truly manifested in Jesus. Without some concrete demonstration of Jesus' power over sin and evil, his words would lack credibility.

The Meaning of the Miracles

This chapter takes a close look at the meaning of Jesus' miracles. The discussion focuses on these three interrelated questions:

1. What did the *Gospel writers* intend to teach about Jesus and his Kingdom through the miracle stories?
2. What did *Jesus* intend to reveal through his miracles?
3. How are *we* to understand Jesus' miracles today? The last question may be the most critical of the three. No feature of Jesus' life and ministry is more debated, confusing, or subject to interpretation than his miracles. And unless we come to a credible, contemporary understanding of Jesus' miracles, we may not be able to "hear" what the Gospel writers—and Jesus—were trying to teach.

For Review

- Identify and describe the kinds of miracles found in the Gospels.
- Why are Jesus' miracles of special significance?

F • O • C • U • S
John: Signs of God in Jesus

Chapter 7 noted that the synoptic Gospels include parables as a major part of the teaching style of Jesus, but the Gospel of John excludes the use of parables altogether, instead it uses allegories to explore the message of Jesus. Likewise, John's use of miracle accounts differs from what we see in the synoptics. The following points are the most significant differences:

1. John includes just seven miracles in his Gospel, far fewer than in the Gospels of Matthew, Mark, or Luke. However, John describes those seven miracles in much greater detail than the synoptics describe theirs. For example, John often follows the story of a miracle with a lengthy discussion about its deeper meaning among those who witnessed it.

2. In the synoptic Gospels, the miracle stories are often presented in groups, one right after another. This can make the miracle stories seem set off from the main part of the Gospels. John's Gospel has a more structured flow than the synoptics do, so the miracle stories are more directly woven into John's portrait of Jesus.

3. Four of the seven miracles in John's Gospel do not appear at all in the synoptic Gospels. John's miracle stories are listed below. Those that are unique to his Gospel appear in bold type.

- **Changing water to wine at Cana (2:1–12)**
- Restoring health to the royal official's son (4:46–54)
- **Curing on the Sabbath (5:1–18)**
- Multiplying the loaves (6:1–15)
- Walking on the water (6:16–21)
- **Healing the man born blind (9:1–12)**
- **Raising Lazarus (11:1–44)**

  John, chapter 21, includes a miracle about a great catch of fish, but that chapter is not considered an original part of the Gospel.

4. The synoptic Gospels refer to Jesus' miracles as acts of power intended to demonstrate that the Kingdom of God is being established in Jesus. John's Gospel centers, instead, on Jesus himself as the Son of God, the One in and through whom the Father is fully revealed. Jesus' miracles are "signs" that through Jesus, God's creative and transformative power is present in all aspects of life.

5. The synoptic accounts focus on the miracles themselves, whereas John's accounts focus on the symbolic meaning of the miracles. Physical miracles in John's Gospel symbolize deeper spiritual truths and realities. For example:
- The health restored to the royal official's son is a sign of the Spirit that will be given through the death and Resurrection of Jesus (5:21–24).
- The primary intent in curing the man born blind is not the matter of giving physical sight. Rather, it is the matter of giving spiritual insight into the real identity of Jesus (9:35–41).
- The raising of Lazarus illustrates not only God's power over life and death but also Jesus' own identity as "the resurrection and the life" (11:25–26).

Cana, in Galilee, is the scene of a wedding where Jesus turned water into wine (John 2:1–11). *Photo:* The city of Cana today.

Why Are the Miracles So Challenging?

Perhaps no image of Jesus both captures our imagination and challenges our mind more than that of Jesus as "the miracle worker." Our imagination is caught up with scenes of power and awe—people raised to life with a simple word, blindness cured with a touch, sickness and disease rendered powerless in the presence of Jesus. These same scenes have moved millions of people to faith throughout the history of Christianity. Yet the notion of miracles often presents the logical and scientific mind of today with serious, disturbing questions rather than faith-strengthening signs of hope. Why might this be so?

Miracles in the Modern World

The way we view the world today is drastically different from the way the Jews viewed it in Jesus' day. We expect and want proof, evidence, and logical explanations for virtually everything we encounter.

■
Photo: **The road leading to Nain in Galilee. It was on the road to Nain that Jesus raised a widow's son from the dead (Luke 7:11–17).**

The Typical Responses

Two extreme responses to Jesus' miracles are typical of our time, given our contemporary expectations: people either "take 'em or leave 'em."

Take 'em. Some of today's Christians simply accept all the Gospel miracles at face value. And in doing so, they feel forced to reject many of our modern scientific and biblical findings. These people are often referred to as fundamentalists, and they opt for a literal interpretation of the Bible. That is, they do not accept any part of the Scriptures as symbolic or open to various interpretations.

Leave 'em. At the other extreme, many people —both Christians and non-Christians—reject any possibility of the miracles. Miracles are, by definition, phenomena that go beyond the laws of nature and point directly to the hand of God as their cause. Those who deny Jesus' miracles consider these Gospel accounts to be illusions of a primitive people or fables of some kind.

Another Option

Today's Christians can hold a middle ground between the two extreme positions on Jesus' miracles. It is not necessary, for example, to lump all the miracle accounts together and treat them the same way, giving one as much factual validity or significance as another. But if we get too bound up with whether an individual event occurred exactly the way the Gospels describe it, we risk completely missing the truth that the story can reveal to us. Certainly all these marvelous stories have something true and valid to teach us about Jesus and his proclamation of the Kingdom. **2**

Jesus Did Work Some Miracles

The Christian who takes the middle ground on the issue of miracles can be sure that Jesus did, in fact, work *some* wonders. Much evidence, and even common sense, upholds this. Consider the following points about Jesus' miracles:

Supported by historical records. Some non-Christian historians of ancient times referred to Jesus as a wonder-worker. So it is evident from historical records that Jesus greatly impressed the crowds with his actions.

Not denied by the Pharisees. Even the Pharisees in the Gospels do not deny that Jesus worked many wonders. Instead, the Pharisees charge him with doing so through the power of the devil (see Matthew 12:24 and Luke 11:15). Biblical scholars claim that this charge by the Pharisees would have been too unusual, too unexpected, to be included

2
Draw a horizontal line. At the far left end of the line, write, "All the Miracles Exactly as Described." At the far right end of the line, write, "None of the Miracles." Mark on the line where you think most young people stand in terms of believing in the Gospel miracles. Then mark where you stand. Follow up with a brief explanation of your responses.

■
In Matthew 8:14–15, Jesus enters Peter's house and cures Peter's mother-in-law of a fever.
Photo: The ruins of a house in Capernaum, believed to be the home of Peter.

in the Gospels if it were not based on an actual incident.

Affirmed by eyewitnesses. An undeniable historical fact is that many eyewitnesses to the works of Jesus—many of whom were still alive when the Gospels were written—believed so firmly in him and his message that they became committed followers. Many even freely chose to die rather than deny faith in him. Such devotion certainly lends great weight to the claims made about Jesus by the Gospel writers. Also, if the Gospel claims had not been based on actual happenings, serious objections would likely have been raised by the eyewitnesses themselves.

Jesus seems to have worked many wonders. The task of sorting out which miracle events occurred just as the Gospels describe them continues to be a major challenge to biblical scholars, and it is certainly beyond the scope of this course. Again, the major concern of this chapter is to understand the meaning of the miracles.

A Persistent Problem

One significant problem is unavoidable in trying to understand the meaning of Jesus' miracles. It is a difficulty even for those who accept a literal interpretation of the Gospels. This persistent problem centers around the fact that the Gospels themselves seem to disagree with one another about the same events. Some miracle accounts show definite signs that each Evangelist offered his own imaginative details. For instance, the miracles tend to intensify, magnify, and even multiply from one Gospel to the next, from the earliest one (Mark's) to the later ones. Consider these examples:

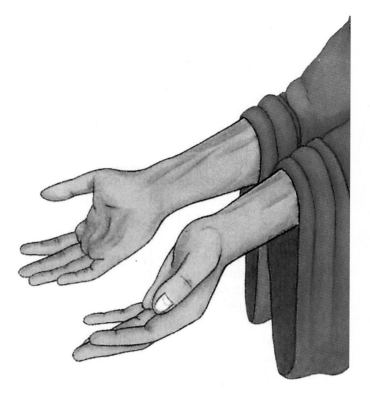

- The Gospel of Mark says that Jesus "cured *many* who were sick" (1:34), while the Gospel of Matthew says that Jesus "cured *all* who were sick" (8:16).
- In Mark's Gospel, a man named Jairus approaches Jesus and pleads, "My daughter is at the point of death" (5:23). In a parallel scene in Matthew's Gospel, Jairus says, "My daughter has just died" (9:18).
- The healing of one blind man in Mark's Gospel (10:46–52) becomes the healing of two in Matthew's Gospel (20:29–34).

It is conceivable as well that a tendency to exaggerate existed in the early community of faith before the Gospels were written.

■

Illustration: **With the touch of his hands, sickness and disease were rendered powerless in the presence of Jesus.**

The possibility of exaggeration and elaboration in the miracle stories raises two questions: On what basis can we approach and judge the truth of the miracles? How are we to understand them if they cannot always be understood as historical events reported with complete accuracy by the Evangelists? The remainder of this chapter will offer several possible answers to these questions.

For Review

- What is the fundamentalist response to the Gospel miracles?
- Why should Christians avoid extreme positions regarding the historical accuracy of the miracle accounts?
- Briefly summarize the evidence given to uphold the conviction that Jesus did work some miracles.
- What persistent problem regarding the miracles exists even for those who accept them all literally?

The Jews and Miracles

A Different View

One way to understand the miracle stories is to recognize that the people of Jesus' day viewed the world around them differently than our modern culture does.

Now Versus Then

People in our modern Western culture tend to rely on science to explain the world. That is why miracles are typically thought of as events that contradict the laws of nature, the scientific explanation of the way nature works. People in our culture also tend to view God as remote and not actively involved in the world.

The Jews of Jesus' day, however, explained everything in their world in terms of the power and presence of God. They did not think of miracles as special interventions in the laws of nature

■
Ancient Jews believed the breeze was God's breath passing over the earth.
Photo: A wheat field in Galilee.

Jesus' Miracles in the Synoptic Gospels

	Matthew	Mark	Luke
Cleansing of a leper	8:1–4	1:40–45	5:12–16
Healing of a centurion's servant	8:5–13		7:1–10
Curing of Peter's mother-in-law	8:14–15	1:29–31	4:38–39
Calming of a storm	8:23–27	4:35–41	8:22–25
Healing of the Gadarene demoniac(s)	8:28–34	5:1–20	8:26–39
Healing of a paralytic	9:1–8	2:1–12	5:17–26
Jairus's daughter and the woman with a hemorrhage	9:18–26	5:21–43	8:40–56
Healing of two blind men	9:27–31		
The man with a withered hand	12:9–14	3:1–6	6:6–11
First miracle of the loaves	14:13–21	6:30–44	9:10–17
Raising of the widow's son			7:11–17
Walking on the water	14:22–33	6:45–52	
Curing of the Canaanite woman's daughter	15:21–28	7:24–30	
Healing of a deaf man		7:31–37	
Second miracle of the loaves	15:32–39	8:1–10	
The blind man of Bethsaida		8:22–26	
Healing of a boy with a demon	17:14–20	9:14–29	9:37–42
Cleansing of ten lepers			17:11–19
Healing blindness at Jericho	20:29–34	10:46–52	18:35–43
The barren fig tree **3**	21:18–22		

3
Select one of the miracle stories above that has three Gospel versions and read all three. Write a description of how the versions differ and what the underlying message of all three versions is.

because they believed that God caused everything in nature anyway, not that nature ran itself according to a set of laws. The rain and the breeze were the direct results of God's activity—the rain was released through the floodgates that God opened, and the breeze was God's breath passing over the earth. The Jews accepted miracles as acts of God, too, if somewhat unusual ones. They were understandably awed by works of wonder, but not terribly surprised by them.

In the ancient Jewish view, everything was an expression either of God's creative power or the power of evil in the world. While good things like rain or a soft breeze were caused by God, all illness —from blindness to leprosy to death itself—was the result of evil. Any cure, therefore, was an exorcism, because it "cast out," or conquered, evil.

More Miracles and Miracle Workers

Given the ancient Jewish view of the world, it is not surprising that people recognized various events as miracles more readily than we do, even though we might be looking at similar events. When unusual or extraordinary events occur today, we search for, and often find, a scientific explanation. The Jews already had their explanation for things they could not understand: those things were the activities of God, the creator of the universe.

Not only were there more events identified as miracles in Jesus' day, but there were also more miracle workers, persons who appeared to have strange powers over people and events. We know from sources other than the Gospels, for example, that other rabbis at the time of Jesus were also considered to be wonder-workers, able to cure people of their afflictions. Miracle workers were

also commonly found in the Greek culture of the time. **4**

Seeing the Hand of God Today

Today's Christians do not need to choose between the modern scientific or the ancient Jewish faith-based understanding of the world. Rather, Christians can gain a greater sense of appreciation and awe for the creative power of God through the discoveries of science. Some scientists, for example, study the origins of the universe and come to a strong conviction that a loving God was the source of it all. Surgeons occasionally claim to experience a miracle in the operating room when a patient survives against all odds. We ourselves might spy a single flower blooming in a garden and be overwhelmed with the wonder of creation.

Such encounters teach us that sacred Mystery is present within all our life experiences, and help us understand the worldview that dominated the minds and hearts of the ancient Jews. **5**

A Different World

Another way to understand Jesus' miracles is to remember the rather gruesome aspects of the world that Jesus encountered, a world very different from the one most of us experience.

Common Scenes

The people of Jesus' day had no hospitals and no institutions for those who were mentally disturbed or insane. Medicine was primitive. It was common to see blind and crippled beggars along the roadways and at the gates of the cities. People with diseases like leprosy were forced to roam in

---

4
List at least ten of your everyday experiences that the Jews of Jesus' day might have considered miracles.

5
Write either a pro or a con reaction to this statement: *It is much more difficult to believe in God today than it was during Jesus' time.*

F • O • C • U • S

Modern Miracles: Signs of God's Presence Today

The evening of 25 January 1949 started out like any other for the cook at the Catholic parish in Ribera del Fresno, Spain. As she did every evening, she began preparing dinner for the children at a nearby orphanage and some of the town's poor families.

Unfortunately, this evening there was not nearly enough rice and meat in the pot to feed sixty children and the families. Not knowing what else to do, the cook prayed that Blessed John Macías, the town's patron, would ask God to do something about the situation.

Not long after, she noticed the rice boiling over. She ladled some of it into a second pot. But the rice filled the second pot and continued to overflow the first, so she began filling a third. Amazed, she called others to witness the multiplying food. By the end of the evening, everyone had been fed, and there was more than enough food left over. The last ladleful of

rice was just as fresh as the first, even though it had been boiling for four hours.

Later, a special panel of experts hired by the Vatican examined the leftover rice and interviewed twenty-two witnesses to the event. A report was drafted and debated by experts and church theologians. Together they decided that there was no natural explanation for the phenomenon—in other words, the multiplication of rice at Ribera del Fresno was a miracle. (Based on Woodward, *Making Saints*, pages 209–210)

That is just one of the hundreds of miracles approved by church officials in the last century alone as part of the process of naming saints. Clearly, the church believes that God continues to work miracles, even in our modern world. Beyond church-approved miracles, stories of healings, apparitions of the Virgin Mary, crying statues, and the like also abound. In considering such claims of divine works, it can be helpful to keep the following points in mind.

First, an extraordinary event does not have to be approved by the church to be a miracle. In fact, the church does not even investigate most miracle claims. But the church is very cautious about approving the miracles it does investigate: the official report on a miracle can be more than a thousand pages long and take years to complete. The vast majority of claims of miracles are never approved.

Individual believers need not be quite so strict, but it is best to be prudent, rather than blindly accepting a claimed miracle. Some cases might

Photo: A miracle such as the claim of multiplying rice in Ribera del Fresno can be a sign of God's abundant grace.

be better explained by natural causes, and some cases could even be made up, the result of wishful thinking or outright deception.

Second, it is not necessary to believe in any particular miracle—even ones approved by the church—in order to be a faithful Catholic. That is because everything essential to the Catholic faith has already been revealed by God in the Bible and church Tradition. Nothing needs to be added, including miracles.

Still, the church believes that miracles are special gifts from God that call us to a deeper faith. For instance, a miracle such as the one in Ribera del Fresno reminds us that God's grace overflows in our lives, nourishing our spirits just as rice nourishes the body. Miraculous physical healings lead us to pray for the spiritual healing of our hearts. Jesus says that his works of wonder are signs that "the kingdom of God has come to you" (Matthew 12:28). Today's miracles are also signs of the Kingdom.

Even so, if we focus too much on extraordinary miracles, we risk missing the reality of God's grace all around us. As Christians mature in faith, they find they do not need extraordinary evidence of God's presence. Instead, they begin to notice surprises from God everywhere—in beauty, in a new friendship, and even in what seems to be the tragedy of death. When we open our eyes to God's constant presence in our lives, we find miracles are an everyday occurrence. **6**

■
Millions of pilgrims still make their way to the grotto at Lourdes, France, to seek healing of the body and soul in the waters of its spring. Mary, the mother of Jesus, is said to have appeared to a fourteen-year-old illiterate peasant girl named Bernadette Soubirous at the grotto in 1858.

6
Why is the church so cautious about approving certain events as miracles? Write your opinion in a paragraph.

bands throughout the countryside because they were forbidden to enter the cities. Insane people were chained in caves, and their screams could be heard through the days and nights. And not surprisingly, all these ill people were banned from worshiping in the Temple.

Cruelty or Fear?

Our tendency might be to condemn the ancient Jewish society for its cruel treatment of the physically and mentally ill, but we must remember why the society acted as it did. Sickness, insanity, and disease were often seen as the direct manifestation of the power of evil. So healthy people were at times terrified of those who were sick, fearful of being contaminated by them, especially with contagious diseases like leprosy. In other words, fear more than meanness motivated people to reject and banish those in need.

Some Jews even felt that sickness was a punishment from God for personal sins or the sins of one's ancestors. This was a terribly difficult belief for those who held it, however, because it was clear that good people seemed to suffer as much, some-

■

Illustration: **In Jesus' day, blind and crippled persons could be seen begging at the gates of the cities.**

times even more, than apparent sinners. (Jesus talks about this in Luke 13:1–5, assuring his listeners that those who suffer accidents and other misfortunes do not do so because of their sins.)

The Reign of God: No More Evil

If, as most Jews believed, all illness and other human suffering were the result of the power of evil in the world, then common sense indicated that the Reign of God would not be truly present until all these manifestations of evil were overcome. It was precisely this belief about God's Reign that the Gospel writers sought to address in telling about Jesus' life and ministry, especially his miracles.

- Through Jesus, God was destroying evil in all its forms and expressions.
- Because God was using Jesus in this way, Jesus was truly the Messiah, the One sent by God to establish the new Kingdom that the Jews had been waiting and praying for.

Now as Then

Though we today need not adopt every aspect of the ancient Jewish understanding of evil, that understanding does have some truth to teach us about reality. Just as we might see the goodness of God operative in the wonders of creation, we can also understand much of the pain and suffering in the world as a result of the power of sin and evil. And whenever good conquers evil—whether in world affairs or in our own relationships—we, like the ancient Jews, can recognize the hand of God at work. In other words, Jesus' vision of the Kingdom of God can be as real to us today as it was to his first followers two thousand years ago. **7**

For Review

- How do the differences between the modern Western worldview and that of the ancient Jews help to explain the ancient Jews' understanding of miracles?
- Why would the ancient Jews have viewed any cure of illness as overcoming the power of evil?
- Why should we hesitate to condemn the ancient Jews for their treatment of physically and mentally ill people?
- What did the Gospel writers try to say about Jesus through the miracle stories?

7
Major catastrophes—earthquakes, tornadoes, floods, and even diseases like AIDS—are viewed by some as being directly caused by God for a specific reason, such as punishment of the victims. Write a short response to this view.

■
Photo: Whenever good conquers evil—whether in world affairs or in our own relationships—we, like the ancient Jews, can recognize the hand of God at work.

Understanding Jesus' Miracles Today

Despite the validity of seeing wonders in everyday life, some of the events that are considered miracles in the Gospels do not have to be seen as such during our time. We understand, for example, the incredible power of the human brain to effect change in the body. We talk about psychosomatic illnesses, which seem to disappear when patients' attitudes change. And we know of the remarkable power of suggestion that is demonstrated through hypnosis. These phenomena may account for some of the exorcisms recorded in the Gospels, in which emotionally distraught people are calmed by the strength of Jesus' character.

Other accounts of Jesus' cures may be explained in part as exaggeration by the Evangelists. Exaggeration was characteristic of the writers in Jesus' culture, who sometimes sought to emphasize their points by stretching the historical facts.

But these insights do not explain all the miracles of Jesus. Nor do they negate Christianity's solid tradition of accepting miracles throughout its history—a history that Christians believe has been guided by the Holy Spirit, the spirit of truth. Ultimately, when trying to understand the meaning of Jesus' miracles, we are dealing with both a faith question and a faith answer.

■
Trying to understand the meaning of Jesus' miracles involves both a faith question and a faith answer.
Photo: **This painting by a Nicaraguan peasant of the multiplication of loaves and fishes illustrates the miracle's meaning for the artist's own time and culture.**

F • O • C • U • S

A Modern Miracle: From Death to New Life

Reverend Ann Holcomb had been pastor of Our Savior's Lutheran Church for only six weeks when the tragic news spread through the community: at thirty-five, she had been diagnosed with incurable cancer. Many members of the congregation expected her to move back to her former parish, where closer friends could help her through the inevitable pain and loneliness she faced. But Pastor Ann said: "God has called me to this parish at this time. I want to dedicate my life to service as your pastor. It looks like I might serve you only by facing my own death with you."

Over the next months, the transformation of the congregation was remarkable. People who hardly knew one another became deeply bonded by their concern for Pastor Ann. Worship services became the center of parish life as people gathered in sincere prayer. Especially touching were those services when Pastor Ann, seated in a wheelchair, would join the community, with an oxygen tank nearby to help her breathe as the cancer slowly sapped her body of strength. She even managed to distribute diplomas at the eighth-grade graduation.

As Pastor Ann's condition worsened, tension developed among members of the congregation. Some of them gathered weekly to pray for a miraculous cure of Pastor Ann's cancer. Others claimed that praying for such a cure was almost superstitious and would only lead to great disappointment—even a loss of faith for some people—when Pastor Ann inevitably died.

Pastor Ann had the perfect response to both sides: "I firmly believe that God has a miracle in store for me," she told the people. "God may decide to heal my body of this cancer. Or God may choose to work a greater miracle and call me into everlasting, resurrected life. I'm ready for either one."

A year from her installation as pastor, Ann Holcomb died in her own parsonage bedroom, remaining to the end among the people she had promised to serve. Her funeral service drew an overflowing crowd. Parishioners may have experienced a more profound depth of faith in her dying than if she had lived. Many commented that Pastor Ann had been absolutely right: God had worked a miracle. The miracle for Pastor Ann was resurrected life. But another miracle had taken place—in the hearts of the members of Our Savior's Lutheran Church. **8**

8

Write a response to this opinion:
Miracles that take place in people's hearts are as significant as dramatic, physical cures.

A Faith Question and a Faith Answer

What Do the Miracles Mean?

Christians are not expected to blindly accept irrational claims. Rather, they are asked to recognize and accept the real significance of the miracles—their religious meaning—in light of faith in Jesus. In other words, yes-or-no questions about the historical reality of individual miracles are not of prime concern. The question to be posed repeatedly is this: What do the miracles *mean?* And this question can be answered only from the perspective of faith.

Faith: The First Requirement

The requirement of faith for accepting Jesus' miracles was as necessary for the people who actually witnessed these events as it is for us today. Over and over again the Gospels mention that Jesus required belief in him and faith in God before he would cure one who was ill. In fact, Jesus could not cure those in his home region:

They said, "Where did this man get all this? What is this wisdom that has been given to him? What deeds of power are being done by his hands! . . ." And they took offense at him. . . . And he could do no deed of power there, except that he laid his hands on a few sick people and cured them. And he was amazed at [the prevailing attitude of] unbelief. (Mark 6:2–6)

The Father's Business

Recall from the earlier discussion of Jesus' temptation in the desert that Jesus refused to try to impress people with his power. He was not in show business. Rather, he was wholeheartedly involved in the "business" of his Father—that is, the task of revealing God's nature and relationship with people by revealing and establishing the Kingdom.

Miracles and the Kingdom

The key to understanding the miracles of Jesus is grasping their relationship to his proclamation of

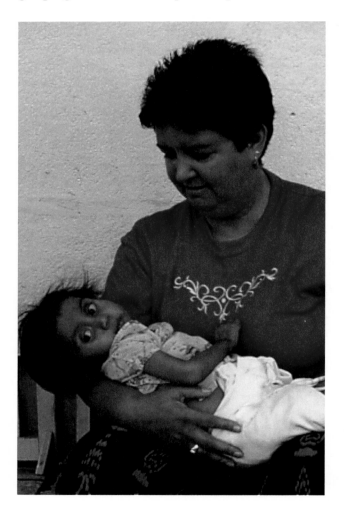

Jesus' miracles reveal God's promise of unconditional love and commitment to the poor and outcasts of society.
Photo: Maryknoll sister Delia Smith cares for an HIV-positive child in Guatemala. Christians are called to reveal God's love by bringing healing to the world.

the Kingdom of God. At the core of that proclamation—and therefore at the core of the miracles—are these realities:

- God's promise of unconditional love
- God's commitment to poor people and outcasts of society
- God's complete control over the power of sin and evil
- God's offer of complete reconciliation
- God's presence incarnated in the Jesus of History **9**

The Force of Love

Jesus did not just speak of his Father's love. He lived out that love in his actions. Love, not a desire to impress the crowds, made Jesus heal people and work wonders. The Gospels are clear on this: Jesus healed because people needed to be healed. He healed out of compassion. In Mark 1:41, for example, he is moved with pity for a leper who begs to be cured. In Luke 7:13, sorrow touches Jesus when he meets the widow of Nain, whose son has died.

Special Signs

Kindness was not Jesus' only motive for working wonders, however. In the synoptic Gospels, the most common word used for miracles and cures is *power*. In John's Gospel, the word used most often for these works is *sign*. Jesus' miracles, therefore, were signs intended to show God's power over all creation and, in a special way, over the forces of sin and evil. Ultimately, the miracles were meant to lead people to belief in Jesus.

The healing miracles. In the Gospels, we see Jesus relieving people of their physical suffering and even bringing some people back from the dead. Wherever evil and its effects are most direct-

ly and dramatically evident in the lives of people —in their suffering, their pain, their death—Jesus heals and restores fullness of life.

The casting out of demons. The chief lesson of the exorcisms, in which Jesus casts out evil spirits, is the extent of God's power. The Evangelists are showing us that God, in and through Jesus, can confront the power of sin in its most direct forms and conquer it.

The forgiveness of sins. Many of Jesus' miracles reflect a far deeper and more important level of healing than the "mere" healing of the body. For in the context of his miracles, Jesus frequently mentions that the physical healing of individuals is directly linked to their acknowledgment of their sin and Jesus' forgiveness of it. Matthew's Gospel, for instance, tells of some scribes who attack Jesus for claiming the authority to forgive the sins of a paralyzed man. Jesus responds to them by showing them that all of his authority comes from God:

"Why do you think evil in your hearts? For which is easier, to say, 'Your sins are forgiven,' or to say, 'Stand up and walk'? But so that you may know that the Son of Man has authority on earth to forgive sins"—he then said to the paralytic—"Stand up, take your bed and go to your home." And [the man] stood up and went to his home. When the crowds saw it, they were filled with awe, and they glorified God, who had given such authority to human beings. (9:4–8)

The nature miracles. The nature miracles reveal the same basic message that the other miracles do: God's Reign over all creation is present in this man, Jesus, and is being revealed to the world through him.

9
Read another miracle story listed under "Jesus' Miracles in the Synoptic Gospels," on page 178. Using the list of Kingdom realities above as a guide, write an essay on the connections be- tween the miracle story and Jesus' proclamation of the Kingdom of God.

- Just as God drew order out of chaos in the creation of the world (Genesis 1:1–2), so God in Jesus now overcomes all chaos in the world.
- Just as God parted the waters of the sea to allow the safe passage of the Israelites (Exodus 14:15–31), so God in Jesus calms a storm and walks on water.
- Just as God offered the special food manna to his people as they roamed in the desert (Exodus

16:12–35), so God through Jesus multiplies the loaves and fish to feed the multitudes.

For Christians, all miracles are signs of the healing and redeeming power of God's love, a loving power present in and revealed by Jesus. No wonder those who walked with Jesus, who watched him touch people, were convinced that he truly was a man of extraordinary power and force! **10**

■
Just as God parted the waters of the sea to allow safe passage of the Israelites (Exodus 14:15–31), so Jesus, through God's power, calms a storm and walks on water.

Photo: **A storm on the Sea of Galilee.**

10
Write about an incident in your life (or in the life of someone you know) that could be considered a modern miracle, a sign of God's loving power.

The Gospel Understanding of Jesus the Miracle Worker

To be consistent with the image of Jesus portrayed in the Gospels, we must avoid viewing him as some kind of biblical superman or magician. Jesus constantly refused any such designation. He worked miracles almost reluctantly, and it is notable that he often instructed those he had cured to tell no one what he had done for them (see, for example, Mark 1:44). Jesus even became angry with those who actually expected miracles as proof of his power (see Mark 8:12). Why?

Because he did not want his miracles to cloud or confuse the far more important reality—that "the Kingdom of God is among you!"

Liberator of the Heart

Once people have faith in Jesus and his message, a real miracle has already begun in their heart. The physical cure they experience becomes an expression of an interior reality, a conversion, a change of heart. The cure of their body represents a deeper, more profound change within them. Therefore, they are liberated not only from lameness but also, for example, from legalism. They are liberated not only from a crippling deformity but also from a closed mind. They are liberated not only from physical blindness but also from the inability to recognize the needs of their neighbors. Ultimately, Jesus liberates people from sin and death to goodness and life. **11**

For Review

- Why can the meaning of the miracles be explained only from a faith perspective?
- What is the key to understanding the miracles of Jesus? What realities are at the core of the miracles?
- Name two things that motivated Jesus to perform miracles.
- What happens once people have faith in Jesus and his message? Give an example to illustrate your answer.

■
Illustration: Just as God offered manna to the Israelites as they roamed in the desert, so Jesus multiplied the loaves and fishes to feed the multitudes.

11
Write a short essay comparing what you thought about Jesus' miracles before you studied this chapter with what you understand about them now.

F • O • C • U • S

A Modern Miracle: From Frightened Stutterer to Popular Speaker

Until the eighth grade, Tom was an average kid—a decent student, a fair athlete, generally outgoing and popular. Oh, he made his share of poor decisions, like most kids do. In the seventh grade, for instance, he stole some beer from his dad for a party with his friends. But most people thought Tom would turn out okay. Then things changed.

In the eighth grade, Tom developed a speech problem. For some reason he became very self-conscious when asked to speak in front of the class, and he would begin to stutter and stammer. The rest of the class laughed. The teacher thought all Tom needed was practice, so he began asking Tom to read aloud on a regular basis. The problem, however, only grew worse, and Tom became even more embarrassed and withdrawn.

After graduation from the eighth grade, Tom went to a Catholic senior high school. There he tried to hide his problem by making new friends, staying away from anyone from grade school who knew about his stuttering. He never achieved his potential in the classroom because he avoided any situation in which he would have had to speak to everyone. He also began to drink, arranging almost weekly beer parties as a way to gain some "respect" from his friends. Several times Tom was caught in the act—either by his parents or by other adults, and on a couple of occasions by the police. His reputation as a troublemaker grew.

One day the principal of the high school called Tom to his office. Once again the police had contacted the school about Tom. The principal told him that he was going to be expelled from school if he didn't shape up. Tom wouldn't show it, but he was scared.

That same day, Tom was approached by a teacher who had heard about his trouble. Rather than criticizing or threatening Tom, the teacher stunned him by asking him to join a Christian youth group. Tom, much to his own surprise, accepted the invitation. That was the start of an amazing transformation.

Tom became an active member of the youth group. By the end of his senior year, he decided to try out the religious life by joining the Christian Brothers (the order of brothers who taught at his high school). He stayed only five months, but while he was with the brothers, he began to deal with his speech problem for the first time since it had begun five years earlier. After he left the religious life, Tom became involved in church youth programs as a volunteer leader. Later, after completing college, he decided to make youth ministry his occupation. He wanted to help other young people who, like himself, needed someone to turn to at difficult times in their lives. Perhaps most amazingly, Tom became known for his public speaking, and was often asked to make presentations at youth retreats and conferences.

Eventually Tom was hired by a publisher of materials for religious education and youth ministry. The book you are now reading was written by him. In fact, three days before this little story was written, Tom Zanzig gave a talk at a youth convention attended by 2,300 high school students. Nobody who had seen him stuttering in front of his eighth-grade class some twenty years before would have believed it!

Like Pastor Ann, Tom responded in trust to God's goodness and power, which Jesus proclaimed nearly two thousand years ago. There are many miracles in each person's life. Some are dramatic, like those relayed here. Others are so ordinary that they might easily be missed. Jesus teaches us that in order to see any of them, we need the eyes of faith.

On the Way to the Cross

It is difficult to comprehend how someone as dedicated to works of love and compassion as Jesus was could become a source of great conflict, an object of hatred and fear. Yet surely no single event in the story of Jesus is more etched into the hearts, minds, and emotions of Christians than his agonizing death on the cross. How can we make sense of the horribly brutal execution of such a good man? The next chapter will seek an answer.

In the synoptic Gospels, after Jesus predicts his Passion and death, Peter, James, and John go with him to the top of a mountain and witness Jesus' appearance transformed in glory (Mark 9:1–10). This Transfiguration affirms for believers that Jesus in his earthly existence truly is the Son of God, and that glory follows the Passion.

Photo: Mount Tabor, the site traditionally suggested as the scene of the Transfiguration.

9
The Cross:
The End or a Beginning?

THEY went to a place called Gethsemane; and [Jesus] said to his disciples, "Sit here while I pray." He took with him Peter and James and John, and began to be distressed and agitated. And [he] said to them, "I am deeply grieved, even to death; remain here, and keep awake." And going a little farther, he threw himself on the ground and prayed that, if it were possible, the hour might pass from him. He said, "Abba, Father, for you all things are possible; remove this cup from me; yet, not what I want, but what you want." He came and found [Peter, James, and John] sleeping; and he said to Peter, "Simon, are you asleep? Could you not keep awake one hour? Keep awake and pray that you may not come into the time of trial; the spirit indeed is willing, but the flesh is weak." And again he went away and prayed, saying the same words. And once more he came and found them sleeping, for their eyes were very heavy; and they did not know what to say to him. He came a third time and said to them, "Are you still sleeping and taking your rest? Enough! The hour has come; the Son of Man is betrayed into the hands of sinners. Get up, let us be going. See, my betrayer is at hand." (Mark 14:32–42)

The Road to the Cross

"Enough! The hour has come." With those simple but chilling words, the drama that was Jesus' earthly life moved toward its horrifying climax. It was probably the year 30 C.E. Jesus was a man of some thirty-five years, and his life was about to end abruptly and violently. He had preached for no more than three years, and perhaps less than one. He had proclaimed good news about a kingdom of love, joy, peace, and harmony. But it had all led to this—the road to the cross.

This chapter takes a close look at the events that immediately preceded and surrounded Jesus' death on the cross: What actually happened and why? And what does it all mean, especially for Christians?

A Man of Peace, a Source of Conflict

Certainly Jesus was committed to peace, and we are right to remember most strongly his acts of love and compassion. But we must remember as well that he seemed to cause conflict and tension wherever he went. His words were often challenging, even threatening, to his listeners. Consider the following:

- On virtually every important issue of his day— marriage, authority, the role and meaning of the Law, the Temple and worship—Jesus' opinion conflicted with that of people in positions of power.

Just as Jesus poured out his love through his suffering and death, so too all Christians are called to "take up their cross" by giving themselves to others with unlimited love.

Photo, facing page: **The Kidron Valley and the Mount of Olives. The Garden of Gethsemane, where Jesus began his Passion, is located on the Mount of Olives.**

Background: **"After twisting some thorns into a crown, they put it on his head" (Matthew 27:29).**

- Jesus made the outcasts of society the very cornerstone of his message about God's Kingdom.
- Jesus claimed for himself a position of authority above that of both the religious and the political powers of his day.

All this and more brought Jesus to an unavoidable confrontation with the Jewish and Roman authorities. He was a very real threat to religious tradition and political stability.

So in many ways, Jesus' violent end was the price he paid for living a life committed to the One who sent him. For Jesus, to have lived otherwise would have been not only a betrayal of his Father but also of his own Dream, his own vision and values. For Christians, the historical event of Jesus' death is significant—but not just because a man was willing to die for his beliefs. As will be discussed shortly, Jesus' death has a larger, more profound meaning. **1**

The Nature of the Passion Accounts

In order to better understand the following discussion of the events surrounding Jesus' death, take time now to read at least one, but preferably all, of the synoptic accounts of the **Passion** of Jesus: Matthew, chapters 26 and 27; Mark, chapters 14 and 15; and Luke, chapters 22 and 23.

Next, turn to John's account of the last days of Jesus, which begins with chapter 13 and runs through chapter 19. The description of Jesus' arrest, trial, and execution in John's Gospel (chapters 18–19) is quite similar to the descriptions found in the synoptic Gospels. However, John precedes these events with an extended discussion of Jesus' last meal with his disciples. This discussion includes what are referred to as Jesus' Last Supper discourses (chapters 14–17). Reading these discourses will prove valuable later, when looking at the meaning of the Last Supper. **2**

Central Events in the Gospels

As we might expect, the arrest, trial, and Crucifixion of Jesus are the most extensively reported events in the Gospels. (Even the non-Christian historians mentioned earlier in this book reported that Jesus died by crucifixion.) The Gospels seem keyed to these events, as if everything in the Gospels is intended to prepare the reader for Jesus' execution. Even the writing style of the Passion accounts is much different from that of the Gospels' typical stories and short sayings. For instance, we find many more details in these accounts than in other parts of the Gospels. This is so for several reasons:

- The **death** and **Resurrection** of Jesus are at the heart of the Christian story. His **Crucifixion** had to be very carefully explained to the members of the early community of faith.
- What happened to Jesus was totally contrary to what the people had been expecting for their Messiah. Their desire for a great deal of information about these events would have been natural and intense.

■
Jesus often encountered the hostility of the scribes and Pharisees when he taught in the Temple.
Photo: **A scale model of the Temple, which is surrounded by the Court of the Gentiles.**

1
Write a short piece about a time in your life (or in the life of someone you know) when doing good became a source of conflict and tension.

2
Draw four columns and label each one with the name of one of the Gospels. As you read the four accounts of the Passion, take brief notes on how events unfold, and compare accounts.

- The Evangelists were writing to and for the early followers of the risen Jesus. These people would confront almost immediate persecution for their faith in him. The reminder that Jesus had suffered persecution and death would be a constant consolation to them.

The Passion accounts were probably among the first stories about Jesus to take on a consistent form. They may well have been part of the worship of the early faith community even before they were committed to writing.

Reconciling the Differences

We find a lot of detail in the Passion accounts, but we also find signs of editorial work by the Evangelists. Naturally, the Evangelists were trying to provide theological insights into the meaning of the Crucifixion. Matthew's Gospel, for example, is the only Gospel that mentions the eruption of graves at the point of Jesus' death (27:52–53). This may well be a case of symbolic imagery that was added to the basic account of the Passion. Also, the Gospel accounts differ—sometimes a great deal—on a number of other points. By concentrating on what most or all of the Gospel accounts have in common, we can arrive at a reasonably clear idea of the historical facts surrounding the arrest, trial, and Crucifixion of Jesus.

For Review

- Why is the image of Jesus as a man of peace, love, and compassion not a complete one?
- What are the literary characteristics of the Passion accounts in the Gospels?
- Why did the Evangelists use a style different from their typical stories and sayings to tell the story of Jesus' death?

■
Photo: **The road to Jerusalem from the Mount of Olives, where Jesus was arrested at the Garden of Gethsemane.**

Jesus' Final Days

The Last Supper

All three synoptic Gospels give an account of what has come to be known as the **Last Supper.** Interestingly, the earliest recorded account of the actual institution of the Eucharist—that is, the blessing of the bread and cup—is found in Paul's First Letter to the Corinthians (11:23–26). For some reflections and insights on John's version of the Last Supper, see "John: The Last Supper," on page 198. The following discussion focuses on the three synoptic accounts.

A New Covenant Is Made

As the synoptic Gospels relate, on the evening before he was crucified, Jesus hosted a meal for his disciples, in a room loaned to them by a friend in Jerusalem. Jesus followed the normal Jewish custom of his day, giving thanks to God for the meal.

But then he took the bread, handed it to his disciples, and said: "This is my body, which is given for you. Do this in remembrance of me" (Luke 22:19). Likewise, after they had eaten, he took the cup, saying, "This cup that is poured out for you is the new covenant in my blood" (Luke 22:20).

According to the Gospels, the Last Supper took place near the time when the Jewish people were celebrating Passover, one of their greatest religious feasts. Recall that during this feast, the people remembered how God had delivered them from slavery in Egypt many years before and how, in gratitude, the people of Israel had pledged their loyalty to God. Ever since that time they had been known as the People of the Covenant. Thus, when Jesus identified his actions as representing a "new Covenant," he was linking those actions to a reality that was at the heart of Jewish history. **3**

"Do This in Remembrance of Me"

Jesus' words and actions at the Last Supper were packed with meaning. The synoptic Gospels suggest these two main points:

- Jesus had his approaching death in mind as he gathered his disciples for that meal.
- Jesus made a real connection between the meal itself and his death on the cross.

When Jesus stood up to do his customary duty as host in saying the blessing over the cup and bread, he startled his disciples by saying that the cup and bread were to be recognized as signs of his own death. At the time, the disciples did not understand what he was talking about. They believed that he had come to Jerusalem to assume his role as king, not to die!

Only later—after Jesus' death and Resurrection—did the early community of faith recall that meal and begin to use the words and gestures of Jesus as a continuing reminder of his death. Nearly two

---

■

Illustration: **After the meal, Jesus took the bread and cup and gave them to his disciples as signs of his own life poured out for them.**

3
Using an encyclopedia or other sources, write a short essay on the origins and major characteristics of the Passover meal.

thousand years later, Christians all over the world gather in their communities, solemnly repeating those words and gestures—still recalling in this special way the life, death, and Resurrection of Jesus.

Is Jesus Really There?

The various Christian churches today have differing convictions about the way the risen Jesus is present in the consecrated bread and wine of the Eucharist. Although all Christians who celebrate the Lord's Supper today believe that the blessing of the bread and wine at that ritual is done in memory of Jesus and as a symbol of his giving himself to others, Catholics and Orthodox Christians go further. They believe that in this symbolic action Jesus is truly and fully present; Jesus' body and blood are present in the consecrated bread and wine. Some other Christian denominations hold a similar, but not identical, belief to that of Catholics, and this is the subject of much interdenominational dialog.

■

Illustration: **In John's account of the Last Supper, Jesus washes the feet of his disciples to show that loving service of others is at the heart of his message: "Just as I have loved you, you also should love one another."**

John: The Last Supper

John's account of the last meal Jesus shared with his disciples is rich in imagery, poetic in expression, and deeply touching in its portrayal of the human Jesus. Here are a few of the major features that distinguish John's account from the synoptic accounts:

The Lamb of God. The synoptic writers agree that Jesus celebrated the Last Supper as a Passover meal, but John situates the meal on the day before that religious feast. It seems obvious, nevertheless, that John did want to link Jesus' death with the Passover.

Recall that a major part of the Passover ritual was the slaughter of lambs in the Temple; the meat of the lambs was then consumed during the Passover meal. The lambs were slaughtered in memory of the Exodus, the time of the original Passover, when the Israelites were brought out of slavery. In his account, John links Jesus' death with the killing of the paschal lambs. That way, Christians can see Jesus as the new paschal lamb, "the Lamb of God, who takes away the sins of the world" through his death on the cross.

The washing of the disciples' feet. Very significantly, John does not include the institution of the Eucharist in his description of the Last Supper. Instead, John has Jesus perform a ritual not found in any of the synoptic Gospels. Jesus washes the feet of the disciples as a sign of the centrality of his message about service to others (13:1–17). The connection John seeks to make is this: Christians can fully celebrate the Eucharist only when committed to loving service to others. **4**

The Last Supper discourses. As noted previously, John includes a series of Last Supper discourses by Jesus. Here we discover such memorable statements as the following:

- "I give you a new commandment, that you love one another. Just as I have loved you, you also should love one another" (13:34).
- "I am the way, and the truth, and the life. No one comes to the Father except through me" (14:6).
- "Abide in me as I abide in you. . . . I am the vine, you are the branches. Those who abide in me and I in them bear much fruit, because apart from me you can do nothing" (15:4–5).
- "No one has greater love than this, to lay down one's life for one's friends. . . . I do not call you servants any longer, . . . I have called you friends" (15:13–15).
- "Very truly, I tell you, if you ask anything of the Father in my name, he will give it to you. . . . Ask and you will receive, so that your joy may be complete" (16:23–24).

4
List as many ways as you can that teenagers in your school or parish serve others.

"Thy Will Be Done": The Agony in the Garden

At some time or another, each of us has felt the ache of loneliness, the feeling that no one understands or cares about us. Perhaps it is because we all have felt this pain that the image of Jesus in the Garden of Gethsemane can touch us so deeply.

We might try somehow to soften the pain of Jesus at Gethsemane with thoughts of how, as the Son of God, he could heroically accept the pain of his impending death, sure that his Resurrection awaited him. But the Gospels are clear on this: Jesus' agony in the garden was a time of sheer human terror and darkness. He knew the time was fast approaching when all the conflicts surrounding him would build to a breaking point.

Jesus Could Read the Signs of the Times

Toward the end of his life, did Jesus realize that he was about to die? We do not have to imagine that Jesus foresaw his future by the revelation of some divine inner voice. For Jesus could read the signs of the times. That is, he could foresee his future just by looking at what was happening around him.

The building hostility. Jesus was definitely aware of the building hostility of all the people who opposed him, which included members of nearly every faction of Judaism—Pharisees, Sadducees, Zealots. In a rare situation indeed, all the leaders who normally disagreed with one another were united against Jesus.

The situation in Jerusalem. Jesus had freely chosen to go to Jerusalem. He probably realized that great tension, if not violence, would result from his presence there. Scholars debate whether certain details of the Gospel accounts of Jesus' tri-

umphant entry into Jerusalem (remembered today as Passion, or Palm, Sunday) are historically accurate. However, it is reasonable to assume that Jesus' arrival in the holy city did cause some sort of stir. And Jesus would have been aware that the authorities—both Jewish and Roman—would not tolerate such emotionally charged happenings during the already intense season of Passover.

The fate of a prophet. Jesus probably recognized himself as a true prophet of Israel, as one led by the Spirit. Because Israel had repeatedly rejected the prophets, Jesus would have had a growing expectation of his own rejection as well. At one point earlier in his ministry, he had cried out over the city of David, "Jerusalem, Jerusalem, the city that kills the prophets and stones those who are sent to it! . . ." (Matthew 23:37). Jesus would

■

Photo: **Jesus' agony in the garden was a time of sheer human terror and darkness.**

F • O • C • U • S

Judas: Betrayer of Jesus?

During the Last Supper, Jesus predicted that one of his disciples was about to betray him. The disciples were shocked at the thought and vigorously denied the possibility. But among them sat one man whose story is probably far more ambiguous, and perhaps more touching, than we are usually inclined to believe. The man was Judas.

The widely accepted understanding of Judas has been that he was a greedy, weak man who "sold out"—betrayed Jesus for thirty pieces of silver. But perhaps it is not quite that easy to assess Judas's motives.

Matthew, for instance, is the only synoptic writer who even bothers to mention the payment of silver. Matthew also says that Judas, even before the official condemnation of Jesus, is filled with remorse when he realizes that Jesus will probably be executed. Judas throws the money down before the chief priests and elders and then goes out and hangs himself in despair (27:3–5). It is difficult to mesh the stereotyped image of the greedy Judas with Matthew's image of a man filled with sadness, despair, and apparent surprise at what is happening to Jesus.

Some scholars propose that Judas was actually trying to force Jesus to respond to the official charges of the chief priests and others. These scholars contend that Judas figured Jesus would do so by revealing his power and assuming the role of king. In other words, maybe Judas did not expect or intend Jesus' execution at all, but rather was trying to pressure Jesus into the expected role of Messiah. This is all guesswork, of course, but perhaps it will keep us from too quickly or too harshly judging Judas—or anyone else, for that matter.

■

Photo: **An ancient olive tree in the Garden of Gethsemane.**

have seen at least the possibility, if not the likelihood, of his having to suffer and even die for his proclamation of the Kingdom.

The faithful love of God. Throughout their history, the Jews had recognized that often God was most with them in times of despair—that somehow the greater their suffering, the more vividly was God's love revealed to them. Jesus was certainly aware of this tradition and must have drawn strength from it.

He Could Have Run Away

In the face of the possibility of a violent death, Jesus could have run away. This would seem to have been the most human thing to do. Yet Jesus stayed, because he was firmly committed to doing the will of the One who sent him: "Abba, Father, for you all things are possible; remove this cup [that is, death] from me; *yet, not what I want, but what you want*" (Mark 14:36, italics added).

Jesus' free acceptance of his death is central to all of Christian theology. Christians believe that Jesus saved all people from sin and death only because he lovingly gave, or sacrificed, his whole being to God. Jesus' death would not have had the effect of saving the world from sin and death if he had run away after realizing he was about to be killed. In that case, his life would have been *taken* by others, not freely and lovingly *given.*

Scholars debate exactly what and how much Jesus foresaw about his death and Resurrection. But it seems likely that Jesus did not *know* that he would be raised from the dead in three days with the same kind of clear and sure knowledge that God did. After all, something that is given away with the expectation that it will eventually be received back is only a loan, not a gift. It seems more likely that Jesus foresaw his Resurrection

only in the sense that he had complete *trust* that God had a unique plan for him, and would not abandon him in death. That Jesus feared his death, but accepted it anyway, made his choice a powerful act of love.

The account of Jesus' agony at Gethsemane is a dramatic departure from other stories of martyrs that were popular among the Jews during and before the time of Jesus. In those stories, as in many modern TV shows and movies, the martyr faced death with courage and firm resignation, hardly showing a sign of fear. Jesus, however, was no such fictional character, no actor playing out a dramatic role. He was totally immersed in our human experience and, like us, felt loneliness and fear. But he found—as do many of his followers—consolation, strength, ultimate hope, in the one he called *Abba,* his Father. And it was in his commitment to his Father's will that Jesus found the courage to accept what was to come. **5**

For Review

- With what historical Jewish event is the Last Supper linked? What two main points do the synoptic Gospels make about Jesus' words and actions at the Last Supper?
- What is the Roman Catholic conviction regarding the presence of Jesus in the Eucharist?
- Explain the meaning of this statement: *Jesus could read the signs of the times regarding his death.*
- Why is Jesus' free acceptance of his death central to all of Christian theology?

5
Compose a personal letter to Jesus as you imagine him facing his last days. Base your words on your own experiences of loneliness and fear.

Jesus' Final Hours

Appearing Before the Great Sanhedrin

At the Great Sanhedrin, the Jewish leaders met as a "court of inquiry" to determine what charge to level against Jesus in the trial to be held before the Romans. Although the Jewish leaders clearly wanted Jesus dead, they did not have the authority to carry out the death penalty while they were under Roman control.

The Fateful Question

During Jesus' examination by the Sanhedrin, Caiaphas, the high priest, raised the question that would eventually lead to Jesus' execution. Caiaphas, becoming frustrated with Jesus' refusal to answer the questions of the other priests, asked Jesus directly, "Are you the Messiah, the Son of the Blessed One [God]?" (Mark 14:61). Jesus answered,

I am; and
  "you will see the Son of Man
  seated at the right hand of the Power,"
  and "coming with the clouds of heaven."

(Mark 14:62)

In this scene, Jesus not only accepts the title *Messiah* (*Christ*) from Caiaphas, but even expands that to say that he is uniquely in touch with divinity, with God. Jesus' response draws an immediate charge of blasphemy from Caiaphas (Mark 14:63–65). (For parallel scenes of Jesus before the Great Sanhedrin, see Matthew 26:57–68 and Luke 22:66–71.)

A Charge That Would Stick

Blasphemy means "showing a lack of reverence toward God" or, more specifically in Jesus' case, "claiming for oneself a dignity due to God alone." It was not Jesus' claim of being the Messiah that gave rise to the furor among the Jewish leaders. Other men had made that claim before him, and others would make it after his death. According to the Gospel accounts, what totally shocked and appalled the members of the Sanhedrin was Jesus' apparent claim—which he expressed through the striking imagery of the Scriptures—that he himself was somehow divine. By making such a claim, Jesus had gone too far. He had taken the final step toward virtually guaranteeing that he would be executed.

Appearing Before Pontius Pilate

To carry out the death penalty against Jesus, the Jewish leadership needed the help of the Romans. However, the Roman procurator Pontius Pilate could not accept the charge of blasphemy as a sufficient reason for execution. Blasphemy was a religious offense, not a political one that in any way threatened the Roman state. The Jewish priests and elders then offered several alternative charges against Jesus: inciting the people to revolt against their Jewish leaders, opposing the payment of taxes to Caesar, and claiming to be the Messiah or a king (see Luke 23:2). Pilate was unmoved by those charges. **6**

Pilate: Looking for a Way Out

Luke's Gospel includes a scene that is not contained in either of the other synoptic Gospels or in

6
Imagine yourself as the prosecuting attorney at the trial of Jesus. Write a brief summary of the charges you would bring against him to "prove" he deserved execution.

the Gospel of John: In front of Pilate, the Jewish leaders persist in their angry accusations about Jesus. Eventually Pilate learns that Jesus is from Galilee, and this gives Pilate the chance to pass responsibility for Jesus' case to Herod Antipas, the Jewish leader appointed by Rome who had authority over Galilee. By sending Jesus to Herod, who happened to be in Jerusalem at the time, Pilate could avoid both the responsibility of condemning Jesus, whom he knew was innocent of any crime deserving death, and the risk of further infuriating the Jews during the already emotionally intense time of Passover.

But Herod Antipas did not want to condemn Jesus either. Instead, according to Luke's Gospel, "when Herod saw Jesus, he was very glad, for he had been wanting to see him for a long time, because he had heard about him and was hoping to see him perform some sign" (23:8). When Jesus refused to respond to this expectation, an angry Herod Antipas sent him back to Pilate.

"I Am Innocent . . ."

As the angry cries of the Jewish leaders intensified, Pilate was left with only one more option. In accordance with the common practice of the Romans to release a Jewish prisoner during major religious feasts, he offered the Jewish leaders a choice: he could release either Jesus or Barabbas, a "notorious prisoner" who was accused of murder and of participating in a rebellion.

The Jewish leaders were adamant about what they wanted—that Jesus be crucified. Pilate realized that the situation was hopeless. In a gesture described only in Matthew's Gospel, Pilate washed his hands in front of the crowds and said, "I am innocent of this man's blood; see to it yourselves" (27:24). The "official" Roman charge against Jesus was that he had incited a revolt among the Jews.

Pilate's simple washing of his hands, of course, could not truly cleanse him of the guilt he was to share for the execution of Jesus. Some have tried to minimize his role in the trial, and the authors of the Gospels may have done so in an attempt to identify the Jewish leaders as the people chiefly responsible for Jesus' death. But the evidence is that Pilate, under extreme pressure from an angry mob, condemned to death by crucifixion a man he knew to be innocent. **7**

The Antonia Fortress, just outside the Temple area, housed Roman troops. Jesus' trial before Pontius Pilate probably took place in its central courtyard.

Photo: A scale model of the Antonia Fortress

7
In writing, briefly express the degree to which you think each of the following was responsible for Jesus' death: Judas, the Jewish leaders, Caiaphas, Pontius Pilate. Give reasons for your answers.

Being Scourged and Crucified

After all the building tension and conflict—the touching and tragic encounter at Gethsemane, the hurried but complex inquiry and eventual trial—the Gospels give a brief but stark description of the execution of Jesus.

"King of the Jews"

Before he was crucified, Jesus was first ridiculed by Roman soldiers for his claim to kingship, and he was given a soldier's scarlet cloak as a mocking tribute. A "crown" formed from a thorny plant was pressed onto his head. He was then the object of scourging, a beating often given before a crucifixion. During the scourging, Jesus was whipped with leather straps that had either bone or metal chips attached to them. Scourging was terribly brutal, many times leading to the death of prisoners as their flesh was literally torn from their body. Jesus survived.

Then Jesus was given a heavy wooden crossbeam to carry—not an entire cross, as so many paintings have depicted it. He was led to a place called Golgotha, meaning "the skull," perhaps because of its shape. There he was placed on his back, with his arms

Illustration: **Scourging was a terribly brutal punishment, often leading to the death of prisoners as flesh was torn from their bodies.**

F • O • C • U • S
A Word About Anti-Semitism

By this point in the course, it should be clear that Jesus and his followers were thoroughly Jewish. Throughout history, however, some Christians have blamed "the Jews" as a whole people for the death of Jesus. This is historically inaccurate: only a small group of Jewish leaders sought Jesus' death, and it was the Roman authorities who actually carried out his execution.

Unfortunately, too many people have used the Crucifixion of Jesus as an excuse for discriminating against Jews, a practice known as anti-Semitism. Anti-Semitism has even led some Christians to kill Jews, as in the Holocaust during World War II.

In recent decades, the Catholic church has emphatically stated that the Jewish people are not to be blamed for Jesus' death. In fact, the church teaches that Christians reject and "crucify" Jesus whenever they act against his way of love, such as when they hold anti-Semitic views. Rather, Christians are called to love the people of the Jewish faith, just as Jesus did.

stretched across the crossbeam he had been carrying. Through his wrists he was nailed to the crossbeam, which was then lifted and attached to an upright beam that stood permanently in the ground. After being elevated, Jesus' body was tied to the cross with ropes around his arms, legs, and stomach, in order to keep his body from tearing free of the nails that held it. The cross also had a small "seat" built into the upright beam, on which the body could rest to ensure longer life and therefore greater suffering.

A small sign was nailed to the beam above Jesus' head, bearing not the official charge for which he was being executed, but rather the mocking title "King of the Jews." And he was left to hang there, between two crucified thieves, until he died.

A Spear in His Side

Crucifixion was the method of execution reserved for non-Roman citizens and slaves. (Capital punishment for Roman citizens was through the more "humane" method of beheading.) Sometimes a man would hang for a week or more on the cross before finally dying from bleeding, choking, inability to breathe, or even more hideous, being attacked by wild dogs during the nights. According to the Gospel accounts, Jesus died in six hours or less, surprising both Pilate and the guards.

According to John's Gospel, it was against the Jewish religious laws to have a body on a cross during the Sabbath, so the Jews asked that the legs of the three crucified men be broken to hasten death. (If a crucified man's legs were broken, he could not hold himself up to breathe.) But by the time the soldiers approached Jesus, he had already died.

Only John's account mentions that a soldier then pierced Jesus' side with a spear to guarantee his death before the Sabbath observance (John 19:31–37). Out of this wound, according to John, flowed blood and water. For John, water was a

■
Jesus was crucified along with two criminals at a place called Golgotha, which was just outside the city of Jerusalem.
Photo: **David's Citadel, seen from outside the walls of Jerusalem.**

symbol of the Spirit. By adding this detail, he may have intended to show that Jesus' death was the source of a great "outpouring" of the Spirit. Some ancient church theologians suggested that the blood and the water were symbols for the Christian sacraments of the Eucharist (blood) and Baptism (water). **8**

Jesus' Last Words

The Gospels provide differing versions of the words Jesus spoke on the cross before his death. Two of his statements, however, are particularly memorable:

"My God, my God . . ." According to both Mark and Matthew, Jesus uttered this statement, which is frequently recalled by believers and debated by scholars: "My God, my God, why have you forsaken me?" (Matthew 27:46; see also Mark 15:34). Believers are touched by the statement because it reflects such deep loneliness and anxiety on the part of Jesus as he approaches his death. The debate of scholars centers on whether the words do in fact reflect a sense of deep despair. If the answer is yes, this in turn would seem to suggest that Jesus had a certain lack of faith in his Father's love for him.

Most scholars rightly point out that these words of Jesus are the opening line of Psalm 22. Faithful Jews traditionally memorized psalms in their entirety. By placing the first line of Psalm 22 on the lips of Jesus, the Evangelists were likely suggesting that the entire psalm was being recalled by Jesus. Scholars point out that although the psalm begins with a cry of distress and anguish, it ends with a strong statement of faith in God. While acknowledging the importance of this interpretation, we should not ignore the fact that the cry of Jesus on the cross reflects his undeniable humanity, which

F • O • C • U • S

The Power of the Cross

Most of the Gospel stories come alive and take on more meaning for us when we try to identify with the main characters. However, when looking at the story of Jesus' Crucifixion, this seems impossible. How can we possibly identify with Jesus as he faced his horrifying death on the cross?

As the following true story illustrates, we *can* identify with—and certainly draw strength from—Jesus' experience of the cross, including his deep faith and total trust in his Father. The story is a first-person account by the author of this textbook, Tom Zanzig.

> A couple of years ago, I was asked to address a group of young people who were attending a weekend youth conference. My task was to prepare the group for the Mass that would close the conference. The day was Palm Sunday, and the themes of the liturgy readings were pain, suffering, death, and the crucified Jesus.
>
> I would much rather have talked about something more joyful than the fact that pain and suffering are a central and necessary part of life and the Gospel. But I stuck to my task, and I was almost brutally honest at times. "If we're lucky," I said, "our pain is periodic and temporary, but for some people it is permanent state. During painful times, we cannot help but ask, If life is so terribly difficult, how can we believe in a good God? Where do we find our meaning? How do we cope?"

8

Create a prayerful meditation on the scourging and Crucifixion of Jesus and the meaning of those events for you.

Then I proceeded to tell the gathering of six hundred young people about a recent incident in my life:

I had been going through a particularly difficult time in almost every area of my life. I was so wracked with loneliness that I was rarely able to sleep. Even prayer seemed useless, empty.

About three o'clock one morning, I gave up on sleep and went to the family room. Sitting in my rocking chair, I felt totally alone, overwhelmed by the seeming hopelessness of my situation. I started to weep.

Then, as if a small voice came out of my past, I remembered the words, "Father, into your hands I commend my spirit." I silently said those words, not as an act of faith but out of sheer desperation. Something stirred in me as I said them, so I said them again. "Father, into your hands . . ." Then I started to whisper them over and over, ". . . into your hands . . . into your hands . . ."

Finally, I'm not sure how long after that, I got up and went back to bed. That night I fell into the deepest sleep I had had in years. When I awoke the next morning, I knew that I had experienced a fundamental change in my life.

At the youth conference, hearing me share my experience, was a young woman named Susan. Shortly before the conference, Susan had felt so miserable about her life that she wanted to kill herself. Searching for some way to help, Susan's youth minister talked her into attending the conference, in the hope that she would find a better answer there.

Once at the conference, however, Susan only became more depressed. Everyone else was so happy. They all felt close to God, and she didn't. They all talked about love, and she felt that no one cared for her. They all laughed and sang and danced, while she became more lonely. On the Saturday night of the conference, Susan decided that when she got home, she would end her life.

Then she heard me speak. She was stunned that anyone "who seemed to know a lot of stuff" could feel so lonely and sad. Maybe she wasn't so messed up after all. Maybe life is supposed to include some pain and heartache, even though people seem to deny that all the time.

Susan shared all this with me by phone about a month after the conference, at the urging of her youth minister. She told me that she had started to say that prayer, "Father, into your hands . . . ," and it was keeping her alive.

About a year after I received the call from Susan, I heard from her youth minister that Susan was attending college and studying to be a youth minister. She wanted to specialize in counseling suicidal adolescents.

Photo: "Father, into your hands I commend my spirit" (Luke 23:46).

included moments of profound doubt and distress.

"Father, into your hands . . ." Of the three synoptic writers, only Luke specifically mentions Jesus' final words before he died. Matthew and Mark say that Jesus cried out in a loud voice and breathed his last (Matthew 27:50; Mark 15:37). John records Jesus' closing words in this way: "When Jesus had received the wine, he said, 'It is finished.' Then he bowed his head and gave up his spirit"; that is, he died (19:30).

The words that Luke places on Jesus' lips, if not actually spoken by Jesus, no doubt reflect the attitude he carried with him to his death: "Father, into your hands I commend my spirit" (23:46). **9**

For Review

- The high priest Caiaphas asked Jesus if he was the Messiah. What was significant about Jesus' answer?
- Why did the Jewish leaders bring their charges against Jesus to the Romans?
- Why did Pontius Pilate not accept the Jews' first charge against Jesus?
- Why do scholars debate the meaning of Jesus' utterance on the cross, "My God, my God, why have you forsaken me?"

Understanding the Cross

Throughout its history, the church has struggled to explain Jesus' death in a way that adequately reflects its profound and complex significance for Christians. That struggle is reflected in the wide variety of expressions, symbols, and theological interpretations the church has used to explain the cross.

The fact that there have been so many different approaches to understanding the cross is a hint that, to a certain extent, its full significance is too great for words. Although it would be possible to settle on just one explanation, that would greatly limit our understanding of the meaning of the cross. With that in mind, let's look at some of the varied language and images the church has used in talking about Jesus' death.

Jesus' Sacrifice: Freeing Us from Sin

Jesus, the Suffering Servant

When the first Christians wrote about Jesus' death and Resurrection, they often referred to the sacred Scriptures of Judaism to show how all that Jesus did had always been part of God's plan for humanity. Devout Jews would take the word of their Scriptures more seriously than even the Apostles' eyewitness accounts of Jesus' post-Resurrection appearances. Perhaps nowhere was the link between God's plan and Jesus more clear and powerful than in the "suffering servant" passages in the book of the prophet Isaiah.

The passages, written hundreds of years before the birth of Jesus, describe an unnamed servant of the Lord who suffers greatly—not as punishment for his own sins but to save the people from theirs.

9
Which quotation of Jesus' last words is most significant to you—the one provided by John or the one provided by Luke? Explain your choice in a paragraph.

Christ of St. John of the Cross, by Salvador Dalí. Glasgow Museums: The Saint Mungo Museum of Religious Life and Art

■ Christians believe that through his death, Jesus bridged the separation between God and humanity that is created by sin. *Photo: Christ of St. John of the Cross*, by Salvador Dalí. Jesus was fully human, and his death was a real historical event. But he was also fully divine, so his death goes beyond time to affect all people.

The servant has been given God's spirit, and his mission is to bring justice to the nations. He is subject to insults and derision, he is beaten, and his face is spat upon. He is spurned and avoided by the people, who think God is punishing him for his sins.

However, Isaiah points out that in reality, "he [the suffering servant] was pierced for our offenses, / crushed for our sins" (53:5, NAB). The servant is compared to a lamb that is led away to be slaughtered. But in the end, because he "poured out himself to death . . . [and] bore the sin of many," ultimately he is glorified by God (53:12). (The complete passages are found in Isaiah 42:1–4; 49:1–6; 50:4–9; 52:13—53:12.)

The early Christians saw in this passage a foretelling of the mission of Jesus, and an explanation for the suffering he went through in the Crucifixion. The prophecy also helped the first believers understand that through his death on the cross, Jesus freed us from sin. **10**

Jesus, the Paschal Lamb

Recall that the Evangelist John linked the death of Jesus with the killing of the paschal lambs, which were slaughtered as part of the celebration of Passover. John's Gospel refers to Jesus as the new paschal lamb, "the Lamb of God who takes away the sin of the world" (1:29).

During the first Passover, the blood of the paschal lambs was the sign that spared the Israelites from death, led to their liberation from slavery, and began their journey to the Promised Land. By calling Jesus the new paschal lamb, the Evangelist was suggesting that Jesus' death on the cross constituted a "new Passover" for those who believe in Jesus. Just as the blood of the paschal lambs saved the Israelites from death and slavery, so too does Jesus' death and Resurrection save all humanity from death and slavery to sin. **11**

Jesus, a Ransom for Many

Explaining Jesus' death in terms of the suffering servant or the paschal lamb made sense when the first Christians were addressing Jews. But Gentiles did not have the necessary background in Jewish culture to understand these explanations. The Gospel of Mark, which was written for a Gentile audience, offers another insight into Jesus' death. In Mark 10:45, Jesus states that "the Son of Man came not to be served but to serve, and to give his life [as] a ransom for many."

In the Roman world, a ransom was the price paid to release a slave, and it was often paid by someone other than the slave. The payment was made in front of a shrine to a local god, to indicate that the slave was becoming the property of that god

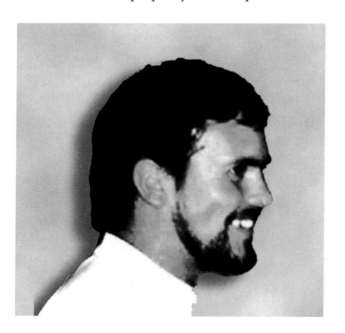

■
Even today, Christians around the world continue to follow Jesus' radical example of love by giving up their life for others.
Photo: Twenty-five-year-old Miguel Angel Quiroga Gaona was a brother in the Society of Mary in Colombia. He was shot and killed in 1998 when he spoke up against a paramilitary group that was threatening people from the rural community he served.

10
To suffer because of others' sins, not one's own, may seem terribly unfair. Write your opinion on this statement: *Life is not always fair, but that does not mean God does not love us.*

and could no longer be owned by another person. The idea of ransom can help us understand the cross if we recognize Jesus' death as liberating us from our slavery to sin. His death sets us free by demonstrating the incredibly freeing power of a love that knows no limits.

Ultimately, a Sign of God's Love

"Jesus Died for Our Sins"

Although all these explanations use different metaphors, each has a common understanding of the meaning of the cross: when Jesus gave up his life for our sake, he freed us from sin.

This is often expressed by saying, "Jesus died for our sins." Unfortunately, this wording can convey an image of God that is far removed from the one Jesus revealed to the world. Such a statement can give a sense, for instance, that Jesus had to die in our place because an angry God demanded payment for past offenses. This image of God runs directly contrary to Jesus' message—that God is totally loving and forgiving.

A better way of describing what it means to say that Jesus died for our sins is to say that through his death, Jesus bridged the separation between God and humanity that is created by sin. In doing so, he also freed us from the ultimate consequence of sin—death. (We will discuss Saint Paul's teachings about salvation and sin later in this course.)

The Power of Love

At the core of the Christian understanding of the cross is this truth: through the death and Resurrection of Jesus, God poured out unlimited, complete love for all people.

11
Besides their role in the Passover story, name some characteristics of lambs that make the lamb a fitting symbol of Jesus.

■
Photo: Jesus' death frees us with the incredible power of a love that knows no limits.

Christians believe that God loves us so much that God became one of us in Jesus, giving totally of Self to us. Although human beings rejected and attempted to destroy God's gift of love by crucifying Jesus, God responded not with anger but by offering new life to anyone who would accept it.

So the cross and the Resurrection form the new Covenant (or special relationship) that God made, through Jesus, with all people. In that covenant, the cross is a sign of how much God loves us, giving the divine Self to us completely not only on the cross but always. The Resurrection, in turn, is a sign of how God overcomes *all* sin, no matter how great—for what sin could be greater than the rejection of God through the Crucifixion of Jesus? Our part in the new Covenant is to accept God's love as it is expressed in Jesus.

Viewing the cross as a sign of great love makes it easier for Christians to understand what Jesus meant when he said that they must "take up their cross and follow me" (Matthew 16:24). Just as Jesus poured out his love on the cross, Christians are called to give themselves to others with unlimited, unconditional love—the sort of love that involves personal sacrifice. **12**

As the Evangelist John would say years after Jesus' death:

Whoever does not love does not know God, for God is love. God's love was revealed among us in this way: God sent his only Son into the world so that we might live through him. In this is love, not that we loved God but that he loved us and sent his Son to be the atoning sacrifice for our sins [that is, the sacrifice that would take away our sins]. Beloved, since God loved us so much, we also ought to love one another. (1 John 4:8–11)

For Review

- Explain the differences and similarities between these metaphors for Jesus' death on the cross: *suffering servant, paschal lamb, ransom.*
- The statement that Jesus died for our sins is important, but to what confusion can it lead?
- What did Jesus mean when he said that his followers should take up their crosses and follow him?

12
Consider one situation in your life in which loving someone or some group unconditionally would require great personal sacrifices. Reflect in writing on how willing and prepared you would be to make those sacrifices.

Only in Light of the Resurrection

The fact that the Resurrection has already been mentioned in our discussion of the cross demonstrates that we cannot really understand the death of Jesus until we understand what followed it—Jesus' being raised from the dead by his Father. None of the Gospels end with Jesus' Passion and death on the cross. Rather, we see Jesus' total trust in God at the moment of his death—"Father, into your hands I commend my spirit." That trust in God would prove to be well founded in light of the Resurrection.

■
Photo: **The full meaning of the cross can only be understood in light of the Resurrection.**

10
The Resurrection:
God Is Victorious! Jesus Is Lord!

In This Chapter . . .

- The Resurrection of Jesus
- What Does the Resurrection Mean?
- Recognizing the Risen Jesus Today
- The Ascension of Jesus
- Pentecost

WHEN the sabbath was over, Mary Magdalene, and Mary the mother of James, and Salome bought spices, so that they might go and anoint [Jesus' body]. And very early on the first day of the week, when the sun had risen, they went to the tomb. They had been saying to one another, "Who will roll away the stone for us from the entrance to the tomb?" When they looked up, they saw that the stone, which was very large, had already been rolled back. As they entered the tomb, they saw a young man, dressed in a white robe, sitting on the right side; and they were alarmed. But he said to them, "Do not be alarmed; you are looking for Jesus of Nazareth, who was crucified. He has been raised; he is not here. Look, there is the place they laid him. But go, tell his disciples and Peter that he is going ahead of you to Galilee; there you will see him, just as he told you." So they went out and fled from the tomb, for terror and amazement had seized them; and they said nothing to anyone, for they were afraid. (Mark 16:1–8)

The Resurrection of Jesus

The Gospels themselves—indeed, Christianity as a recognized religion—would not even exist were it not for what happened *after* the death of Jesus. The last days of Jesus' earthly life—his arrest, trial, and death by crucifixion—have been recalled and passed on for some two thousand years only because they were followed by an event that gave them meaning. That event, of course, was the Resurrection, Jesus' being raised from the dead by God, his Father, on Easter.

Curiously, the Gospel accounts of the Resurrection of Jesus are brief compared with those of the final days of Jesus' life. The quotation from Mark's Gospel at the opening of this chapter is typical of the accounts found in the other Gospels—straightforward, offering little detail, with no attempt to further explain what happened. Many of us might like to ask the Evangelists a few of the following questions:

- What did Jesus look like when he was raised from the dead by God?
- Did anyone actually see Jesus come out of the tomb?
- If no one saw him, how do we know that he was really raised? Maybe somebody just stole the body to make people *think* he was raised.
- How can people today be expected to believe something so incredible, something that is almost unbelievable?

All of these are good, reasonable questions. This chapter attempts to provide some satisfying answers. **1**

Photo, facing page: **The garden tomb where Jesus was laid, according to some Christians** *Background:* **Butterflies are symbols of the Resurrection's power to transform creation, both physically and spiritually.**

1

In writing, give any ideas you have in response to the four questions listed above. Write down any questions you have that are not listed on this page.

What Happened?

Each Gospel tells of the burial and Resurrection of Jesus and some of his appearances to his disciples and others after the Resurrection (see Matthew 27:62–66; 28:1–20; Mark 15:42–47; 16:1–20; Luke 23:50–56; 24:1–53; and John 19:38–42; 20:1–31; 21:1–25). Despite a number of differences between these accounts, we can arrive at a basic sense of what occurred that remarkable Sunday morning long ago.

Jesus Was Buried in a Tomb

All four Gospel accounts agree that after Jesus died, his body was claimed by a wealthy disciple of Jesus' named Joseph of Arimathea. Joseph had asked Pilate for the right to take the body and give it a decent burial. He took the body, wrapped it in a burial cloth called a shroud, and laid it in a tomb hewn out of stone. (The full preparation of the body for burial according to Jewish custom had to wait until after the Sabbath, which was already beginning on the evening of the Friday Jesus died.) A large, round, flat stone was then rolled into place at the entrance of the tomb. Matthew's Gospel states that Pontius Pilate assigned Roman soldiers to guard the tomb, to prevent Jesus' disciples from stealing the body. The Jewish leaders were concerned that the disciples would steal the body and then claim that Jesus had risen from the dead as he had predicted he would.

Other Common Points in the Gospel Accounts

After describing Jesus' burial, each Evangelist offers his own version of what happened. However, the accounts do have these points in common:

- Various people go to the tomb and discover that the body of Jesus is no longer there.

- The people who go to the tomb find out—either on their own (in John's Gospel) or through one or more messengers of God (in the synoptic Gospels)—that Jesus is no longer dead but alive, and that he will reveal himself to them again soon.
- The initial reactions of the witnesses are, quite naturally, shock and then fear. But soon they experience Jesus among them in such striking ways that there can be no doubt it is he—alive again, and yet somehow very different from when he walked among them before his death. Jesus has risen, and everything he claimed is proved true by this fact! **2**

2
Imagine yourself as one of the disciples, first hearing the news of Jesus' Resurrection. In writing, briefly describe how you, as a disciple, might react to this news.

■
Illustration: **Considerable historical evidence—including the empty tomb—supports the Christian conviction of Jesus' Resurrection.**

Focusing on the Larger Picture

Beyond the common points listed on the previous page, a number of differences in the Gospel accounts of the Resurrection are easily recognized with just a quick reading of those accounts. However, remember this basic lesson about the Gospels: The small details in the accounts are not significant or essential to what is being revealed through them. The truths expressed through the accounts far surpass any inconsistency that might be apparent in them.

Evidence for Accepting the Resurrection

Saint Paul, in his First Letter to the Corinthians, states, "If Christ has not been raised, then our proclamation has been in vain and your faith has been in vain" (15:14). No element in Christian faith is more central to our understanding of the Christ of Faith than the Resurrection. Ultimately, recognizing the risen Christ is a matter of faith. Yet considerable historical evidence supports the Christian conviction of the Resurrection of Jesus by his Father.

A Consistent Belief in the Early Church

The Resurrection was a consistent belief in the early church. The letters of Saint Paul, sermons contained in the Acts of the Apostles, and all four Gospels mention it. In the Acts of the Apostles, we see that experiencing the risen Jesus was even considered a key qualification for being accepted as one of the Apostles (1:15–22).

The Empty Tomb

The empty tomb also testifies to the reality of the Resurrection. All accounts of the Resurrection agree that the tomb was empty on the morning the women went to prepare Jesus' body for burial. Surely the Romans would have produced Jesus' corpse if they could have found it. Publicly displaying his dead body would have destroyed any stories of his Resurrection that might have been falsely created by his disciples, quickly putting an end to the movement Jesus started.

But one might ask, Could the disciples have somehow stolen Jesus' corpse and then either hidden or destroyed it? The problem with this proposition is that several of the disciples would eventually choose to die as martyrs rather than deny their faith in a resurrected Jesus. Would they have freely died for a hoax, knowing that Jesus had not really risen?

Moreover, the Gospels identify women as major witnesses to the empty tomb. In ancient Jewish society, women were not accepted as legal witnesses. Therefore, an author seeking to convince an audience of something untrue would never have chosen women as primary witnesses; they were not perceived as credible.

Jesus' Post-Resurrection Appearances

Though no one actually witnessed the Resurrection itself, many claimed to have experienced the risen Jesus later. And though the Gospels disagree on who saw him where and when and under what circumstances, the appearances do follow a common pattern:

- Everyone to whom the risen Jesus appears is downcast, distressed, clearly convinced that he is dead.
- Jesus then takes the initiative and reveals himself to them, usually greeting them with the statement that they should be unafraid and at peace.

"Although the doors were shut, Jesus came and stood among them and said, 'Peace be with you'" (John 20:26).
Photo: An Italian Renaissance artist's depiction of Jesus appearing to the Apostles after the Resurrection.

- Finally, Jesus often gives a command, such as "Go therefore and make disciples of all nations" (Matthew 28:19) or "Go into all the world and proclaim the good news to the whole creation" (Mark 16:15). The knowledge of Jesus risen is not to be kept secret, as a private revelation. Those who know him are clearly called to share that knowledge with others.

Note how the empty tomb and the apparitions of Jesus are consistent with, and thus firm up and solidify, each other. Without the empty tomb, the appearances of Jesus could be regarded as hallucinations, as the fantasies of depressed people. Without the appearances, the empty tomb could be considered a trick.

A Courageous Community

One final piece of evidence can be offered to support the reality of Jesus' Resurrection: a thoroughly shattered band of Jesus' followers was transformed into a community of courageous witnesses after the Resurrection. This may be the most important evidence of all. The total conviction with which the disciples proclaimed the risen Jesus as a sign of joy and hope is undeniable. After all, only such a conviction—and the commitment to share the faith motivated by that conviction—can explain the beginning of the church. **3**

Proclamations of Faith

The Gospel accounts of the Resurrection, we must always remember, are more than just attempts to record in historical detail what occurred the day we call Easter. This does *not* mean that the Resurrection did not happen. On the contrary, the risen Jesus is the most consistently proclaimed reality in the entire New Testament. And the Resurrection is the most pivotal event proclaimed by the Gospels. Only if God actually raised Jesus from the dead is the truth of both Jesus and his message confirmed. Only then is the Gospel proclamation truly Good News, not a lie, a hoax, or a fantasy to be rejected.

As proclamations of faith rather than historical documents, the Gospel accounts and their inconsistent details should not be a stumbling block to believing in Jesus' Resurrection. The Resurrection simply was not a historical event in the usual sense. The death of Jesus was historical in that even nonbelievers would have been able to see Jesus crucified. But only people of faith experienced Jesus after his Resurrection. The risen Jesus could not have been scientifically proven to exist. The Resurrection, in other words, goes beyond history as we know it.

What Was the Risen Jesus Like?

What did the risen Jesus look like? Exactly how did the disciples experience him? What seems certain yet mysterious in the Gospel accounts is that Jesus was truly transformed through the Resurrection. He was experiencing an utterly new kind of existence. The risen Jesus was not a person who had been asleep and then suddenly awakened, nor was he a corpse that had somehow come back to life. He was the same Jesus and yet completely different.

Resurrected life is not merely a continuation, after death, of the kind of earthly life we experience. It is, rather, an entirely new way of living, a new relationship in and with God, something completely beyond our imagination. How can we explain this kind of life? The simple answer is, we

3
Write your own evaluation of the four pieces of evidence given on pages 217 and 219 to support the reality of the Resurrection.

On the Road to Emmaus

Luke's Gospel contains a particularly beautiful and insightful story about an appearance by the risen Jesus to his disciples (24:13–35). Pause and read the story as Luke tells it.

In this apparently simple story, Luke manages to sum up the entire Good News of Jesus. But he also provides us with insights into what it means to be a follower of Jesus today, as well as a member of the community that professes faith in Jesus.

In the story, two confused and distressed disciples are joined by the risen Jesus as they walk along the road to Emmaus. The disciples are so wrapped up in their grief about Jesus' recent Crucifixion, however, that they do not recognize him. Jesus does not force himself on them, nor does he dramatically reveal his identity. Instead, he just walks with them, sharing their journey and listening to their story. They tell him of Jesus of Nazareth, who proved he was "a prophet mighty in deed and word before God and all the people"; of how they had hoped he would be the one to set Israel free from its oppressors; of how he had been crucified; and of the stories they have just heard about his being alive again.

Jesus listens. "Then beginning with Moses and all the prophets, he [interprets] to them the things about himself in all the scriptures." Still the two disciples do not recognize him, though they will recall later that their hearts burned within them as they listened to him speak.

As the three approach the town of Emmaus, Jesus begins to move ahead. Now it is the disciples' turn to take the initiative, to show at least some degree of openness to what he can offer them. And they do so by requesting that Jesus stay with them. Jesus, of course, accepts their invitation. When they gather that evening for a simple meal, he takes the bread, as he did just a few days earlier, and he blesses it, breaks it, and hands it to them. "Then their eyes [are] opened, and they [recognize] him."

The Emmaus story is about what it means to recognize the risen Jesus, a task that ultimately confronts all who would choose to follow him. The word *recognize* is significant, coming from the prefix *re-*, meaning "again," and the Latin word *cognoscere,* meaning "to know." In the act of recognizing, we come to know something or someone again. We rediscover or renew our awareness of a reality we have experienced before.

This is what happened to the disciples at Emmaus. In the act of blessing and breaking bread, Jesus was recognized. Suddenly the disciples rediscovered him, and all the memories of what they had shared before his death flooded back on them. They came to the powerful realization that Jesus was alive, present with them! The joy and excitement that overwhelmed them was typical in the witnesses to whom Jesus appeared.

Photo: **The Emmaus story is about recognizing Jesus along the road of life.**

can't! Nonbelievers have suggested that the authors of the New Testament imagined or intentionally created a vision of resurrected life. But it would seem that the Gospel evidence supporting the Resurrection of Jesus is too complex and too thorough to have been created by any one author, let alone several authors working independently of one another.

For Review

- According to Matthew's Gospel, why did Pontius Pilate assign Roman soldiers to guard the tomb of Jesus?
- Summarize the common points in the Gospel accounts of Jesus' Resurrection.
- List and summarize the four pieces of evidence given to support the reality of Jesus' Resurrection.
- Why was the Resurrection of Jesus not a historical event in the usual sense?

What Does the Resurrection Mean?

For the first Christians, understanding the meaning and significance of Jesus' Resurrection from the dead was of greater concern than proving that it actually happened, or explaining exactly how it happened. As the early believers considered Jesus in light of his message and their sacred Scriptures, they began to realize the enormous implications the Easter events had for all of humanity. Let's look at the critical meaning of those events for Christian faith.

Jesus Recognized as the Son of God

For the first believers, and for Christians today, the Resurrection demonstrated the truth of Jesus' divine claim. As we will see shortly, the first Christians quickly began calling Jesus *the Christ* (which is the Greek translation of *messiah*) and *our Lord*. All these titles pointed to Jesus' divine nature as the Son of God, and not just a great, good man with a marvelous but unrealistic Dream.

Many people want to give a halfhearted, incomplete assent to Jesus and his message. They are willing to admit that he was a special person, perhaps the greatest in history, and certainly one worth imitating. But the Messiah, the Lord? That is going too far, they say.

The Resurrection of Jesus, together with the church's constant commitment to belief in the Resurrection as *the* central characteristic of Christian faith, makes it unacceptable for Christians to see Jesus as merely an extraordinary human being. As bluntly stated earlier in this book, Jesus was one of three things: a lunatic, a con artist, or exactly who he professed to be. The Resurrection favors the last option: Jesus was and is the Divine One sent by God to redeem the world.

Affirmation of the Truth of Jesus' Teachings

If the Resurrection reveals the truth of Jesus' divine claim, then it also shows the truth of his other claims and teachings about God.

- In his claim about God's unconditional love for each of us, Jesus spoke the truth.
- In his promise that we can find fulfillment in loving God and others, Jesus spoke the truth.
- In his rejection of empty religious ritual and his commitment to a prayerful and personal relationship with God, Jesus spoke the truth.
- In his conviction that forgiveness of one another will always be more life-giving and enriching than revenge, Jesus spoke the truth.
- In his call for respect and special affection for the outcasts of society, Jesus spoke the truth.

- In his teaching that the rich must share with the poor, Jesus spoke the truth.
- In his absolute refusal to accept anything that would separate people from one another—social status, sexual or racial discrimination, economic standing, political affiliation, even religious beliefs—Jesus spoke the truth.

All of this is affirmed by the Resurrection. **4**

From Death to New Life

If Jesus' mission had ended on the cross, it would have been impossible for his followers to find any meaning in his death. Indeed, if Jesus' story had ended with the cross, there would be no Christian religion today. But in light of the Resurrection, the cross takes on new significance. Because of the Resurrection, Christians can claim that Jesus' death freed humanity from sin.

Through the Resurrection, God poured out new life for humanity—not just the life after death in heaven that Christians believe they will experience because they share in Jesus' death and Resurrection, but also a new way of living right now.

That way of living is the way of the Kingdom of God, which Jesus' life, death, and Resurrection established. Christians continue to reveal the Kingdom of God when they imitate Jesus' example and work together to make the world the just and peaceful place that God always meant it to be.

Transforming Life as We Know It

For Christians, the Resurrection of Jesus completely transforms the understanding of all human life. Because of the Resurrection, Christians know that happiness and fullness of life are not accomplished merely through rigid religious practices or through some new self-improvement

---

■

The Resurrection demonstrated the truth of Jesus' divine claim. *Photo:* **The sun begins to emerge from an eclipse. "The light shines in the darkness, and the darkness did not overcome it" (John 1:5).**

4

Read over the list of Jesus' teachings that were shown to be the truth by the fact of the Resurrection. Which of those teachings or truths do you most need to pay attention to now?

Reflect on your choice in a paragraph.

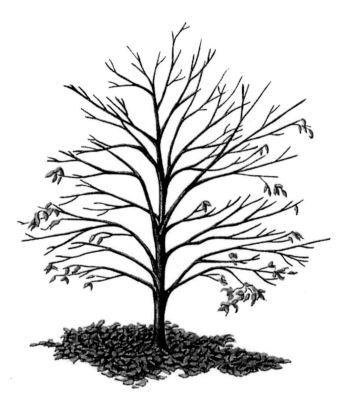

chal lamb," established a new Passover. This new Passover saves us from death, frees us from the slavery of sin, and starts us on a journey toward the "Promised Land" of new life. It is a mystery in the way that love is a mystery—a deep reality to be lived rather than a problem to be explained.

The Paschal Mystery in Everyday Life

Christians see the paschal mystery in their own lives whenever they see the power of new life being released from an experience of suffering or death. The themes of dying and rising in everyday life help Christians understand the redemptive meaning of the paschal mystery.

In nature. Much of nature reflects a repeating cycle of death and rebirth. For example, many plants flourish during the summer, then wilt and "die" in the fall and winter, only to bloom again each spring. Animals are born, grow to maturity, generate new life, and then die, only to decay and provide nourishment for new life. People too, of course, reflect this biological pattern.

In pain experiences. The redemptive meaning of the paschal mystery can be witnessed in personal ways as well as in the cycle of nature. Christians believe, for example, that much of the pain encountered in life—whether physical or emotional—can serve as an invitation to and opportunity for new growth, when seen with the eyes of faith. When a friend is suffering, an act of love on our part can bring new life to our friend and to ourselves. When a person hurts us through an unkind word or careless action, a gesture of forgiveness from us can renew the relationship and bring it to new depth.

This is not to say that pain and suffering should be sought. Enough of it comes inevitably with life. Through the Resurrection, God lets us know that

program. Rather, happiness and fullness of life come from a new center, a new life force, a new source of power. That new source of power is nothing less than God, the God that is revealed in and through Jesus Christ. "I live now not with my own life," said Saint Paul, "but with the life of Christ who lives in me" (Galatians 2:20, JB).

The Paschal Mystery

The whole series of events by which Jesus saved humanity—from his giving the Eucharist at the Last Supper, through his death and Resurrection, to the outpouring of the Holy Spirit on the first Christians (an event called *Pentecost*)—is known by the church as the **paschal mystery**. It is *paschal* because through those events, Jesus, the "new pas-

Illustration: **The meaning of the paschal mystery can be found in many facets of everyday life. In nature we see how death precedes and brings forth life.**

Recognizing the Risen Jesus Today

If Only We Could See Him Too

Some people today, as they struggle to decide whether to accept Jesus and Christianity's proclamation about him, make this point: It would be so much easier if only we could experience the risen Jesus the way his disciples did—or like Doubting Thomas did, placing our hand in the wounds of the risen Jesus and knowing that in him God has conquered death (see John 20:24–29). Then we could believe also. It was easy for them. How could they *not* believe?

But those who hold the notion that it was easy for the first disciples to believe in the risen Jesus do not understand the depth of faith of those first disciples. That same depth of faith is required of Christians today if they are to "see" Jesus and recognize him as the Christ. Ultimately, nothing *forces* people to believe, nothing compels them to accept Jesus as Redeemer. However, a great deal about Jesus *invites* individuals to freely accept him and his message, which were proved worthy of trust by God's raising him from the dead. **6**

ultimately, pain and suffering are not what life is about. When responded to with faith, hope, and especially love, pain and suffering can provide the ground from which new life springs. Then the paschal mystery is again made real. **5**

From death to resurrection and new life—the paschal mystery seems to permeate all of life for those with "the eyes to see and ears to hear" (see Mark 8:18). Perhaps only when the paschal mystery is lived out in the actions and attitudes of daily life can the full meaning of Jesus' death and Resurrection make sense for the Christian.

For Review

- What fact about the Resurrection is of most significance to Christian faith?
- Why is viewing Jesus as just an extraordinary man rather than the Christ an unacceptable position for Christians?
- What is the origin and meaning of the term *paschal mystery?*

How Do We Encounter Jesus?

When Christians accept Jesus and his message, they find and experience the risen Jesus in ways that can be as meaningful as the Apostles' encounters after the Resurrection. Through their faith encounters with Christ, Christians share in the transforming, saving power of his death and Resurrection. Today's Christians can encounter

---

■
Illustration: A tree could not bloom brilliantly in spring without its apparent death the previous autumn.

5
Copy and complete this statement: *In my own life, I see the paschal mystery most clearly reflected in _____ because _____.*

6
Read the story of Doubting Thomas in John 20:24–29. Then imagine yourself as Thomas and write a letter to another disciple who has asked for help in dealing with doubts about Jesus.

Christ in the same ways that Christians have throughout time.

In the Eucharist

Catholic faith teaches that Jesus is encountered in a special way in the **Eucharist,** or the Mass. The Eucharist is the central saving act for Catholics, the core of the church's life in Christ. Catholics believe that because Jesus told us at the Last Supper, "This is my body, which is given for you. Do this in remembrance of me" (Luke 22:19), the bread and wine truly become Jesus himself during the Mass.

In the celebration of the Eucharist, the church re-enacts the paschal mystery—Jesus' sacrifice of himself for all of humanity on the cross, and then his rising from the dead. In the Eucharist, Jesus' sacrifice is not repeated, because he died once and for all and does not die again. Rather, the saving power of Jesus' sacrifice is made present to us. In this way, the Eucharist brings Jesus' death and Resurrection right into the midst of the community of believers.

In celebrating the Eucharist, the community of believers brings all the sacrifices that its members make when they follow Jesus' example in their daily lives—their praise, suffering, prayer, and work—to be offered in the celebration, along with the bread and wine. Like the bread and wine, those sacrifices, and the people who offer them, are transformed. In sharing Jesus' body and blood, the people are meant to *become* Jesus—becoming hope, life, and joy for the world today. The food and drink of the Eucharist gives the people the strength to live as Jesus did.

By celebrating the Eucharist with the believing community, Catholics are reminded of a constant reality—that the risen Jesus is with us. They can leave the eucharistic celebration with "new eyes," a renewed capacity to see Jesus present in many other ways in their daily life.

The opposite, however, is also true. Those who make little or no attempt to recall and live out the message of Jesus, who make no effort to reach out in love to others in their daily life, have a difficult time fully experiencing Jesus as present in the

In Matthew 25:31–46, Jesus teaches that we encounter him whenever we comfort the poor and suffering.
Photo: Christ in the Breadline, by Fritz Eichenberg.

Eucharist. The Eucharist is no more magical than the Resurrection itself. In both cases, only "those with the eyes to see" will see.

In the Community of Believers

Jesus told his disciples, "Just as you did [a compassionate deed for] one of the least of these who are members of my family, you did it [for] me" (Matthew 25:40). Christians discover Jesus in their loving relationships with one another. Jesus also said, "Where two or three are gathered in my name, I am there among them" (Matthew 18:20). Christians discover Jesus within the community of believing Christians, those gathered "in his name," the church. Every loving relationship we experience—especially one in which we love without demanding love in return—is an encounter with the risen Jesus.

In Remembering and Living Out Jesus' Dream

Memory is a complex and powerful human capacity, and it is especially helpful in understanding how Jesus is with us today.

We can treat some memories as "dead and gone," as events and experiences that no longer influence us. Other memories, however, can be treated just the opposite; they can be "alive and present" and help shape every moment of our life.

We get a hint of the power of memory when a fragrance or a popular song first experienced several years ago creates within us today the emotions associated with the original experience. If this power is true of the memory of aromas and sounds, how much more true it is of the memory of important people in our life. Perhaps we remember a good friend or relative who died when we were much younger. We never truly forget such people. They continue to live within us, sometimes in very real and powerful ways.

In living out the Dream of Jesus, Christians encounter Jesus in very real and powerful ways. They do more than simply recall or remember a past event—that is, the historical life and ministry of Jesus. They consciously make Jesus, and everything that is associated with him, present again. **7**

The Mark of a True Christian

In summary, then, to fully encounter the risen Jesus today, Christians must not only gather together and break bread in his memory, they must live every day in accordance with his Dream of the Kingdom of God. In fact, the key criterion for being a Christian is whether the person is willing to let his or her life be shaped and led by the power of Jesus' life and message. This openness to a lived faith is of far greater importance than an intellectual grasp of the Resurrection.

The risen Christ is revealed in and through loving Christians, who say along with Saint Paul, "I live now not with my own life but with the life of Christ who lives in me" (Galatians 2:20, JB). After all is said and done, living out one's faith is what it means to discover and know the risen Jesus and to meet God in and through him.

For Review

- Why do some Christians have difficulty experiencing Jesus as present in the Eucharist?
- In what sense can a memory be "alive and present"?
- What is the key criterion for being a Christian?

7
In writing, describe an incident from your life that stands out as an encounter with the risen Jesus.

The Ascension of Jesus

What happened to Jesus after his Resurrection and his appearances to the disciples and others? Our immediate inclination is to respond that he "went to heaven." But where and what is heaven? And how did he get from here to there? These are perhaps obvious questions, but they have anything but obvious answers. **8**

What the Scriptures Tell Us

Numerous parts of the New Testament refer to Jesus' presence with the Father "in heaven." For example, Jesus is said to be "seated at the right hand of God." However, specific references to the **Ascension** of Jesus into the presence of his Father are fewer in number.

- A specific description of the Ascension of Jesus as a historical event is made only in Luke's Gospel (24:50–53) and in the second part of Luke's work, which is called the Acts of the Apostles. (1:9–11)
- Matthew's Gospel doesn't mention the Ascension at all, and the brief mention of the event in Mark 16:19 may have been added to Mark's original Gospel.

8
Write a description of what you hope heaven will be like.

■
Jesus is said to be with God "in heaven." But where and what is heaven?
Photo: A twelfth-century artist's conception of Jesus in heaven, entitled *Christ in Majesty,* painted on the dome of a church.

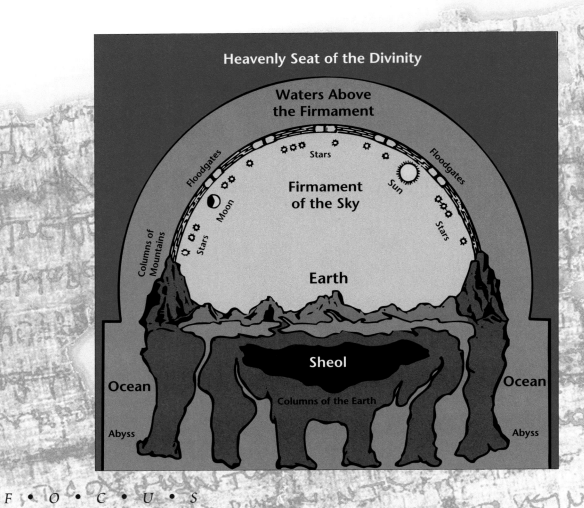

Heavenly Seat of the Divinity

Waters Above
the Firmament

Floodgates

Stars

Floodgates

Firmament
of the Sky

Sun

Moon

Stars

Columns of
Mountains

Stars

Earth

Sheol

Ocean

Columns of the Earth

Ocean

Abyss

Abyss

F • O • C • U • S
The Worldview of the Ancient Jews

This illustration represents the concept of the universe held by Jews of the first century.

According to this worldview, God resided in the heavens, above the upper waters. The sky, or *firmament*, lay below these upper waters and was visualized as an overturned bowl supported by columns of mountains. The firmament had floodgates that opened to let the upper waters fall to earth in the form of rain or snow. The earth was thought to be a platform that sat upon columns. The lower waters surrounded the columns supporting the earth and the surface of the lower waters formed the oceans. All that lay beneath the earth was called the *abyss,* and therein was the home of the dead, or *Sheol.*

- Only two brief references to the Ascension can be found in all the epistles (1 Timothy 3:16; 1 Peter 3:22).

In his Gospel account of the Ascension, Luke says, "[Jesus] led them out as far as Bethany, and, lifting up his hands, he blessed them. While he was blessing them, he withdrew from them and was carried up into heaven" (24:50–51).

According to the account given in Acts, Jesus promised his disciples, "You will receive power when the Holy Spirit has come upon you" (1:8).

When he had said this, as they were watching, he was lifted up, and a cloud took him out of their sight. While he was going and they were gazing up toward heaven, suddenly two men in white robes stood by them. [The men in robes] said, "Men of Galilee, why do you stand looking up toward heaven? This Jesus, who has been taken up from you into heaven, will come in the same way as you saw him go into heaven." (1:9–11)

An Event Beyond Human Comprehension

As was true of the earlier Gospel accounts, contradictions and differences are evident in the various scriptural references to the Ascension. These contradictions and differences are understandable, given that the writers of the Christian story were dealing with an event beyond human comprehension. A happening of this magnitude stretches our ability to express it within the limits of language.

A Problem of Space and Time

We, as humans, cannot escape images of space and time in our speaking, writing, and even thinking. For example, we automatically think of heaven as a place "up there." This notion may have been inherited from the people of Jesus' day, who had a simplistic view of the universe.

The ancient Jews viewed the universe as consisting of several layers: the earth itself; the firmament above it, which included the sky and the stars; and the abyss, which lay beneath the earth. The people imagined the realm, or world, of God as existing beyond the sky and the waters above the sky. It was natural for the scriptural writers, therefore, to express their recognition of Jesus as the risen Messiah through these images of time and space, stating that Jesus was "carried up into heaven" at a particular time and place.

In spite of our limited understanding of Jesus' Ascension, we can get a handle on the meaning the scriptural authors intended to express through their description of this event.

Right Here, Right Now

The main lesson that the scriptural authors wished to teach by describing the Ascension was this: Following his Resurrection, Jesus passed totally into the presence of God, and in doing so, he moved beyond our experience of space and time. What this actually means—strangely enough—is precisely the opposite of what we often assume it means. When we speak of the risen Jesus as "going to his Father," we naturally think in terms of Jesus' being removed from our earthly realm, of his being separated from us. But when we reflect on where God is (in light of Jesus' teachings about his Father), we realize that it is not right to speak and think of God as "out there" somewhere. The entire message of Jesus hinges on precisely the opposite realization—that the Kingdom of God is among us, that God is not "out there" but rather "right here."

Even small children acknowledge God as "being everywhere." But think of what this implies: If God is totally present, if God is right here and right now, then by "going to the Father," Jesus was actually becoming more truly *present* to us than he could possibly have been as he walked the roads of Palestine! Now free of the limitations of space and time, Jesus can be totally with us. He is no longer tied down to one place at one time, talking about one thing to one particular group of people—as was true two thousand years ago. Rather, he is free to be everywhere, with everyone, for all time, loving and caring and calling us to his Father. This is the marvelous reality of the Good News! **9**

For Review

- What human limitation makes it difficult to understand the Ascension?
- What was the main lesson that the scriptural authors wished to teach by describing the Ascension?

Pentecost

The Gift of the Spirit

In the Acts of the Apostles, immediately before the account of the Ascension, the disciples ask Jesus if he is going to restore Israel to its former power as a kingdom. Jesus tells them that only the Father knows what the future holds. Then he says to them, "But you will receive power when the Holy Spirit has come upon you; and you will be my witnesses in Jerusalem, in all Judea and Samaria, and to the ends of the earth" (1:8).

Following Jesus' Ascension, another incident occurs, this one during the Jewish feast of Pentecost. For Christians, this event that followed ten days after the Ascension is itself called **Pentecost.** At that time, the gift of the Holy Spirit was poured out upon the frightened disciples, suddenly transforming them into courageous witnesses of the risen Jesus.

When the day of Pentecost had come, [the disciples] were all together in one place. And suddenly from heaven there came a sound like the rush of a violent wind, and it filled the entire house where they were sitting. Divided tongues, as of fire, appeared among them, and a tongue rested on each of them. All of them were filled with the Holy Spirit and began to speak in other languages, as the Spirit gave them ability.

Now there were devout Jews from every nation under heaven living in Jerusalem. And at this sound the crowd gathered and was bewildered, because each one heard [the disciples] speaking in the native language of each. Amazed and astonished, [the people] asked, "Are not all these who are speaking

9

List at least five implications that the following statement has for the lives of young people: *God is not "out there" but rather "right here."*

Galileans? And how is it that we hear, each of us, in our own native language? . . ." All were amazed and perplexed, saying to one another, "What does this mean?" But others sneered and said, "They are filled with new wine." (Acts 2:1–13)

The Birthday of the Church

Pentecost is often referred to as the birthday of the church because at the first Pentecost, the disciples began a whole new way of living in communion with one another.

The story of the first Pentecost is filled with marvelous imagery—a powerful wind, tongues of fire, people moved to speak in foreign languages, and observers moved to total amazement. The disciples were apparently filled with such joy that people accused them of being drunk! But the message of the story is essentially this: When disheartened and frightened people encounter the Spirit of the risen Jesus, they are transformed by the experience. As the remainder of the Acts of the Apostles powerfully points out, the early believers were so moved by the experience that they went

Illustration: **After the Ascension and before Pentecost, the disciples and Jesus' mother, Mary, gathered anxiously in an upper room in Jerusalem.**

out with joy and courage to share the Good News with others.

Thus, a shattered band of disciples who had followed Jesus during his lifetime was transformed into a community of faith through Jesus' death, Resurrection, Ascension, and gift of the Spirit. So it was that the church was born, and from that small but striking beginning some two thousand years ago, the church has grown to a worldwide community numbering approximately two billion people—about a third of the human race.

Jesus Proclaimed as Lord

The gift of the Spirit at Pentecost allowed the early believers to recognize on an even deeper level who

■

The church was born at Pentecost because it was then that the disciples were transformed into a community of faith through Jesus' death, Resurrection, Ascension, and gift of the Spirit.

Photo: **A window in a Catholic church on the Mount of Olives, Jerusalem.**

Jesus truly was. Jesus' identity as God was of such significance that people could only gradually come to any understanding of it. As will be discussed in chapter 13 of this course, it would take nearly three hundred years for the Christian church to develop a detailed explanation of Jesus' identity. But the desire and need to struggle with Jesus' true identity was strong for the earliest believers, and their struggle is reflected in their use of various titles for Jesus. Three titles reflect the core of the early Christian community's post-Resurrection, post-Pentecost understanding of Jesus: *the Christ, the Son of God,* and *our Lord.*

The Christ

Recall from earlier in this course that the title *Christ* is based on the Greek translation of the Hebrew word *messiah,* and it means "anointed one." Because of the roots of the title *Christ* in Jewish history, it is not surprising that it was popular among the writers of the New Testament. It was initially used as a kind of adjective to describe Jesus after his Resurrection, and he was referred to by believers as "Jesus the Christ." This wording quickly, and perhaps unfortunately, became shortened to the point that Christ became almost a surname, or family name, for Jesus, and he was referred to as "Jesus Christ," a title commonly used for him today.

The Son of God

The title **Son of God** had been used in reference to the kings of the Israelite nation, and it was not unheard of for the Jews to refer to any particularly good man as a son of God. The first-century writers of the New Testament, though occasional-ly using the title in this broad sense, often fundamentally changed the significance of the term by referring to Jesus as "*the* Son of God," indicating his divine relationship to the Father. It would be several hundred years before the church would explain that relationship in its official teaching by describing Jesus as one of three divine persons—Father, Son, and Holy Spirit—in the one God. That explanation, formally proclaimed at the Council of Constantinople in 381, is now known to Christians as the doctrine of the **Trinity.**

Our Lord

For the early community of believers, no phrase summed up all of Christian faith as fully and beautifully as the proclamation, "Jesus is Lord!" The Jewish people avoided speaking the name of God, *Yahweh,* by substituting the word *Lord* and other expressions or words for God's name. Using the word *Lord* for God is common in many parts of the New Testament as well. Many times the title is used by Jesus himself in speaking to or about God, his Father. But rather quickly after Jesus' death and Resurrection, believers popularly referred to Jesus as *the Lord* or *our Lord.*

By giving Jesus this title, the early Christians—particularly the ones who were loyal and faithful Jews—were taking an almost unbelievably radical step. During prayer, the Jewish people often proclaimed: "Hear, O Israel! The Lord our God, the Lord is one. . . ." The oneness of God was a central belief of the Jewish people. Calling Jesus *Lord* seemed to some Jews to be saying that Jesus was a god separate from the one true God. For by calling Jesus *Lord,* they were proclaiming a divine identity for Jesus, a unity with God that was then—and in a real sense, remains—absolutely beyond understanding.

The title *Lord* summed up faith in Jesus so thoroughly that it was used in the closing words of the Bible:

The one who testifies to these things says, "Surely I am coming soon."

Amen. Come, Lord Jesus!

The grace of the Lord Jesus be with all the saints. Amen. (Revelation 22:20–21) **10**

For Review

- Why was the first Pentecost a significant happening in the life of the early church? What is the message of the Pentecost story?
- What three titles for Jesus reflect the early Christian community's post-Resurrection, post-Pentecost understanding of him?
- What does the church teach about Jesus in terms of the Trinity?
- Why was referring to Jesus as *the Lord* or *our Lord* a radical step for early Christians?

10
List at least five titles or names for Jesus that reflect the meaning he holds for you, or list at least five titles or names for Jesus that might appeal to young people in general.

■
The early church, spreading out from Jerusalem, proclaimed the Good News of Jesus.
Photo: **A view from Jerusalem.**

Insights from Paul's Story

To this point in the course, the focus has been primarily on the Gospel accounts of Jesus' life, death, and Resurrection. In those works of sacred literature, we encounter the Jesus of History recognized by Christians as the Christ of Faith. However, many of the other books of the New Testament can offer us insights into the meaning of Jesus and his message. The Acts of the Apostles tells the story of the early church as it begins to proclaim the Good News of Jesus. And in that book we also meet a man whose ideas have powerfully influenced the church's understanding of Jesus throughout history. That man is Saint Paul. In chapter 11, we will turn to his story.

11

Paul:

Apostle to the Gentiles

In This Chapter . . .

- A Brief Review
- Getting to Know Paul
- The Damascus Experience
- Paul's Missionary Work
- Understanding Paul's Letters

MEANWHILE Saul, still breathing threats and murder against the disciples of the Lord, went to the high priest and asked him for letters to the synagogues at Damascus, so that if he found any who belonged to the Way, men or women, he might bring them bound to Jerusalem. Now as he was going along and approaching Damascus, suddenly a light from heaven flashed around him. He fell to the ground and heard a voice saying to him, "Saul, Saul, why do you persecute me?" He asked, "Who are you, Lord?" The reply came, "I am Jesus, whom you are persecuting. But get up and enter the city, and you will be told what you are to do." The men who were traveling with him stood speechless because they heard the voice but saw no one. Saul got up from the ground, and though his eyes were open, he could see nothing; so they led him by the hand and brought him into Damascus. For three days he was without sight, and neither ate nor drank.

Now there was a disciple in Damascus named Ananias. The Lord said to him in a vision, "Ananias." He answered, "Here I am, Lord." The Lord said to him, "Get up and go to the street called Straight, and at the house of Judas look for a man of Tarsus named Saul. At this moment he is praying, and he has seen in a vision a man named Ananias come in and lay his hands on him so that he might regain his sight." . . . So Ananias went and entered the house. He laid his hands on Saul and said, "Brother Saul, the Lord Jesus, who appeared to you on your way here, has sent me so that you may regain your sight and be filled with the Holy Spirit." And immediately something like scales fell from [Saul's] eyes, and his sight was restored. Then he got up and was baptized, and after taking some food, he regained his strength.

For several days he was with the disciples in Damascus, and immediately he began to proclaim Jesus in the synagogues, saying, "He is the Son of God." All who heard him were amazed and said, "Is not this the man who made havoc in Jerusalem among those who invoked [Jesus'] name? And has he not come here for the purpose of bringing them bound before the chief priests?" Saul became increasingly more powerful and confounded the Jews who lived in Damascus by proving that Jesus was the Messiah. (Acts of the Apostles 9:1–22)

A Brief Review

Before going any further, it will be helpful to review what this course has already said about Jesus. After the review, the course will make a major shift in its study of Jesus, his message, and the meaning of both.

■
Paul was instrumental in spreading the Gospel message beyond Palestine and Judaism into the Gentile world, in which people worshiped pagan gods.

Photo, facing page: The ruins of the temple of Apollo, a god of the Greeks and the Romans, in Corinth, Greece, where Paul founded a Christian community.

Background: A map of ancient Greece. Although Paul managed to establish a Christian community at Corinth, he was unsuccessful in converting the Athenians.

From the Jesus of History to the Christ of Faith

The early part of this book focused heavily on the Gospel portrait of the Jesus of History, the divine Son of God as he walked the earth in the person of a first-century Palestinian Jew. Although the Gospel portrait of Jesus expresses the first Christians' faith in him as Lord, it is also an attempt by the early church to preserve and pass on information about Jesus' life and ministry. The Gospels tell the story of his cultural and religious background, his preaching and marvelous works, the growing opposition to him by the leaders of his day, and, finally, his execution on the cross.

With the discussion of the Resurrection in chapter 10, the focus of this course began to move beyond presenting a portrait of the Jesus of History. The concentration for the remainder of this course will be on the Christ of Faith—Jesus as the one Christians profess as the eternal Son of God, present to all people throughout all time. The context for this discussion will be the books of the New Testament other than the Gospels, especially the epistles of Paul.

The Resurrection as a Pivotal Event

The event that turns the focus from the Jesus of History to the Christ of Faith is the Resurrection. We can see why this is so by tracing the development of the disciples' and the early church's understanding of Jesus' identity.

"Is Not This the Carpenter's Son?"

This course began by focusing on Jesus as an "ordinary" first-century Palestinian Jew, the son of a carpenter, Joseph, and his young wife, Mary. Many people of Jesus' day also began their assess-

ment of him with this view. Later, in response to his works and wonders, they would ask, "Is not this the carpenter's son?" (Matthew 13:55).

As his ministry grew, Jesus gradually became recognized as a teacher with particular power and insight—so much so that many faithful Jews eventually accepted him as a new prophet sent by God. Only near the end of Jesus' ministry did some people come to place their hope in him as the Messiah they had been waiting for.

That hope, however, was apparently dashed by Jesus' gruesome execution on the cross. The Jews

Photo: After the Resurrection, the early followers of Jesus were filled with joy.

The Acts of the Apostles: "The Gospel of the Holy Spirit"

The Acts of the Apostles is the second part of Luke's two-volume work, the first part being his Gospel.

The First Half of Acts

Acts begins with a description of Jesus' Ascension into heaven and moves on to the story of Pentecost. It then describes the early days of the church as the Good News of Jesus spread throughout the Roman Empire. Because Acts always attributes the growth of the church to the workings of the Holy Spirit among the believers, it is often referred to as the Gospel of the Holy Spirit.

Roughly the first half of the book focuses on the life of the first Christian community living in Jerusalem—the works of various Apostles and disciples there, emerging conflicts between Christians and Jews, and so on—all leading up to the conversion of Paul. (Paul, in the story of his conversion, is referred to by his Jewish name, *Saul*.)

The Second Half of Acts

The second half of Acts is dominated by the personality, preaching, and missionary travels of Paul and his coworkers. The focus shifts from the growth of the church in Jerusalem to Paul's spreading the Gospel message beyond Palestine and to the Gentiles of the Roman world. Acts ends with Paul reaching Rome, which at that time was considered "the ends of the earth." Luke apparently felt that once the Gospel had been preached in Rome, the story was complete.

What Acts Tells Us About Jesus

Beyond the description of Jesus' Ascension into heaven, Acts does not tell us anything new about Jesus. What is particularly interesting, however, is that we see how the Apostles began to explain—or better, proclaim—their experience of Jesus to various audiences. Acts includes eighteen discourses, or speeches, by various characters—eight of them by Paul. Acts is filled with high drama and action-packed, fascinating stories that tell about the spread of the Gospel of Jesus Christ throughout the world.

viewed death by crucifixion as a certain sign that the one crucified had been cursed by God. The earthly life and ministry of the Jesus of History appeared to have been a miserable failure.

But Then Came Easter

With the Resurrection, the followers of Jesus realized that Jesus was far more than they had imagined. They began almost immediately to refer to him as *the Christ, the Son of God,* and *Lord*—all titles indicating a profound unity between Jesus and the people's God. Then, as the church continued to reflect prayerfully on and debate the meaning of Jesus' union with God, it eventually articulated the doctrine of the Trinity, which proclaimed Jesus as one of three divine persons in one God.

The development of the church's understanding of Jesus was gradual and occurred in fits and starts rather than in a clearly defined pattern. When summarized in a simplified fashion, the progression of understanding looks like this:

Jesus of Nazareth
▼
Special Teacher
▼
Prophet
▼
Messiah or Christ
▼
Risen Lord
▼
Son of God
▼
Second Person of the Blessed Trinity, equal with God the Father and the Holy Spirit **1**

Keeping Things in Perspective

Saint Paul and Others

This chapter and the next look at the life and missionary work of Saint Paul—one of the most influential figures in Christian history. These two chapters also briefly examine some of the non-Gospel books of the New Testament—that is, the Acts of the Apostles, the Pauline epistles, the catholic epistles, and the Book of Revelation. The discussion deals primarily with the writers' treatment of Jesus as the Christ of Faith, even though the prime concern of the writings themselves is more often the growth of the church and the personal spirituality of the early Christians. Remembering the early church's evolving sense of Jesus' identity and the nature of the various writings about him will help keep this discussion in proper perspective.

F • O • C • U • S
The Pauline Epistles

Thirteen epistles in the New Testament were either written by or attributed to Paul. The practice of claiming an important person as the author of a work, even if that person did not write it, was common in Paul's time. Often the individuals or groups responsible for the writing were disciples of the person named as the author. By attributing the authorship, they showed their respect for that person, and their work gained immediate credibility and stature.

Most scholars agree that Paul wrote seven of the thirteen epistles credited to him:
• Romans
• 1 Corinthians
• 2 Corinthians
• Galatians
• Philippians
• 1 Thessalonians
• Philemon
Three epistles that are credited to Paul were actually written by his followers:
• Colossians
• Ephesians
• 2 Thessalonians
Three other epistles that are attributed to Paul but are now believed not to have been written by him are often collectively called the pastoral epistles:
• 1 Timothy
• 2 Timothy
• Titus
The word *pastoral* describes the kind of care and guidance that a shepherd might show for a flock. The primary purpose of the pastoral epistles was to offer guidance to two of Paul's coworkers, Timothy and Titus.

1

Looking at the diagram above, list the understandings of Jesus held by the church, in the order those understandings developed. Next, match the following persons with the understanding of Jesus they would most likely hold: a fifth grader, a senior high student, an atheist, a non-Christian Jew of Jesus' day, the pope, yourself.

The Epistles Came First

Because this course began with a Gospel portrait of Jesus, it might seem that the Gospels were the first part of the New Testament to be written, followed by the epistles, which explored the "deeper" issues of Jesus' divinity. But this was not the case. The first Christian writings were letters that Paul wrote to various church communities. In fact, Paul wrote most of his letters about twenty years after the death of Jesus, and that was more than ten years *before* the first Gospel was written.

Other points about the epistles should be noted as well:

A common means of communication. Keep in mind that the epistles represent a different kind of writing than the Gospels. The Gospels were a special literary form that emerged to preserve the story of Jesus and his message, but an **epistle**, or letter, was a common means of communication of the day.

Paul would not have expected his letters to be preserved as part of a treasury of sacred Christian literature because he shared the widespread belief that Jesus would return in glory within a generation, at which time the world as people knew it would end. Although the first Christians likely recognized Paul's letters as particularly valuable, the church would only later recognize his letters as sacred and worthy of the title *Scriptures*.

A focus on Jesus' divinity. The non-Gospel books of the New Testament offer little about the actual words and actions of Jesus while he walked the roads of Palestine. Also, the epistles do not retell the story of Jesus, because the writers could presume that their readers already knew the story. Rather, these books focus on the attempts by the early church to come to terms with the *meaning* of

Jesus. This meaning was seen in light of his Resurrection and Ascension into glory as Lord, as Son of God.

For Review

- How did the ancient Jews view death by crucifixion?
- Which writings of the New Testament were produced first?
- In what ways do the epistles differ from the Gospels?
- Why would Paul not have expected his letters to be preserved?

■
After the experience of Pentecost, the Apostles began to spread the Gospel in Jerusalem and beyond.
Photo: A street in old Jerusalem.

Getting to Know Paul

Paul is second only to Jesus himself as a central figure in the New Testament. It was Paul who—through a unique combination of faith, personality, and cultural characteristics—spread the early Gospel proclamation beyond the Jewish realm and into the Gentile world. The worldwide Christian church that eventually grew from a small seed in first-century Palestine is a lasting monument to the work of God's Spirit in and through Paul. **2**

Sources About Paul

Virtually all that we know of Paul is found in the New Testament. The story of his conversion (see the quotation at the opening of this chapter) and his career as a missionary is given in the Acts of the

---

■

Illustration: **The image we have of Paul from the New Testament is of a person unimpressive in physical stature but so on fire with conviction that he could not help but impress people.**

2
Read any one of Paul's epistles. Based solely on that epistle, jot down your impressions of who Paul was and what kind of person he was. Then compare your impressions with what is said about him in this course, briefly noting any similarities and differences.

F • O • C • U • S
The Catholic Epistles

In addition to the thirteen Pauline epistles (either written by or attributed to Paul) and the Letter to the Hebrews (written by an unknown author), the New Testament includes seven writings attributed to Apostles and commonly referred to as letters, or epistles:
- Three are attributed to John.
- Two are attributed to Peter.
- One is attributed to James.
- One is attributed to Jude.

Together, these are referred to as the catholic epistles.

For the Whole Church

The word *catholic* means "universal," and it is applied to the writings listed above because they seem intended for the entire, or universal, church rather than for a particular local community. Several of the letters do not have the characteristics of ordinary letters of the day, and a few of them are so short (see 2 John, 3 John, and Jude) that we may wonder why the church ever decided to include them in the New Testament.

In fact, the ancient church was quite reluctant to accept the catholic epistles as part of the New Testament. Serious doubts existed about whether they were actually written by the Apostles identified as their authors. Such objections, however, were overcome by the fifth century, and all the letters were accepted as worthy of inclusion in the Bible.

What Do We Learn About Jesus?

For the purposes of this study of Jesus, the catholic epistles are not particularly helpful. A number of them focus on the ethical conduct of believers, warn against false teachers, offer encouragement in light of suffering, and so on. However, the Second Letter of Peter does present a vigorous defense of the belief in the Second Coming of Jesus, apparently in response to Christians who had become doubtful because of the long delay in Jesus' return. And the letters of John include some beautiful passages in defense of basic teachings about the humanity and divinity of Jesus.

Apostles, written by the Evangelist Luke as a continuation of his Gospel. But we learn more about Paul's personality and his understanding of Jesus from Paul's own writings. At times there are differences between what Luke tells us about Paul and what Paul claims about himself.

This chapter is offered as a brief sketch of Paul's distinctive personal and cultural background and relies in part on what Luke tells us about him in the Acts of the Apostles.

Both Jew and Roman

Like Jesus, Paul cannot be understood outside his culture and history. Read the description that Paul gives of himself:

Circumcised on the eighth day, a member of the people of Israel, of the tribe of Benjamin, a Hebrew born of Hebrews; as to the law, a Pharisee; as to zeal, a persecutor of the church; as to righteousness under the law, blameless.

Yet whatever gains I had, these I have come to regard as loss because of Christ. . . . For his sake I have suffered the loss of all things, and I regard them as rubbish, in order that I may gain Christ and be found in him, not having a righteousness of my own that comes from the law, but one that comes through faith in Christ. (Philippians 3:5–9)

Paul of Tarsus

Paul was born a Jew in Tarsus, the capital city of the Roman region called Cilicia, in Asia Minor, now known as southern Turkey. Tarsus was a thriving, prosperous city situated at the intersection of major trade routes. Although the region he lived in was part of the Roman Empire, Greek culture was still dominant. Living there, Paul was educated in the philosophies of Greek culture. He learned to speak and write in a style that was familiar to the Greek-speaking people of his time. Paul's family, though devout Jews, had been granted the rare privilege of Roman citizenship. This unique background gave Paul the skills needed to pass on the Gospel message to the Gentile world.

Paul . . . or Saul?

Paul's combination of Jewish faith and Roman citizenship accounts for the fact that he has two names in the New Testament. (For example, in the reading at the opening of this chapter, he is referred to not as Paul, but as Saul.) Some have mistakenly claimed that this use of two names is of some religious significance, connected with Paul's conversion experience. The fact is that Paul's Jewish name, the one used within the Jewish community, was *Saul*, while his name in Roman or Greek circles was *Paul*.

■
Paul was a Jew of the Diaspora, born in the city of Tarsus in what is now known as southern Turkey. *Photo:* **A fresco of Saint Paul, from a seventh-century church in Turkey.**

Paul the Jew

A Member of the Diaspora

Recall that at the beginning of the Exile in Babylon, about six hundred years before Jesus, many Jews fled the kingdom of Judah to settle in small colonies along the Mediterranean Sea. These people were called the Diaspora, from a word meaning "dispersion." Paul was raised in just such a Jewish colony, or neighborhood, in Tarsus. In his later missionary work, he would encounter and frequently experience conflicts with colonies of the Diaspora throughout the Roman Empire.

A Pharisee

Paul became an enthusiastic and deeply committed member of the Pharisees, whose sincere but often rigid commitment to the Law made them respected among the common folk but also brought them into serious conflict with Jesus. In Paul's Letter to the Philippians, quoted in part on pages 243–244, Paul says that he was such a devout Pharisee that "as to righteousness under the law, [he was] blameless." According to the Acts of the Apostles, Paul had received training in Jewish Law and theology under the most respected rabbi in Jerusalem. Paul's writings thoroughly reflect his deep understanding of and commitment to the Jewish Law. He also had some background in Greek philosophy.

A Tent Maker

Despite his impressive educational background, Paul was not a rabbi or a lawyer. He was a tent maker by training, and in that role he probably worked with leather in a variety of ways. (You may remember from the discussion of Jewish daily life in chapter 4 that tanners of leather were looked down on because they smelled bad.) Even after he began his missionary work—something for which the other Apostles were often paid—Paul insisted on continuing to earn a living as a tent maker. In part, he did this to avoid the accusation that he was preaching the Gospel message as a way to make money.

A Man on Fire

Virtually nothing is known about what Paul looked like, and some of the hints found in the New Testament seem contradictory. In the Acts of the Apostles, for example, Luke suggests that Paul was a captivating speaker. But Paul himself, while acknowledging that his letters may be impressive, suggests a different sense of his speech-making capabilities: "I do not want to seem as though I am trying to frighten you with my letters. For they say, 'His letters are weighty and strong, but his bodily presence is weak, and his speech contemptible'" (2 Corinthians 10:9–10). On other occasions, Paul seems to allude to some illness or physical deformity

Illustration: **Paul was trained as a tent maker, and continued to work in that profession during his missionary years.**

that afflicts him throughout his ministry. In any case, the basic image we have of Paul is of a person small and unimpressive in physical stature but so on fire with conviction that he cannot help but impress people.

A Man Who Never Knew the Jesus of History

It is important to note that Paul never met the earthly Jesus, the Jesus of History. However, as an educated and devout Pharisee, he may well have heard a great deal about Jesus and his followers and then watched Jesus' popularity grow throughout Palestine. Everything that Paul might have learned about Jesus would have led him to despise Jesus and his message, for they were a direct threat to the Pharisaic Judaism that Paul so deeply treasured.

Paul: Persecutor of Christians

Following the death and Resurrection of Jesus, the powerful movement now known as early Christianity started to emerge. Jesus' followers began to proclaim him as the risen Lord. Conflicts between the Christians and both Jewish and Roman authorities began almost immediately. Not surprisingly, Paul the Pharisee enthusiastically supported any condemnation of the Christians.

At the Feet of Saul

The Acts of the Apostles includes the story of the first Christian to die rather than give up faith in Jesus. He was Stephen, a man who courageously proclaimed his faith when he was brought before the Sanhedrin. (For the entire story of Stephen, see Acts 6:8–15; 7:1–60.) The high priest and other members of the Sanhedrin were so enraged at Stephen's testimony that "they dragged

him out of the city and began to stone him" (7:58). Stephen confronted his own death with the heroic love first demonstrated by Jesus himself: "While they were stoning Stephen, he prayed, 'Lord Jesus, receive my spirit.' Then he knelt down and cried out in a loud voice, 'Lord, do not hold this sin against them.' When he had said this, he died" (7:59–60).

A chilling detail is noted in the account of Stephen's martyrdom: "The witnesses laid their coats at the feet of a young man named *Saul*" (6:58, italics added). Some scholars suggest that Paul may have been attending the execution of Stephen as an official witness and representative of the Sanhedrin. This passage refers to Paul as a young man. Scholars believe that Paul would have been about twenty years old when Jesus was executed (in about 30 C.E.), and a few years older when he watched the stoning of Stephen.

Illustration: At the stoning of Stephen, the first Christian martyr, "witnesses laid their cloaks at the feet of a young man named Saul."

From Persecutor to Apostle

As revealed in the passage that opens this chapter, Paul was so opposed to the Christian movement that he requested permission from the high priest to arrest any Christians (who at first were called followers of "the Way") he might find in Damascus and bring them back to Jerusalem in chains for punishment. It is doubtful, however, that Paul could have been granted such authority by the high priest, who had no authority over Damascus. Luke, who wrote the passage, may have been exaggerating a point to illustrate Paul's deep hatred for Christians. Nevertheless, it seems clear that Paul was almost fanatical in his desire to destroy the early church.

Despite the hostility Paul showed toward Jesus' followers, Christians today claim that Paul is one of the most outstanding figures in all of Christian history. He is second only to Jesus in the way he dominates the New Testament. What can account for this? The answer lies in the story of what happened to Paul on the road to Damascus.

For Review

- Briefly describe Paul's significance in the development of the Christian church.
- Why would Paul have felt at home among both Jews and Gentiles? Why does he have two names in the New Testament?
- What connection can be made between Paul and the Diaspora?
- Describe Paul's initial relationship with the Christian church.

The Damascus Experience

What Happened?

In the passage from the Acts of the Apostles quoted at the beginning of this chapter, Luke tells the dramatic story of Paul's experience on the road to Damascus. In fact, Luke was apparently so impressed by what had happened to Paul that he told the story two more times (see Acts 22:6–16 and 26:12–18), though in those cases Luke portrayed Paul himself as retelling the story. Remember, though, that Luke and Paul do not always agree in their discussions of Paul's life and ministry.

In Paul's Words

Curiously, in his letters to the early church communities, Paul tells almost nothing about what happened to him on the road to Damascus. The following passage by Paul includes a brief mention of the event and then summarizes what he did afterward.

For I want you to know, brothers and sisters, that the gospel that was proclaimed by me is not of human origin; for I did not receive it from a human source, nor was I taught it, but I received it through a revelation of Jesus Christ.

You have heard, no doubt, of my earlier life in Judaism. I was violently persecuting the church of God and was trying to destroy it. I advanced in Judaism beyond many among my people of the same age, for I was far more zealous for the traditions of my ancestors. But when God, who had set me apart before I was born and called me through his grace, was pleased to reveal his Son to me, so that I might proclaim him among the Gentiles, . . . I

The Book of Revelation: Visions of the Ultimate Victory of God in Christ

The Book of Revelation, the last book of the New Testament, is without doubt one of the most difficult books to understand in the entire Bible. Traditionally, the authorship of this book has been attributed to John, the writer of the fourth Gospel. He supposedly wrote Revelation while exiled on the island of Patmos, a Roman penal colony. In fact, however, the author of Revelation is never identified, and many characteristics in the writing styles of Revelation and the Gospel of John make it doubtful that the same author wrote both of them. Many scholars today suggest that a disciple of the Evangelist John may have authored Revelation.

Not to Be Taken Literally

The Book of Revelation is also referred to as the **Apocalypse**, from the Greek word for "revelation." The spiritual visions and strange beasts that fill this book are typical of a kind of writing that was popular at the time the Bible was developing. In our time, some fundamentalist Christian churches tend to interpret Revelation literally. For instance, based on numbers that appear in the book, they attempt to predict the exact date of the end of the world.

Roman Catholic scholars are unified in the conviction that the Book of Revelation uses mostly symbolic language and cannot, therefore, be interpreted literally. The symbolism is strikingly demonstrated, for instance, when Jesus is portrayed as a lamb with seven horns and seven eyes! Note the meaning behind that image: In the Bible, the number seven signifies perfection. Horns symbolize power, and eyes are a symbol of knowledge. Therefore, this means that the risen Lord is a being of total power and knowledge. On nearly every page of Revelation we find described symbolic numbers, colors, garments, and so on.

Victory over Satan

Some of the language of the Book of Revelation can seem extremely cruel and brutal. For example, Christian martyrs

■
The Book of Revelation tells Christians to remain faithful under persecution, trusting that ultimate victory will be accomplished through Jesus.

Photo: The Colosseum in Rome, where early Christians were publicly tortured and executed by Roman authorities.

cry out for revenge against their persecutors, and God is depicted as filled with rage and violent anger against the forces of sin. Scholars suggest that the book may have been written by early Christians as a response to the ruthless persecution of Christians by Roman authorities. It calls Christians to stand firm in the faith and to trust that God will fulfill the promises made in Jesus. Salvation and ultimate victory will finally be accomplished when Jesus comes again in glory at the end of this age and the forces of Satan are destroyed forever.

Ultimately, this message—one of hope, consolation, and courage—continues to make the Book of Revelation valuable for today's believers. Revelation promises that whatever suffering and persecution they may endure, those who dare to believe can be assured that God will be the final victor, and they will be saved.

went away at once into Arabia, and afterwards I returned to Damascus.

Then after three years I did go up to Jerusalem to visit Cephas [Peter] and stayed with him fifteen days. . . . Then I went into the regions of Syria and Cilicia, and I was still unknown by sight to the churches of Judea that are in Christ; they only heard it said, "The one who formerly was persecuting us is now proclaiming the faith he once tried to destroy." And they glorified God because of me.

Then after fourteen years I went up again to Jerusalem. (Galatians 1:11–24; 2:1) **3**

"Have I Not Seen Jesus?"

Paul offers no further details of his pivotal Damascus experience. Significantly, however, he suggests that he spent many years after the experience reflecting on what had happened to him. On some occasions Paul refers very briefly to the event as proof that he deserves full recognition as an Apostle. (To be recognized as an Apostle in the early church, one had to have a personal relationship with Jesus.) In his First Letter to the Corinthians, Paul asks, "Have I not seen Jesus our Lord?" (9:1).

What Truly Happened?

Scholars have long sought to understand what truly happened to Paul in what is often called the Damascus event or the Damascus experience. Was it strictly an experience in Paul's mind and heart that Luke then expressed through a dramatic story? We cannot say with any certainty. Luke did not write the Acts of the Apostles until approximately fifty years after Paul's experience, so it may be that some elaboration of the story took place as it was told over and over again through the years.

3
In a short paper, compare and contrast Luke's description of Paul's Damascus experience (Acts of the Apostles 9:1–22) with Paul's own description of the event (Galatians 1:11–24; 2:1).

A Profound Encounter with Jesus

We can say without question that whatever happened to Paul on the road to Damascus was such a profound encounter with the risen Christ that it radically changed his life. The experience burned so deeply within him that he spent the next fourteen or more years in prayer, reflection, and study on his own and with other believers, among them the Apostle Peter. Toward the end of this period, Paul began his missionary work, and that ministry ultimately took him to his death in the city of Rome. There, according to tradition, Paul died the death of a martyr, proclaiming his faith until the end—all in the name of the risen Jesus, whom he had met on the road to Damascus.

From Conversion to Vocation

Some scholars describe Paul's experience as a conversion. The word *conversion* can be used to describe the point at which someone who had no faith at all comes to believe in God. But if used in this narrow way, the term does not accurately describe what happened to Paul on the road to Damascus. Paul had never doubted God, and his life reflected a deep and sincere commitment to Judaism. But the term *conversion* can also describe the experience of someone who has had a radical change in, or deepening of, their attitude toward God and religion. In this sense, Paul certainly experienced a conversion.

Out of this dramatic conversion, Paul discovered his driving sense of vocation. The term *vocation* is based on a Latin word meaning "call." Paul felt himself called by God for a specific and significant purpose—to be a missionary to the Gentile world, to bring the Gospel proclamation of Jesus to all the non-Jews of the Roman Empire.

■

Three years after his Damascus experience, Paul met with Peter and the other Apostles in Jerusalem, where Paul had previously persecuted Christians.

Photo: **An alleyway in old Jerusalem.**

A Time of Reflection and Growth

As noted earlier, it apparently took Paul a number of years—fourteen or more—to clarify for himself the meaning of Jesus' life, death, and Resurrection and to come to a full sense of his own vocation to proclaim the Gospel among the Gentiles. During that time, the many small, scattered communities of the early church were springing up steadily. Paul no doubt spent much time with these communities, learning the Good News and deepening his own convictions about Jesus. It was during those years that the stories and teachings that would eventually become the Gospels were being collected and passed on orally. Paul immersed himself in all of this, thereby growing in the recognition that the message of Jesus was intended for all the world, not just the Jews. **4**

As Paul grew in understanding, he pursued the call from God to be a missionary to the Gentiles. And he did so with deepening passion and a growing sense of urgency. According to Paul, God's final day of judgment was near at hand. There was no time to lose.

For Review

- What criterion was required for recognition as an Apostle in the early church? On what grounds did Paul claim to meet that requirement?
- What can be said with certainty regarding Paul's experience on the road to Damascus?
- Define the terms *conversion* and *vocation* and explain their relevance to Paul's Damascus experience.

■ Paul was as zealous in spreading Christianity across the Roman Empire as he previously had been in persecuting it.

Photo: A harbor on the island of Rhodes, where Paul stopped during his missionary travels.

4
Does fourteen years seem like a long time for Paul to have pondered Jesus? In writing why or why not.

F • O • C • U • S

The Adventures of the Apostle Paul

The following summary highlights Paul's missionary work following his conversion experience. It can give you a sense of the magnitude of Paul's impact on the early church.

After the Damascus Event

Damascus. Following Paul's experience on the road (about 33 to 35 C.E.), he lived and carried on his ministry in Damascus for three years.

Jerusalem. Paul then made the first of three significant trips to the holy city of Jerusalem. On this trip, he met with the Apostles Peter and James to establish that he could be recognized as an Apostle too.

Tarsus. After two weeks in Jerusalem, Paul began a mission to Cilicia and Syria, working out of a base in his home city of Tarsus.

Antioch. Paul helped to build a community—the first to be called Christian—in this capital of Syria. The controversy over whether Gentiles had to become Jews before becoming Christians first erupted here.

The First Journey

Cyprus and Asia Minor. On Paul's first missionary journey, he and his coworkers established Christian communities on the island of Cyprus and then in several cities in Asia Minor. Next, Paul returned to Antioch.

The Jerusalem Council

From Antioch, Paul and his coworkers traveled to Jerusalem to meet with the Apostles Peter, James, and John. At the Jerusalem Council, the church decided that Gentiles could convert to Christianity without becoming Jews first.

The Second Journey

Galatia. Paul was traveling through Galatia when he became ill and had to stop. He converted some of his caretakers, and may have founded the Christian communities to which his Letter to the Galatians would later be written.

Macedonia. In Macedonia Paul founded churches in the cities of Philippi and Thessalonica.

Greece. Paul preached to the Greeks in Athens but failed to found a church there.

Corinth. Paul then spent about two years in Corinth, founding his most famous church community in about 51 C.E. This is probably where he wrote his First Letter to the Thessalonians, which is the first of his letters and the oldest part of the New Testament.

Ephesus. Paul stopped in Ephesus while returning to Antioch with two close friends, Priscilla and Aquila, and made some initial contacts.

The Third Journey

Ephesus. After a short rest in Antioch, Paul returned to Ephesus to establish a church. For two years he used Ephesus—a meeting place for eastern and western travelers and traders—as the base for his ministry.

Corinth. It was during his trip to Corinth that Paul wrote his most famous letter, the one to the church in Rome, around 56 C.E.

Final Travels

Jerusalem. Paul returned to Jerusalem in another effort to demonstrate that Gentiles were full Christians. He was mistakenly accused of bringing a Gentile convert beyond the barrier that excluded non-Jews in the Temple. This touched off a riot in the city, and Paul was arrested.

Rome. After two years of imprisonment at the Roman military headquarters in Caesarea, Paul appealed his case to the tribunal of Caesar (on the basis of his Roman citizenship) in order to avoid being sent to Jerusalem to stand trial. He arrived in Rome in 60 C.E. and was kept under house arrest awaiting trial for two years. The captivity epistles—the epistles to the Philippians, Philemon, the Colossians, and the Ephesians —may have been written during this time, although scholars debate whether the letters were actually written from Rome or even by Paul himself. The Acts of the Apostles ends at this point, but scholars believe that Paul never left Rome and was beheaded during the persecution of Christians by the Roman emperor Nero.

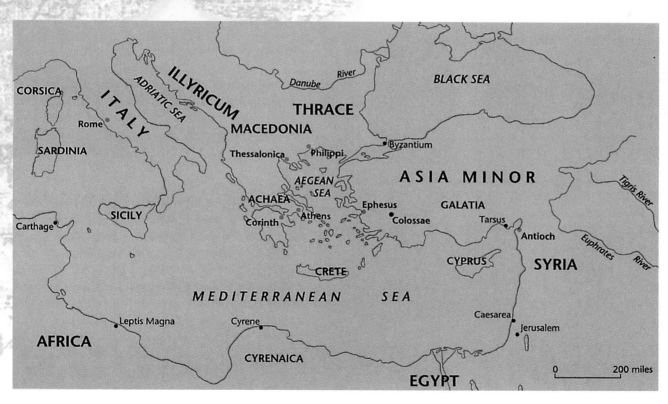

Paul's Missionary Work

The map and summary on pages 252–253 indicates the extent of Paul's impact on the early
Christian church. Clearly, Paul was as zealous in
spreading the Good News of Jesus throughout the
Roman Empire as he had been in persecuting
Christians before his conversion. Paul's story is so
rich and exciting that we may want to discuss it
at great length, but here we will examine it only
as background for understanding his teachings
about Jesus. **5**

Preaching to the Gentiles

The Gentile Question

The very first Christians were faithful Jews who
believed Jesus to be the Messiah only to the Jewish
people. It was not long, however, before the
Apostles realized that God was offering salvation
to the whole world, including Gentiles.

But although Peter and the other Apostles
accepted the mission to the Gentiles, a debate
arose over whether non-Jewish Christians would
be required to follow Jewish laws. The Jewish followers of Jesus argued that the Gentiles had to
become Jews before they could be baptized into
Christianity. Paul and the Gentiles felt strongly
that the Gentiles should be baptized directly into
Christianity.

The Jerusalem Council

The Gentile question came to a head about ten
years after the decision to accept Gentiles as
Christians. Paul and two of his coworkers—
Barnabas, a Jew by birth, and Titus, a Gentile con-
vert—had traveled to Jerusalem to consult with
Peter, James, and John. Both groups wanted to
make sure that they were all preaching the same
Good News.

A controversy erupted, however, when some
Jewish converts demanded that Titus be circumcised, a requirement for Jewish males, before being
accepted as a "complete" Christian. A conference
was called, at which it was decided that Gentiles
would not be forced to become Jews before being
accepted into the church, although they would be
asked to respect certain Jewish laws. This conference is known as the Jerusalem Council.

Even after the Gentile conversion controversy
had been resolved, the tension, at times bitter,

5
Using an encyclopedia or other
sources, write a short paper on
any one of the cities in which
Paul established a Christian community. (See the map and text on
pages 252–253 for city names.)

■
Many ancient Jews despised the
Roman occupation of their land.
But public works projects—such
as roads for travel and aqueducts
for transporting water—made it
possible for Christianity to spread

rapidly throughout the Roman
Empire.
Photo: A Roman aqueduct at
Caesarea, which carried water
from springs thirteen miles away.

lasted for several years and became the focus of much of Paul's writing. Paul's strong stand on the side of the Gentiles during this debate was a leading reason that the Christian faith became a worldwide religion rather than remaining a small Jewish sect.

Paul's Missionary Journeys

The Acts of the Apostles describes three main journeys that Paul took in spreading the Gospel message. Known as Paul's missionary journeys, they spanned more than ten years. The precise details of the journeys are at times unclear. What is very clear, however, is that Paul's travels were anything but easy, as his own description of them illustrates:

Five times I have received from the Jews the forty lashes minus one. Three times I was beaten with rods. Once I received a stoning. Three times I was shipwrecked; for a night and a day I was adrift at sea; on frequent journeys, in danger from rivers, danger from bandits, danger from my own people, danger from Gentiles, danger in the city, danger in the wilderness, danger at sea, danger from false brothers; in toil and hardship, through many a sleepless night, hungry and thirsty, often without food, cold and naked. And, besides other things, I am under daily pressure because of my anxiety for all the churches. (2 Corinthians 11:24–28)

It was in the context of Paul's intense missionary work, and out of his "anxiety for all the churches," that he wrote the letters that have been handed down to us in the New Testament.

■
Some strict Jewish converts refused to share meals with Gentile converts for fear of breaking the ancient purity laws that bound faithful Jews.

Photo: Orthodox Jews in modern Jerusalem clean their cooking utensils to make sure they are *kosher,* that is, ritually fit for use according to Jewish Law.

Understanding Paul's Letters

Just as with all the Scriptures, the key to understanding Paul's epistles is to realize that each was originally directed to people in a particular place, time, and culture, and was composed in a style suited to the needs of that audience. The more we can understand the audience and purpose for a given piece of writing, the more accurate will be our understanding.

For Whom? And Why?

The Early Christian Communities
Paul wrote most of his letters to various small Christian communities that he had founded during his missionary travels. Some of the communities consisted mostly of Gentile believers who were immersed in the Greek worldview and philosophy of their day. Other communities included Jewish converts to Christianity, many of whom were deeply troubled whenever Paul criticized or even discarded religious beliefs and practices that they had long considered sacred.

Responses to Community Issues
Each of the early Christian communities that Paul wrote to had its own problems, conflicts, and concerns. Several of Paul's epistles were written as responses to issues that had emerged within these communities as they grew and developed. In that sense, the epistles are only one side of a two-sided conversation.

Imagine writing a letter to a close friend, offering advice on a tough situation and sharing some of your deepest feelings. Then imagine that a third person, someone who does not know your friend,

For Review

- Summarize the controversy surrounding the entry of Gentiles into the early church. What decision was made at the Jerusalem Council?
- Name two ways Paul contributed to spreading Christianity throughout the whole world.

■
Paul was shipwrecked three times during his missionary travels, which took him across the Mediterranean Sea.
Photo: **The Mediterranean coast of Galilee.**

reads your letter. You will likely feel a great need to further explain yourself, to tell the reader more about your friend so that your letter will make more sense, and so on. We today are in the situation of the third person when reading Paul's letters. We are often forced to read between the lines of the epistles, trying to sort out what was going on in the communities that might have prompted Paul's reactions and insights.

Full of Conviction, Deep Faith, and Love

To each of his audiences, Paul spoke with a profound passion rooted in his own encounter on the road to Damascus with the risen Jesus—or as Paul often referred to Jesus, "Christ crucified." His letters focus on Jesus as Lord, Savior, and Son of God. We must remember that Paul assumed his readers had some knowledge of the Jesus of History. Paul's main concern was how believers were to understand Jesus in light of his death, Resurrection, Ascension, and exaltation as Lord of the universe.

Paul spoke to his audiences with a sense of urgency, demanding that his readers accept Jesus as the risen Lord now or risk eternal damnation. Remember, the early Christians were convinced that Jesus would soon return in glory to conclude the work of salvation and to bring history, as human beings knew it, to an end. For Paul, there was no time to be meek and mild-mannered, no time to mince words.

Paul yearned for those who heard and read his words to experience a new way of living. He knew from personal experience that an encounter with the risen Jesus could shatter one's past convictions and awaken one to an entirely new way of living. "So if anyone is in Christ," Paul wrote, "there is a new creation: everything old has passed away; see, everything has become new" (2 Corinthians 5:17). Paul's letters convey the wide range of emotions he experienced in trying to convince people of his message: conviction, anger, impatience, humility, frustration, sorrow, joy.

But behind these changing emotions, we see two constant qualities in Paul—a sincere love for the people to whom he preached and an unshakable faith in Jesus Christ. Let's look at a few examples from his letters that illustrate those qualities.

Photo: **The ruins of a library in Ephesus. Paul's Letter to the Ephesians was addressed to the Christian community here.**

Letters in Paul's Day

Letters in Paul's day were quite different from what they are today.

A Different Format

Letters in Paul's day were formal and structured rather than "newsy" and free-flowing like our letters today. Paul's letters followed a consistent pattern:

1. a salutation in three parts—naming the sender (Paul), naming the persons addressed, and then offering a formal greeting
2. a thanksgiving to God for the blessings bestowed upon the receivers of the letter and upon Paul
3. the body of the letter, in which Paul took up various matters related to the Good News, the behavior of the people receiving the letter, and problems in the local church
4. final instructions, at times regarding things unrelated to the body of the letter, such as preparations for an upcoming visit by Paul
5. a closing in two parts—final greetings to various people and a concluding word, often in the form of a prayer

Different Materials and Processes

In Paul's day, letters were ordinarily written on parchment (leather prepared for that purpose) or on papyrus (thin slices of the papyrus plant glued horizontally onto a backing formed by thin slices placed vertically). A pen was a split reed or a quill, and ink was a composite of materials like carbon and glue or gum. Creating a letter with these materials was such a tedious and lengthy process, and one requiring such skill, that it was normally done by professional scribes or writers.

In the case of his epistles, Paul would first think through what he wanted to convey to his intended audience. Just formulating his complex ideas may have taken weeks of work, especially in the case of a long letter like the one to the Romans. Then his ideas had to be dictated word by word to a scribe or, as was quite common, be expressed in more general terms, with the scribe acting as a kind of editor as well as a secretary.

A scribe could work no more than two or three hours at a stretch, normally crouched on the ground with a tablet in one hand and a quill in the other. It took the average scribe about one minute to write just three syllables, which comes to about seventy-two words per hour. (A skilled typist today can type about seventy-two words per minute.) The average sheet of papyrus could

Letters in Paul's day were sometimes written on parchment, a durable material made from animal skins.
Photo: Leather stretched on a frame to make parchment.

hold about 140 words. The First Letter of Paul to the Thessalonians, consisting of about 1,500 words, would have required about ten sheets of papyrus and more than twenty hours of work by a scribe. Paul's Epistle to the Romans, with over 7,000 words, would have required fifty sheets of papyrus and nearly one hundred hours of writing time!

Weeks, Not Hours

Any one epistle would have taken weeks, not hours, to complete. That fact may partly explain why some of the letters seem choppy, as if written in bits and pieces. The writing process was no doubt interrupted at times, when Paul would gain fresh ideas and insights. And to be sure, no scribe would have been inclined to go back to edit and polish a letter after it was completed!

The First Letter to the Corinthians

Paul's letters to the Corinthians, for instance, exemplify his love and concern for the people he served. His First Letter to the Corinthians holds strong words for the church there:

It is actually reported that there is sexual immorality among you, and of a kind that is not found even among pagans; for a man is living with his father's wife. And you are arrogant! Should you not rather have mourned, so that he who has done this would have been removed from among you?

For though absent in body, . . . I have already pronounced judgment in the name of the Lord Jesus on the man who has done such a thing. . . . You are to hand this man over to Satan for the destruction of the flesh. (5:1–5)

Paul could be stern when he wanted to be! In some of his writings, in fact, Paul can seem incredibly harsh and judgmental. We must remember that he may have been writing to an audience that had rejected the Gospel message.

Ultimately, Paul always sought to convince his readers to follow Jesus' way of love. The same letter contains Paul's frequently quoted description of love:

Love is patient; love is kind; love is not envious or boastful or arrogant or rude. It does not insist on its own way; it is not irritable or resentful; it does not rejoice in wrongdoing, but rejoices in the truth. It bears all things, believes all things, hopes all things, endures all things.

Love never ends. . . . Faith, hope, and love abide, these three; and the greatest of these is love. (13:4–13) **6**

So although Paul was often stern with the Corinthians and other communities, he could also be quite tender. He would later write a Second

6
Rewrite Paul's famous description of love (1 Corinthians 13:1–13) in language that would appeal to young people today. Use as few of Paul's original words as possible.

Wealthy people had their own private baths for bathing, but common people and travelers like Paul went to the public baths.
Photo: Ruins of the public baths at Corinth.

Letter to the Corinthians in which he would say, "I wrote you . . . not to cause you pain, but to let you know the abundant love that I have for you" (2:4). This balance between "tough love" and tenderness is common in Paul's letters.

The Letter to the Church in Rome

The Letter to the Romans is considered Paul's masterpiece, and some scholars claim that it is one of the most significant Christian writings. Paul's Letter to the Romans was the last of his letters to be included in the New Testament, although it appears first because it is his longest. It was written, perhaps, in 56 C.E.

The letter reflects Paul's lengthy missionary experience, his maturity as an Apostle, his insightful understanding of the meaning of Christian faith, and the stunning depth of personal faith that he had developed. Consider these energizing words:

If God is for us, who is against us? He who did not withhold his own Son, but gave him up for all of us, will he not with him also give us everything else? . . . Who will separate us from the love of Christ? Will hardship, or distress, or persecution, or famine, or nakedness, or peril, or sword? . . . No, in all these things we are more than conquerors through him who loved us. For I am convinced that neither death, nor life, nor angels, nor rulers, nor things present, nor things to come, nor powers, nor height, nor depth, nor anything else in all creation, will be able to separate us from the love of God in Christ Jesus our Lord. (8:31–39)

Romans also contains Paul's strongest statements regarding the relationship between the Jewish Law and the faith of Christians (a theme explored in the next chapter of this course).

■

Photo: **Paul's Letter to the Romans expresses his belief that no misfortune can separate us from the love of Christ. For Paul, times of suffering were times to become closer to God.**

For Review

- In what sense are Paul's letters only one side of a two-sided conversation?
- What issues are most often the main focus of Paul's epistles?
- Why is Paul's Letter to the Romans considered his masterpiece? Where does it appear in the New Testament and why?

The Legacy of Paul's Letters

Paul's life most likely ended in Rome, where he was held for several years under house arrest for the trouble his presence in Jerusalem had caused (see "The Adventures of the Apostle Paul," page 253).

Paul was probably executed during the persecution of the Christians by the Roman Emperor Nero, sometime between 63 and 67 C.E., when he was in his early to middle fifties. As a Roman citizen, he would have been beheaded rather than crucified.

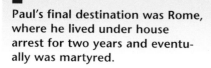

Paul's final destination was Rome, where he lived under house arrest for two years and eventually was martyred.

Photo: Ruins at the Roman Forum, which was the heart of ancient Rome.

The concluding lines of the Acts of the Apostles serve as a fitting summary of Paul's remarkable career as the Apostle to the Gentiles: "He lived [in Rome] two whole years at his own expense and welcomed all who came to him, proclaiming the kingdom of God and teaching about the Lord Jesus Christ with all boldness and without hindrance" (28:30–31).

Paul left behind a church that had spread far beyond the original Jewish community in which it had begun. His letters, originally intended to guide the early church communities, continue to help Christians today understand what it means to follow Jesus. Chapter 12 turns to Paul's understanding of Jesus as the Christ.

12
The Letters of Paul:
Proclaiming Christ Crucified and Risen

In This Chapter . . .

LET the same mind be in you that was in Christ Jesus,

who, though he was in the form of God,
　did not regard equality with God
　as something to be exploited,
but emptied himself,
　taking the form of a slave,
　being born in human likeness.
And being found in human form,
　he humbled himself,
　and became obedient to the point of death—
　even death on a cross.
Therefore God also highly exalted him
　and gave him the name
　that is above every name,
so that at the name of Jesus
　every knee should bend,
　in heaven and on earth and under the earth,
and every tongue should confess
　that Jesus Christ is Lord,
　to the glory of God the Father.

(Philippians 2:5–11)

The Perspective of Paul's Epistles

- While walking through a shopping mall, Yolanda is approached by a young man who bluntly asks: "Have you been saved? Have you given your life to Jesus?"
- With the remote control in hand, Keith casually clicks from one TV station to another, looking for something worth watching. He comes across a religious program in which a preacher, holding a Bible, challenges members of the audience to come forward and "accept Jesus as your personal Lord and Savior or suffer eternal damnation!" Keith giggles uncomfortably and quickly changes the channel.
- Jenny is riding in a car with a friend. They pull up behind another car at a stop sign. A bumper sticker on that car reads, "Jesus Is the Answer!" Jenny's friend turns to her and jokes, "Okay, but what's the question?"

Scenes like these may be familiar to many of us and may even be a routine part of life. But for many others of us, these situations may be relatively new, and often they can make people uncomfortable.

We could debate whether religious programs should be televised or whether street preachers have the right to impose their views on shoppers. However, more important questions lie behind these Christians' methods: What does it mean to be "saved by Jesus"? In what sense must Christians "accept Jesus as their personal Lord and Savior"? What exactly does Jesus save people from . . . or save them for? **1**

■ Paul wrote his letters to small Christian communities such as the one in Ephesus two thousand years ago, yet his words still resound for millions of Christians.

Photo, facing page: **Ruins of the great amphitheater of Ephesus, and the colonnaded Arcadian street.** *Background:* **Paul's letters may have been composed using a quill and papyrus.**

1 Write a paragraph on what being saved by Jesus means to you, based on your current understanding of Jesus' message.

In many of his epistles, Paul attempts to answer these very questions. Biblical scholars admit that for the modern reader, who lives in an extremely different culture than Paul's, the epistles are among the most difficult writings to understand in the Bible. This chapter of the course identifies and briefly explores Paul's major themes, the basic ideas that he repeatedly raised in his letters. A general understanding of these themes can make Paul's epistles easier to comprehend and therefore more enjoyable to read.

Paul's Main Themes: Salvation and the Church

Although Paul's writings are generally concerned with conflicts within the communities and with matters involving personal morality and spirituality among the believers, this chapter focuses on Paul's insights into the nature of Jesus and his message. These insights come through in two primary themes of Paul's letters:

- **Salvation** is found in and through Jesus the Christ.
- The church is the **Body of Christ.**

Paul's experience of the risen Jesus on the road to Damascus forms the background for these two themes. In that experience, Paul learned profound lessons that greatly influenced his life, ministry, and letters.

Justified by Faith

Paul's own experience led him to recognize that the God revealed by Jesus always takes the initiative, meets people right where they are, and can change their life on the spot. According to Paul, it is always God who saves, always God who redeems, always God who reconciles—and God does so through the death and Resurrection of Jesus. The following passage from Paul's Letter to the Romans makes this point strongly:

Since we are *justified by faith,* we have peace with God through our Lord Jesus Christ, through whom we have obtained access to this grace in which we stand; and we boast in our hope of sharing the glory of God. . . .

For while we were still weak, at the right time Christ died for the ungodly. Indeed, rarely will anyone die for a righteous person—though perhaps for a good person someone might actually dare to die. But God proves his love for us in that while we still were sinners Christ died for us. Much more surely then, now that we have been *justified by his blood,* will we be *saved through him* from the wrath of God. For if while we were enemies, we were *reconciled to God through the death of his Son,* much more surely, having been reconciled, will we be *saved by his life.* (Romans 5:1–10, italics added)

■
Photo: What does it mean to be "saved by Jesus"?

In his epistles, Paul uses a number of different expressions for the activity of God in the lives of people—*salvation, redemption, righteousness, justification, reconciliation*. These various terms express slightly different but closely related concepts. For the sake of simplicity, this course uses *salvation* and *saves* as general terms covering all these concepts from Paul.

Jesus Alive in the Body of Believers

Paul's experience on the way to Damascus would teach him a major lesson about Jesus' presence: The unity between the risen Jesus and those who believe in him is so strong and so real that persecuting a believer in Jesus automatically means persecuting Jesus. When confronted by the risen Jesus on the road, Paul asked him, "Who are you, Lord?" And the answer shocked Paul: "I am Jesus, whom you are persecuting" (Acts of the Apostles 9:5). Over time, Paul grew to realize the incredible implication of that revelation: Jesus is alive *in* the body, or whole group, of believers. Eventually this insight led Paul to his teaching that the church is the Body of Christ. With the image of the Body of Christ, Paul was saying that the church is the physical presence of the risen Jesus in the world, just as Jesus, in his own day, was the physical presence of God. **2**

For Review

- What are the two main themes of Paul's letters? What experience forms the background for these two themes?
- List the various expressions Paul uses for the activity of God in the lives of people.

■
Photo: **Paul taught that Jesus is alive in the body, or whole group, of believers.**

2
Paul's writings indicate that a personal encounter with God is possible. In a paragraph, tell about someone—perhaps yourself—who believes he or she has had such an encounter with God.

John: The Letters of John

The three epistles of John are believed to have been written by the same "school" or community of the Beloved Disciple that was the source of John's Gospel. These letters and that Gospel share a poetic style and a focus on the divinity of Jesus.

The First Letter of John: God Is Love

Perhaps the most well known of John's three epistles is the first one. This letter seems in part to respond to various groups who questioned either the humanity or the divinity of Jesus. It takes the strong stance that Jesus was both God and human.

The letter is most recognized, however, for its striking statement that "God is love" and its powerful claim that people can live out their faith in that God only by loving their brothers and sisters.

> Beloved, let us love one another, because love is from God; everyone who loves is born of God and knows God. Whoever does not love does not know God, for God is love. God's love was revealed among us in this way: God sent his only Son into the world so that we might live through him. In this is love, not that we loved God but that he loved us and sent his Son to be the atoning sacrifice for our sins. Beloved, since God loved us so much, we also ought to love one another. No one has ever seen God; if we love one another, God lives in us, and his love is perfected in us. . . .

> God is love, and those who abide in love abide in God, and God abides in them. . . . Those who say, "I love God," and hate their brothers or sisters, are liars; for those who do not love a brother or sister whom they have seen, cannot love God whom they have not seen. The commandment we have from him is this: those who love God must love their brothers and sisters also. (4:7–21)

Photo: "**God is love, and those who abide in love abide in God, and God abides in them.**"

Salvation Through Christ Crucified

Most people in our modern culture, young and old alike, have one of two responses to the question, What does it mean to be saved by Jesus?

- For many people, the notion of being saved means little or nothing, because they have no personal sense of needing to be saved from anything or anyone.
- Others respond to the question with an answer based on their past religious training. For example, they might say, "Being saved means having my sins forgiven by God because of Jesus' death on the cross and, therefore, having the chance to make it into heaven when I die." For them, salvation is in the future ("making it into heaven") rather than in their life now, today.

What is most evident from both of these responses is that for many contemporary people, the idea of salvation has no connection with everyday life. As will be seen in the following discussion, for Paul, salvation had everything to do with everyday life.

Salvation and Sin

The concept of sin underlies Paul's notion of salvation and is the key to understanding Paul's writings on salvation. Sin and its effects struck Paul at the core of his identity, both as an individual and as a faithful Jew of his day. For many people of today, though, sin is an old-fashioned notion that is never mentioned in casual conversation and is frequently ignored even in church settings.

For Paul, being saved from sin and its effects was incredibly freeing. For many of us, it seems virtually meaningless. **3**

Sin: Breaking the Rules?

For many Christians today, sin—if it has any meaning at all—is thought of as "breaking the rules," performing an action that in some way makes one a "bad person." In this view, a person commits sins when she or he acts badly, and perhaps she or he is then encouraged to go to confession (receiving the sacrament of Reconciliation, or Penance) to have those sins forgiven. The impression can be that God is keeping some heavenly tally sheet of people's offenses. Once a person's slate is wiped clean by going to confession and she or he is "good" again, God finds the person lovable again . . . that is, until she or he commits another sin and the whole process is repeated.

Sin: The Breaking of Relationships

Paul would not have agreed with the notion of sin just described. The entire history of his people, the Jews, centered on an intimate, deeply personal relationship with their God.

The story of Adam and Eve. The familiar story of Adam and Eve (see Genesis, chapter 3) was an attempt by the Jews' ancestors to explain how evil entered the world. According to the story, evil had come through the free actions of men and women —represented by Adam and Eve—rather than directly through the will of God. The desire of people to decide for themselves what is right and wrong (to "be like God, knowing good and evil," according to Genesis 3:5) resulted in a break in the relationship between God and the whole human race.

3
Without reviewing what was said about sin earlier, write a brief definition of sin as you currently understand it. Then, using your definition of sin, explain what it means to be saved from sin.

God's desire for reconciliation. Shortly after the story of Adam and Eve, the focus of the Bible turns to the relationship between God and the descendants of Abraham, who shared the human predicament of a broken relationship with the Creator.

Throughout the rest of the Old Testament, God never stops trying to heal that separation, never stops yearning to bring reconciliation to the relationship. At times, God reaches out to the people through an event in their history—such as through the Exodus or the Covenant of Sinai. At other times, God communicates with the Jews through a particular individual—Abraham, Moses, David, or a prophet. God enters the people's lives very personally, cares about them, and sustains them in their trials.

The gift of the Law. The Law, the core of which was the Ten Commandments, was provided to help the people remain reconciled with their God. For the Jews, the Law was not just a cold list of do's and don'ts. Instead, it was a marvelous gift, a sign of God's abiding love for them. In the good times, the people responded faithfully to God and carried out both the spirit and the letter of the Law. In the bad times, the people tried to make it on their own, apart from their relationship with God. They turned their backs on God and abandoned the Law, God's gift to them. When they did that, every part of their lives would start to fall apart, relationships would be shattered, and war and other conflicts would threaten their very existence as a people.

All these events taught the Jews about the essence of sin. Sin was not simply a breaking of rigid rules. Sin was a *rupturing of relationships,* first between the Jews and God and then inevitably among themselves as a people. In his teachings

■
Sin breaks relationships between people and God, one another, and creation.
Photo: In modern Israel, concrete and razor wire separates Palestinians in the Gaza Strip from Israelis.

about salvation, Paul drew upon his Jewish understanding of sin and reconciliation with God and then went beyond it. With his acceptance of Jesus as the Christ, Paul realized that through Jesus, God is calling all people, not only Jews, into reconciliation. This theme—the need for reconciliation between God and people—dominates Paul's writings. (Paul also writes about Jesus as "the new Adam," who reverses the effects of the first Adam's sin. This chapter will offer more on that later.)

Salvation, the Law, and Love

Trying to Earn God's Favor

Over time, some Jews came to a false understanding of the Law and its role in their relationship with God. They started to believe that they could win God's favor by following every letter of the Law rigidly. If they just did everything that the Law dictated (and the Law eventually grew to include over six hundred specific rules!), then God

■
Paul realized that only love could bridge the barriers between people, and that Jesus was the perfect bridge between people and God. *Photo:* **A Maryknoll lay missioner reaches out to villagers in Brazil.**

would have to take care of them. A "good person," according to these Jews, was one who kept the Law "perfectly." The trap that such Jews fell into was this: they started to think that a person could *earn* the favor of God, that people were in some way in control of their own salvation.

Such notions about the Law were held especially by the Pharisees, with whom Jesus frequently came into conflict. (Note that not all Jews in Jesus' time held such legalistic attitudes toward the Law. The fact that Jesus' own popularity grew throughout his ministry was a sign that many Jews agreed with him and did not share the legalism of the Pharisees.) As a Pharisee, Paul would likely have shared a rigid view of the Law prior to his experiencing the risen Jesus. Paul confirms this in his letter to the church in Philippi: "as to righteousness under the law, [I was] blameless" (Philippians 3:6). **4**

Paul's New View of the Law

It is easy to lose perspective. Paul's encounter on the road to Damascus changed his rigid view of the Law. In fact, after that encounter, Paul often had strong words for Jews who had allowed the Law to take the place of God in their hearts. In his writings Paul stressed that people could easily lose sight of the proper and healthy role of the Law (that is, the Law as a guide for proper relationships with God and one another). Following the letter of the Law could become an end in itself, rather than a means to an end.

Love, not the Law, is the goal. With the new eyes of faith in Jesus, Paul saw that the Jewish Law, like all other laws, had its limits. Laws can provide order in a society and help to meet the minimum needs of people, but they cannot meet deeper

human needs, such as companionship, purpose, or happiness. Only love can meet such needs, and laws—even good ones—cannot force people to love one another.

The spirit of the Law, as it was given to the Jews by God, had love as its basis. Paul came to see that after individuals had matured enough to perceive the purposes and deeper meaning of the Law, they no longer needed to follow the exact letter of the Law. In other words, they began to live so in tune with God that they achieved the Law's intentions without even really thinking about it. (See Galatians 3:23–29 for some of Paul's insight.) This understanding of the Law by Paul reflects Jesus' own teaching that the person who loves fully already fulfills everything written in the Law.

Paul strongly preached that the Law had become a barrier, rather than a bridge, between many Jews and God. Paul knew that only love could be such a bridge, and in the crucified Jesus he recognized such love.

In other words, through the Law I am dead to the Law, so that now I can live for God. I have been crucified with Christ, and I live now not with my own life but with the life of Christ who lives in me. The life I now live in this body I live in faith: faith in the Son of God who loved me and who sacrificed himself for my sake. I cannot bring myself to give up God's gift: if the Law can justify us, there is no point in the death of Christ. (Galatians 2:19–21, JB) **5**

The Effects of Sin Are Everywhere

By the time of Jesus, many Jews were convinced that the people's relationship with God was in deep trouble, if not totally cut off. They were, after all, a mostly poor people who had been dominat-

---

4
Write a pro or con response to the following statement: *Most people who follow religious laws do so either to win God's favor or to avoid God's anger.*

5
List the qualities a person needs to possess before she or he can live a good moral life without worrying about laws.

ed by more powerful nations, first the Greeks and then the Romans. The effects of sin were everywhere—poverty, hatred, conflicts among the Jews themselves, foreign domination, hopelessness. Only people like the Pharisees felt "safe" and therefore believed that they did not need to be saved. The majority of the people yearned to be freed from their condition, and they looked for one who could lead them—the Messiah.

This course has attempted to show how Jesus filled the hungers of many of the Jewish people. Through his life, actions, and message—and especially through his death and Resurrection—Jesus restored hope to those who believed in him, and he gave their life an entirely new sense of meaning and purpose. When taking the perspective of the Jews of that time, we might begin to gain some sense of what it meant for them to be saved by Jesus. And in light of that, we might begin to understand the meaning of Paul's preaching to the people of that time. But what about us? What meaning might salvation have for the people of our time and culture?

For Review

- Define the Jewish understanding of sin and briefly summarize its origins.
- What false understanding of the Law surfaced over time among some Jews, and which Jewish group most strongly held this understanding?
- Summarize Paul's new understanding of the Law in light of his faith in Jesus.

■

Photo: Surrounded by the effects of sin, many Jews felt hopeless. Jesus' life and message—and especially his death and Resurrection—brought new hope and meaning.

273

Salvation and Contemporary Culture

Today, understanding and appreciating Paul's notion of salvation hinges on examining our own experience of sin. This, in turn, can lead to recognizing a personal and communal need to be freed from sin and its effects.

In Search of Meaning

Do the following situations sound familiar to you?

- Nina, a ninth-grade girl, is considered attractive by most people in her school. She has a good figure and can afford all the latest fashions. Many of her friends envy her and tell her so. Yet Nina hates her body, her face, her wardrobe. She jumps from one diet to another, even though she is not overweight. She spends hours working on her makeup, hair, and clothes. She is never satisfied with who she is because she constantly compares herself with magazine models. Nina dreams of someday liking the person she sees in the mirror, but she is haunted by the real possibility that she never will.

- Justin has a terrific sense of humor. He gets good grades, though he has some trouble with algebra. He participates in several sports, and he may well be a starter on the basketball team when he's a senior. But Justin is uncomfortable around girls unless they're "just friends." Sometimes he wonders if he's gay, and the thought terrifies him. Though he seems to have a lot going for him, he spends a lot of his private time worrying.

- Geralyn is a loner. Her family life is a mess. She's extremely shy, and she has no friends. Some people do feel sorry for her and try to be friendly, but she is so unsure of herself and so awkward with others that she's hard to be around or talk to.

- Chad's life looks like it is headed toward disaster. Since the breakup of his parents' marriage when he was in the seventh grade, he has been confused and trying to find a group of friends he can feel at home with. A year ago he started to hang around with kids who are into drugs. His entire life now seems caught up in getting drugs and using them. A school counselor tried to confront Chad about this, but Chad just denied that he has a problem. The situation looks hopeless.

- Angela wonders what her future holds. She lives in a poor neighborhood where most kids who finish high school have trouble getting anything but a fast-food job. She's not a star in school, and she could never afford college anyway. It all looks so bleak—why even try?

Photo: **The need for salvation is the need to be freed from whatever imprisons or oppresses our spirit.**

Looking for Something More

You may know young people like those just described. You may even see yourself in them. What will make them truly happy with who they are? What will fill their heart with peace when they are all alone with their thoughts, their fears, and their dreams? They are looking for a deeper sense of meaning. They are searching for something—or someone—who can save them from the pain in their life. **6**

Imagine what Nina, Justin, Geralyn, Chad, and Angela will be like when they become adults. Some of them may be like many of the adults you know now. They may be successful by every common standard of our society—earn a good income, own a nice home, have a happy family—yet they may still be anxious, lonely, frustrated, even depressed. Others of them may live on the edges of society . . . or not really live at all. Why? Because they may still be looking for something deeper in life, something that can make sense of who they are in the world, something that can bring them a feeling of peace and satisfaction, something to sustain them when they are alone with their thoughts and their dreams. They may be looking for meaning. They may be looking to be saved from the pain in their life.

A World in Need of Salvation

The world sometimes seems dominated by obvious evil and the clear effects of sin—war, poverty, sexism, racism. When we allow ourselves to see and acknowledge such evil, we begin to realize that truly the world is as much in need of salvation today as it was at the time of Jesus.

We experience the effects of sin simply by living in this world as social beings who are affected by the actions of others. However, without dismissing the need to understand the social nature of sin, we must look at the personal level of sin in our life if we are to understand the meaning of salvation and redemption the way Paul understood it. On a personal or private level, we often experience the effects of sin as deep loneliness, a lack of hope, or a desperate yearning for meaning. Such feelings are not necessarily caused by our own sin, though at times, of course, that may be the case. **7**

Now Is the Time

The Christian conviction is that Jesus and his message can speak to the part of our heart that we often hide from others, even our closest friends. Sometimes we even hide that part of our heart from ourselves—by filling our life with sounds and activities and relationships, even with studies! Yet when we are alone in bed at night, when the radio has been turned off and darkness fills the room, we

---

6
Choose one of the five young people just described and write an imaginary dialog with him or her. Focus the conversation on what will make the person truly happy.

■
Photo: **Contemporary society offers "salvation in a shopping mall." But true salvation answers life's deepest questions about meaning and purpose, and cannot be purchased.**

7
Write a pro or con response to this statement: *If it were not for the bad influences of society and culture, most people would naturally do what is right and good for themselves and others.*

find ourselves wondering: What does it all mean? How do I fit in? Will anyone ever love me enough to fill the hole in my heart? When we ask such questions, we are dealing with the guts of life and with the central questions of faith. When we have the courage to ask such questions, we are ready to listen to Paul's words about Jesus.

Jesus According to Paul: "The New Adam"

Paul tells the readers of his letters that Jesus shattered the limitations of the Law and brought true reconciliation between humanity and God. According to Paul, Jesus accomplished this by offering his own life in an act of total and selfless love.

The Jewish story of the fall of Adam and Eve was mentioned earlier. Paul explains the role of Jesus in terms of that ancient story. Just as sin had corrupted humanity through the actions of Adam and Eve, so God's saving grace was released through Jesus' life, death, and Resurrection. Therefore, Paul characterizes Jesus as "the new Adam."

The One Who Made Things Right Again

According to Paul, Jesus—as the new Adam—was the one in whom human history would have a new beginning.

If, because of the one man's [Adam's] trespass, death exercised dominion through that one, much more surely will those who receive the abundance of grace and the free gift of righteousness exercise dominion in life through the one man, Jesus Christ.

Therefore just as one man's trespass led to condemnation for all, so one man's act of righteousness leads to justification and life for all. For just as by the

■

Photo: **Will anyone ever love me enough to fill my heart? The Christian conviction is that Jesus can speak to the secret part of us that asks such questions.**

one man's disobedience the many were made sinners, so by the one man's obedience the many will be made righteous. (Romans 5:17–19)

Jesus had made things right again with God. Paul preached often about this "righteousness"—this being right with God—that had been restored by the death and Resurrection of Jesus.

The One Who Was Perfectly Obedient

The opening reading for this chapter of the course, which is from chapter 2 of Paul's Letter to the Philippians, reflects Paul's theme of Jesus as the new Adam. Verses 6 to 11 of the passage are part of a hymn that was likely used in worship services by the early Christians. In the hymn, Jesus is referred to as the one "who, though he was in the form of God," was willing to give up his equality with God to become one with humanity, humbling himself even to the point of death on the cross.

In the Genesis story of the Fall, the attitude held by Adam and Eve is the exact opposite of the attitude held by Jesus. The serpent in the garden tempts Adam and Eve by saying that at the moment they eat the fruit of the forbidden tree, "[their] eyes will be opened, and [they] will be *like God,* knowing good and evil" (Genesis 3:5, italics added). Adam and Eve yearn to be like God, whereas Jesus freely takes on the burdens of being human. Because of their sin, Adam and Eve are banished from the garden, whereas because of Jesus' perfect obedience,

God . . . highly exalted [Jesus]
  and gave him the name
  that is above every name,

. . . .

and every tongue should confess
  that Jesus Christ is Lord.
(Philippians 2:9–11)

Fools for Christ

Paul realized that his message of how Jesus fulfills God's plan for saving humanity would not make sense to nonbelievers. In fact, the meaning of the cross—that life can spring from suffering and death—could be appreciated only by those who had already experienced the power of God in Jesus.

The message about the cross is foolishness to those who are perishing, but to us who are being saved it is the power of God. . . . For Jews demand signs and Greeks desire wisdom, but we proclaim Christ crucified, a stumbling block to Jews and foolishness to Gentiles, but to those who are the called, both Jews and Greeks, Christ the power of God and the wisdom of God. For God's foolishness is wiser than human wisdom, and God's weakness is stronger than human strength. (1 Corinthians 1:18–25) **8**

■ *Illustration:* **Paul cautioned his followers that the meaning of the cross—that life can come from suffering and death—is considered foolishness according to the standards of human wisdom.**

8
Jot down your reflections on Paul's message to the Corinthians about the foolishness of the cross.

Saved from Sin, Freed to Be Fully Human

The preceding quotation, from Paul's First Letter to the Corinthians, gives us a clue as to what salvation in Jesus can mean for Christians today. In his life, death, and Resurrection, Jesus saves us from all the false values and misleading messages of contemporary society. Jesus saves us from society's distorted claims about what it means to be fully human, and he frees us to be fully human in the way God intends us to be—as persons who have God at the center of our life and who love our neighbors as we love ourselves.

The culture of our time tries to sell us a particular vision of what human happiness requires—a sexy body, expensive possessions, freedom from commitment, power over others. When we see all these things through the eyes of Jesus, we recognize how shallow they are, how little happiness they really bring to those who have them. In this way, salvation is as much about freeing us for life as it is about saving us from sin. **9**

Asking the Right Questions

To live fully, we need to ask the right questions, because the questions we ask automatically dictate where we go in search of the answers. Recall from the beginning of this chapter the example of the bumper sticker "Jesus Is the Answer!" and the response it evoked: "Okay, but what's the question?" Both the bumper sticker and the response miss the point of what Jesus and his message are all about. The fact is, Jesus is the Questioner.

When people look at the life and message of Jesus, they must confront the questions on which happiness in life truly hinges. And the questions Jesus asks are drastically different from those posed by popular culture.

- Popular culture asks, How can I acquire a lot of wealth? Jesus asks, How can I share what I have with others?
- Popular culture asks, How can I become popular? Jesus asks, How can I love others, even my enemies?
- Popular culture asks, How can I gain power over others? Jesus asks, How can I serve those in need?

The questions asked by Jesus lead us to drastically different answers than do the questions posed by our culture. And, as Christians believe, Jesus' questions lead us to the right answers—that is, to truth.

■
Photo: Jesus asks, How can I serve those in need? whereas popular culture asks, How can I gain power over others?

9
In a paragraph, explain the meaning of this statement: *Salvation is as much about being freed for life as it is about being saved from sin.*

We Cannot Do It on Our Own

Confronting the questions posed by Jesus is an awesome experience. Clearly, living according to Jesus' values and principles means living contrary to many of the values of modern society. We may be inclined to think that there is no way we can handle that challenge, and Paul would respond, quite bluntly: "You're right. You cannot handle it on your own. But all things are possible with God."

Salvation Is God's Work

Paul constantly reminded the people of his time —and reminds contemporary Christians as well— that people cannot save themselves. The idea of being able to save oneself was what Paul recognized as the primary danger of blind adherence to the Law. People of his time who followed the letter of the Law were tempted to believe that they were earning salvation, that *they* were the source of righteousness. Many modern Christians seem to have the same misunderstanding. They think that if they fulfill their religious obligations, like regularly attending Mass and even giving to charity, then they have paid their religious dues, are assured of going to heaven ("being saved"), and can get on with "more important things" in their life.

Paul's message is that salvation is a gift from God—that is, an act of **grace.** Grace is the total, unconditional, and transforming love of God that is always offered to people regardless of anything they do or fail to do. People cannot turn the flow of God's love on and off as if they control some magical faucet. People are not in charge; God is. All people can do is recognize when grace is offered, accept it as a gift, thank God for it, and celebrate the gift with others. In other words, salvation is God's work and a gift of God's grace, not the result of human effort. This is what Paul means by the expression *justification* (being saved) *by faith.*

Loving Actions:
A Way of Saying Yes to Salvation

If salvation is a gift, then some people might say that our religious observances and loving actions are meaningless, without value, or not necessary. They might ask, "Why pray and serve others if these actions do not necessarily bring about salvation?" Such people would be missing the point

---

Illustration: **Salvation is an act of God's grace, freely given by God and not something we can earn. We cannot turn God's love on and off by our actions. Instead, it flows to us as powerfully and persistently as a waterfall.**

of Paul's—and Jesus'—message. Paul, as noted in chapter 11 of this course, spoke eloquently about the value and power of love. But he did not say that Christians should love others as a way of earning God's love in return. Rather, loving action is the response that flows from accepting God's gift of grace. When people experience the overwhelming and gracious love of God for them, they are given a "new heart," a new power to reach out to others in care and concern. If a person accepts the gift of God's love, she or he inevitably will act differently—more lovingly—toward others.

Loving actions, then, are an essential part of God's work of salvation. If people say they accept the gift of God's loving salvation, but their actions contradict their words, then their words become meaningless. If people do not love one another as Jesus commanded, this is a sign that they have not truly accepted the gift of grace and allowed it to transform the way they live. Salvation is not magic; people can choose to reject it. It requires a personal response, a yes in both word and deed.

The Christian Is "a New Creation"

When people recognize their dependence on God through faith in Jesus, says Paul, they discover the power to live in accordance with the Dream and values of Jesus. The source of their power is not themselves but, rather, the Spirit of the risen Jesus working within them. According to Paul's thinking, the Christian is "a new creation" (2 Corinthians 5:17), guided by the right questions in search of the right answers. And the answers Christians find in Jesus free them to live fully—both now and after death. As Paul puts it: "If the Spirit of him who raised Jesus from the dead dwells in you, he who raised Christ from the dead will give life to your mortal bodies also through his Spirit that lives in you" (Romans 8:11).

■
Photo: In Paul's thinking, the Christian is a "new creation": "If the Spirit of him who raised Jesus from the dead dwells in you, he who raised Christ from the dead will give life to your mortal bodies also through his Spirit that lives in you."

Faith as More than "Me and God"

Paul had another major insight into the way faith in Jesus the Christ gets lived out in the life of the Christian: If salvation consisted only of turning one's life over to God through a personal commitment to Jesus, a person could do that in total isolation from others. But Paul understood that the Christian's salvation in Christ is intimately connected to his or her relationship with the community of believers—the church. The connection is so real, in fact, that Paul called the church the Body of Christ.

For Review

- List some ways we experience the effects of sin, both on a social and on a personal level.
- What is the basic meaning of the term *righteousness?*
- What does Jesus save us from? What does he save us for? How is salvation an act of grace?
- What role do people's loving actions play in salvation?
- What is the source of the power to love in accordance with Jesus' Dream?

The Church as the Body of Christ

Earlier in this course, the point was made that people are bound by their experience to think in terms of time and space. When discussing the Ascension of Jesus, for example, people tend to think of Jesus as going "up there" to heaven, somewhere in space, removed from us. Paul might have had the same temptation were it not for his encounter with the risen Jesus on the road to Damascus.

When Jesus identified himself with the Christians whom Paul had been persecuting, Paul's old way of looking at reality was shattered. With startling clarity, Paul saw that Jesus was alive amid Paul's own experience. Through the image of the church as the Body of Christ, Paul has challenged Christians throughout the ages to live out this vision.

Building on Jesus' Own Words

A central theme of Jesus' preaching was that people live out the Gospel message not just by accepting Jesus but by living as he lived. In a familiar Scripture passage describing the final judgment (see Matthew 25:31–46), Jesus tells his followers that "just as you did [a compassionate deed for] one of the least of these who are members of my family, you did it [for] me" (verse 40). In other words, Jesus saw a direct connection between faith in him and the commitment to serve the needs of others.

When Paul speaks of the church as the Body of Christ, however, he seems to be describing an even more intimate connection between the risen

Jesus and the believing community. Recall from chapter 10 that one of the ways believers are connected to the risen Jesus is through making Jesus' original sacrifice present in the celebration of the Eucharist. For Paul, participation in the celebration of the Eucharist brought the believing community together in Jesus:

The cup of blessing that we bless, is it not a sharing in the blood of Christ? The bread that we break, is it not a sharing in the body of Christ? Because there is one bread, we who are many are one body, for we all partake of the one bread. (1 Corinthians 10:16–17)

Just as the eucharistic bread and wine become Jesus' body and blood, the community of believers is called to become the risen Jesus through its sharing in the Eucharist. The church is called to be the concrete, visible presence of the risen Jesus in the world, just as Jesus, when he himself walked the earth, was the visible manifestation of God. The role of Christians has been expressed this way:

■

Illustration: **For Paul, participation in the Eucharist brings the believing community together in Jesus—no matter how separated they are by distance, time, or culture.**

We are the hands of Christ.
  Where we work, he works.
We are the feet of Christ.
  Where we go, he goes.
We are the heart of Christ.
  When we love, he loves.
Where we are, Christ is.

Each Member Vital to the Whole

At times Paul takes the image of the body to an almost humorous extreme to demonstrate the value of each individual member in the church:

The body does not consist of one member but of many. If the foot would say, "Because I am not a hand, I do not belong to the body," that would not make it any less a part of the body. . . . If the whole body were an eye, where would the hearing be? If the whole body were hearing, where would the sense of smell be? But as it is, God arranged the members in the body, each one of them, as he chose. . . .
  Now you are the body of Christ and individually members of it. (1 Corinthians 12:14–27)

In a similar way, Paul writes of the unique contributions that each member can make to the life of the body as a whole:

Now there are varieties of gifts, but the same Spirit; and there are varieties of services, but the same Lord; and there are varieties of activities, but it is the same God who activates all of them in everyone. To each is given the manifestation of the Spirit for the common good. . . . All these are activated by one and the same Spirit, who allots to each one individually just as the Spirit chooses. (1 Corinthians 12:4–11)

Though Paul mentions the notion of the Body of Christ in several epistles, his longest reflections on the theme appear in his First Letter to the Corinthians (particularly chapter 12 of that letter). The Corinthians were a community with many problems, including much bickering and divisiveness among them. Paul's preaching on the church as the one Body of Christ would have held particular importance for such a community. **10**

Jesus: The Head of the Body

Paul distinctly says that although the church is the Body of Christ in the world, it does not function apart from Jesus. Paul emphasizes that Jesus is the "head" of the body (Ephesians 5:23), the one "in charge," the one whose vision and message must guide the workings of the body.

Paul's vision of the unity of Christians as the Body of Christ, with Jesus as the head, is beautifully summarized in his Letter to the Ephesians:

I . . . , the prisoner in the Lord, beg you to lead a life worthy of the calling to which you have been called, with all humility and gentleness, with patience, bearing with one another in love, making

---

■
Photo: As the Body of Christ, the church is called to be the visible presence of the risen Jesus in the world, just as Jesus, when he walked the earth, was the visible manifestation of God. So we are the hands of Christ; where we work, he works.

10
List other images that express the same reality about the church that Paul's image of the human body does. Pick your favorite image from your list and expand on why you think it works.

every effort to maintain the unity of the Spirit in the bond of peace. There is one body and one Spirit, . . . one Lord, one faith, one baptism, one God and Father of all, who is above all and through all and in all.

. . . The gifts [Christ] gave were that some would be apostles, some prophets, some evangelists, some pastors and teachers, to equip the saints for the work of ministry, for building up the body of Christ. . . . We must no longer be children, tossed to and fro and blown about by every wind of doctrine, by people's trickery. . . . But speaking the truth in love, we must grow up in every way into him who is the head, into Christ, from whom the whole body, joined and knit together by every ligament with which it is equipped, as each part is working properly, promotes the body's growth in building itself up in love. (4:1–16)

Guidelines for a Healthy Body

Paul often spoke of community problems and moral issues out of his strong sense of the church as the Body of Christ. Whenever members of a community were in conflict with one another, Paul saw the Body of Christ in pain. Whenever members of a community worked and prayed together as one, the body was healthy and strong and able to carry on its mission.

Paul's understanding of Christian morality rests on the following basic principle: Christians live out their relationship with Jesus by living well in community with one another. In Paul's Letter to the Romans, Paul describes in perhaps idealistic but uplifting terms what behaviors and attitudes are required if Christians are to live out the Dream of Jesus:

■
Paul believed that Christians live out their relationship with Jesus by working and praying as one. *Photo:* **Young people work together to make friendship bracelets for one another at the** National Catholic Youth Conference.

Let love be genuine; hate what is evil, hold fast to what is good; love one another with mutual affection; outdo one another in showing honor. Do not lag in zeal, be ardent in spirit, serve the Lord. Rejoice in hope, be patient in suffering, persevere in prayer. Contribute to the needs of the saints; extend hospitality to strangers.

Bless those who persecute you; bless and do not curse them. Rejoice with those who rejoice, weep with those who weep. Live in harmony with one another; do not be haughty, but associate with the lowly; do not claim to be wiser than you are. Do not repay anyone evil for evil, but take thought for what is noble in the sight of all. If it is possible, so far as it depends on you, live peaceably with all. Beloved, never avenge yourselves. . . . No, "if your enemies are hungry, feed them; if they are thirsty, give them something to drink. . . ." Do not be overcome by evil, but overcome evil with good. (12:9–21) **11**

The Contributions of Paul: A Second Look

Chapter 11 of this course made several claims about Paul's importance in the history of Christianity:

- He is second only to Jesus himself as a central figure in the New Testament.
- Paul—through a unique combination of faith, personality, and cultural characteristics—spread the early Gospel proclamation beyond the Jewish realm.
- The worldwide Christian church that eventually grew from a small seed in first-century Palestine is a lasting monument to Paul's influence and, of course, to the work of God's Spirit in and through him.

At first, these statements may have seemed to be exaggerations, an attempt to paint an impressive portrait of Paul. It is hoped that the discussion in this and the previous chapter has shown the truthfulness of the claims and confirmed the uniqueness of Paul and his influence in Christian history. In many ways, Paul's influence is a great testimony to the workings of the Spirit in the church. Only the Spirit could transform someone like Paul, who initially hated Christians so much that he hunted them down for persecution, into such a powerful example of Christian faith and hope.

For Review

- Complete this sentence: *Just as Jesus on earth was the visible manifestation of God, so the church is . . .*
- With what imagery does Paul explain the value of each member of the church? Illustrate your answer with an example.
- What does Paul mean when he describes Jesus as the head of the body?
- What is the basic principle behind Paul's understanding of Christian morality?

11
Paul's Letter to the Romans describes requirements for Christians. Select the ten behaviors that you feel are most important. In a short essay, explain your selections.

■
Paul, by opening himself to the Spirit of God, did much to build the early church into a worldwide movement.
Photo: The restored ruins of the interior of a house in Ephesus.

Paul may have stayed in a home like this during his time there.

Throughout history, various interpretations of Paul's notion of the church as the Body of Christ have been popular. Here are two interpretations:

The Perfect Body

Quite commonly, the church has been understood as "the perfect body." With this image, the church is seen as a kind of idealized society in which all the members know, accept, and fulfill their various roles; God's will is always followed; and peace reigns. In other words, the church is seen as the reflection of the resurrected body of Jesus, which has been cleansed of all human imperfection. This view would suggest that if the church suffers at any time, it is because the world beyond the church has been corrupted by sin.

The image of the church as the perfect body was in part the product of the classical Greek culture. The Greeks idealized the human body, almost worshiped it, and this attitude was reflected in much of their art, particularly their sculpture. Not surprisingly, therefore, the converted Greeks applied the ideal of the perfect body to the church as the Body of Christ.

The image of the perfect body has as much appeal today as it did in the early church. We still tend to idealize that which is strong and healthy and reject that which is weak and sickly.

The Broken Body of Jesus

In recent years, some theologians and biblical scholars have suggested that the idealized image of the church as a perfect body is misleading. Personal experience, first of all, teaches us that the church—whether our local parishes or the worldwide community of faith—is hardly perfect. It is a community of people who frequently make mistakes, who are subject to all human weaknesses, and who are in constant need of forgiveness and healing. The church is not subject only to the sin of people outside the community. Rather, the church itself is a community of sinners in constant need of reconciliation.

The church has come to recognize that humanity is in a constant struggle for survival amid often horrifying pain. In this century alone, tens of millions of people have suffered and died as victims of war, disease, racism, poverty, and starvation. Theologians and biblical scholars suggest that if Jesus is to be seen in the world today, he will be recognized in his brokenness, his pain, his suffering. It is not the glorified risen Jesus we see reflected in the world; rather, it is the crucified Jesus we see in the headlines and TV news.

The church, too, is more properly understood as the broken body of Jesus than as the perfect one. This does not mean that the church is powerless to help its own members or to bring healing to the world. On the contrary, Paul would tell us, it is precisely in acknowledging our weakness and turning to God that we find a power beyond comprehension. If we believe in our own invincibility, our own power, we will arrogantly believe we do not need God. It is in confronting our own weakness that we are forced to turn to the Source of all power and healing. Here is how Paul expressed it:

Three times I appealed to the Lord [to relieve me of my pain], but he said to me, "My grace is sufficient for you, for power is made perfect in weakness." So, I will boast all the more gladly of my weaknesses, so that the power of Christ may dwell with me. Therefore I am content with weaknesses, insults, hardships, persecutions, and calamities, for the sake of Christ; for whenever I am weak, then I am strong. (2 Corinthians 12:8–10)

The History of the Church's Teachings About Jesus

With the conclusion of this course drawing near, it is time to reflect on how the church through its history has carried on the mission begun by Paul and the other Apostles. The primary concern of chapter 13 will be the way the church's understanding of Jesus has been passed on from one generation of Christians to the next.

Throughout the discussion of Jesus in this course, the words, teachings, and issues that are commonly associated with Jesus in contemporary religious education have rarely been mentioned. For example, little has been said regarding the doctrines, or official church teachings, about Jesus: teachings about the **Incarnation** (that God became flesh in Jesus), Jesus' relationship to God the Father and the Holy Spirit in the Trinity, the fact that Christians claim Jesus to be "true God from true God, . . . one in Being with the Father," and so on.

The reason that discussion of these matters has been delayed is that they can be reasonably presented and understood only in the context of the church and its history. These matters could not be effectively discussed within a study of the New Testament, simply because they do not appear in those sacred writings in the same sense and with the terminology they have today. The official teachings of the church have developed over hundreds of years of reflection on Jesus' life, death, and Resurrection. Chapter 13 offers a brief discussion of that development.

■
Photo: **The Via Egnatia, near Philippi, was the principal road connecting areas of the Roman Empire. Paul would have traveled this road in his tireless effort to proclaim Christ crucified and risen.**

13
Good News from Age to Age:
The Church's Understanding of Jesus Christ

The Church's History

In This Chapter . . .

THEY [the members of the early church] devoted themselves to the apostles' teaching and fellowship, to the breaking of bread and the prayers.

Awe came upon everyone, because many wonders and signs were being done by the apostles. All who believed were together and had all things in common; they would sell their possessions and goods and distribute the proceeds to all, as any had need. Day by day, as they spent much time together in the temple, they broke bread at home and ate their food with glad and generous hearts, praising God and having the goodwill of all the people. And day by day the Lord added to their number those who were being saved. (Acts of the Apostles 2:42–47)

The above passage from the Acts of the Apostles tells us a number of important things about what the Christian church, in essence, is all about. First, we learn that the **church** is a community of persons who have come to some personal recognition of the risen Jesus in their life. That is, baptized in Christ, they have experienced the transforming power of Jesus, the Son of God, and his message about a God whose love is never-ending and unconditional. The church as a community of believers forms when these individuals, moved and transformed by their experience of Jesus, gather with others to share and celebrate and deepen their awareness of Jesus and his message. We learn from Acts how they express themselves as a community:

- by recalling their past experiences of Jesus and the Apostles' teachings about him
- by committing themselves to care for one another so that everyone's needs are met
- by celebrating Jesus' risen and living presence among them through signs and symbols such as the "breaking of the bread," known as the Eucharist
- by going out as a renewed people to share the Good News with others

These experiences in the first Christian communities set the stage for the gradual development of the church's understanding of Jesus Christ. This chapter picks up where the New Testament leaves off and traces the development of the church's long and complex journey throughout history.

Photo, facing page: **The church's understanding of Jesus has developed with the challenges of each age, like a coastline gradually transformed over time.**

Background: **Throughout the ages, the Holy Spirit kindles, enlivens, and creates enthusiasm as it guides the church in following the way of Jesus.**

A Difficult Journey

One cannot adequately understand the history of the church's thinking and teaching about Jesus without at least some sense of the history of the church itself. Just as the early community of faith gradually grew in its understanding of Jesus following his death and Resurrection, so too has the church gone through constant change, growth, and development from its early days until now.

Moving Out into the World

What was initially a small, loose sect of Jews in Palestine gradually spread out into the world. This meant coming in contact with, and being affected by, diverse cultures and peoples, some of them quite different from what Jesus and the Apostles

were accustomed to. The difficulties encountered by Paul as he went about spreading the Good News were but a preview of what the church would encounter as it moved into the second century. The early Christians soon felt the need to ensure some sense of integrity, cohesiveness, and stability as a community of believers amid all this diversity. For that reason, the church gradually placed more and more emphasis on maintaining certain traditions, preserving right teachings, evolving lines of authority, developing various roles for church leaders, and so on. All this was necessary if the church was to survive in a world that was, especially in the first three centuries of the church's existence, very hostile toward it. **1**

Under the Guidance of the Spirit

Any review of the church's understanding of Jesus through history must constantly affirm a central conviction about the church held by Christians: Their history as a church has been guided by the presence of God's Spirit, who Jesus promised would lead them to all truth (John 16:7–15). As discussed in the previous chapter, Paul expressed this reality by calling the church the Body of Christ, or the visible manifestation of the risen Jesus in the world today. Therefore, while the church is made up of free people capable of making many mistakes, it is also a community that is graced and loved by God.

Over its long history, some leaders and other members of the church occasionally—though perhaps unavoidably—seemed to lose touch with the church's central mission and purpose. There have been times when Christians have lived contrary to the Gospel of Jesus, when their faith has been deeply affected by superstition, misunderstanding, or poor leadership. But through it all the church has survived. It has done so primarily

---

■
Going out into the world to spread the Good News reminded the early Christians of going into a vineyard to reap a plentiful harvest.
Photo: **A vineyard in Israel.**

1
Respond in writing to this opinion: *Belonging to the church was important when Christians were threatened by their society. But today Christians can stay faithful to Jesus even without the church.*

because of the deep and constant faith of so many of its members—people influenced, guided, and supported by the ever-present Spirit of God.

It's Not Over Yet

The development of the church, as well as the development of its understanding of Jesus, continues to this day. For instance, the church must still struggle with balancing the need for unity while respecting a healthy diversity. This is one sure sign that the church's development is not over yet. In fact, struggling for such a balance may be more necessary today than ever before in the church's history. For example, the experiences of the world's oppressed peoples are a growing influence on church teachings. When such developments affect the church's understanding of Jesus and his message, they often radically affect nearly every facet of the church's life as a community of faith. They do so because the church's understanding of Jesus is always at the center of its identity.

The effect of a new insight into Jesus and his message on the church is similar to that of throwing a stone into a calm pool of water. A new insight will strike with various degrees of intensity, but it will always result in a ripple effect of steadily expanding changes. For example, a new insight may change the ways the community of faith expresses its beliefs or the manner in which it celebrates its sacramental life as a community. Christians might also learn new ways of bringing the healing touch of Jesus and his message into a wounded world, such as by participating in the efforts of human rights organizations like Amnesty International or Habitat for Humanity.

Amid change, the constant challenge for members of the church is to attune themselves fully to the Jesus of the Gospels, who is the compass and

■
The experiences of oppressed peoples increasingly influence church teachings and understandings about Jesus.

Photo: A child in a city in Peru, where hunger and poverty are a way of life for many people.

the foundation for understanding their identity as Christians and as the church.

Did Jesus Intend to Found a Church?

Before moving into a discussion of the development of the church's understanding of Jesus throughout history, an important question must first be addressed: Did Jesus ever intend to form a community of faith at all, let alone one like the church as we know it today?

What If He Did . . . or Didn't?

If Jesus did intend to found a church, then it would seem that he wanted his followers to discover him and preserve his teaching in union with one another. This would imply a need for believers to gather with other Christians or, to use more familiar language, to "join a church."

If Jesus did not intend to found a church, then it would seem that individuals have a perfect right to go their own way regarding how or whether they respond to Jesus. In other words, an individual's response would not need to be determined, governed, or subject to evaluation by a broader community of people.

What Do the Scriptures Tell Us?

The question of Jesus' intentions regarding the establishment of a church is a complex one, and a lengthy discussion of various arguments regarding that question is beyond the scope of this course. The Scriptures shed some light on the issue:

- If Jesus ever directly preached or implied the concept of a "church," he would likely not have had in mind all the institutional features that are part of Christians' understanding and experience of the church today, because his experience did not include all those features.

- Nevertheless, many of the Gospel images imply that Jesus' followers shared some kind of communal experience. Parables like those of the shepherd and his flock (John 10:11–18) and the vine and the branches (John 15:1–10) reinforce the imagery of a community nurtured by Jesus. The Gospels' many sayings about the Kingdom convey a similar picture.
- The moral or ethical teachings of Jesus also show a real concern for the communal nature of our actions (Matthew 5:23; 7:3–5).

■

Illustration: **In this parable, Jesus alludes to a community nurtured by himself: "I am the vine, you are the branches. Those who abide in me and I in them bear much fruit" (John 15:5).**

- Jesus' relationship with and training of the Apostles seems to indicate an ongoing role for them as the foundation of some sort of gathering for those who believed in and followed Jesus.

In the Hands of Jesus' Followers

From most indications, then, it seems that Jesus did intend for some kind of community of believers to continue after his death. It was up to the early followers of Jesus themselves, always under the guidance of the Spirit of Jesus, to give the initial community its form and direction. As noted earlier, the church's structure and the way it presents its message about Jesus are inevitably affected by the cultures and times in which the church finds itself. Each generation of Christians has been faced with the challenge of building on the foundation set by the early church and finding the best ways to convey the message of Christ, given the circumstances and needs of the current time and place.

■
Photo: Jesus said, "For where two or three are gathered in my name, I am there among them" (Matthew 18:20).

Two Persistent Tensions in the Church's Thinking

To comprehend the historical developments in the church's understanding of Jesus, we also need an awareness of two persistent and related tensions in the church's thinking throughout its history:

Balancing Jesus' Humanity and Divinity

The church has struggled to find some balance in its treatment of the humanity and divinity of Jesus. The danger always exists that in emphasizing one dimension of Jesus over the other, an accurate understanding of him can get confused. In this brief review of church history, the tension of overemphasizing either Jesus' humanity or his divinity will be recognized again and again.

Balancing the Intellectual and the Emotional

A related tension exists between an intellectual, academic approach to understanding Jesus and a more emotional approach, which is often reflected in the popular piety of ordinary, devout Christians. Again, the challenge here is to find proper balance, not to choose one perspective at the expense of the other. The church's understanding of Jesus can and should respond to both the emotional and the intellectual needs of the believer.

The tension between emphasizing either the humanity or the divinity of Jesus and the tension between emphasizing either the intellectual or the emotional dimensions of Christian faith are both understandable and even healthy realities in the church. Perhaps one of the surest signs of the working Spirit within the community of faith is that anytime the church seems to be losing its sense of balance in these matters, something happens—the rise of a religious movement or the emergence of a great Christian thinker, for example—to restore a proper perspective.

Throughout the following discussion, occasional reference is made to these twin tensions and to the ways the Spirit keeps bringing the church back into balance. **2**

For Review

- Briefly, how did the early church form?
- What do Christians believe has been the guiding force behind the church's journey through history?
- What importance does the question of whether Jesus intended to found a church have for individual Christians? Briefly summarize the evidence supporting the claim that Jesus intended to found some kind of continuing community.
- Name the persistent tensions in the church's historical struggle to understand Jesus and his message.

Understanding Jesus in the Early Centuries

In the Beginning: What Was Going On?

A number of significant things were happening in the early church as it began its search for a full understanding of Jesus. It is particularly important to remember the following points:

The early Christians believed the risen Jesus would come again soon. Following the death, Resurrection, and Ascension of Jesus, and the gift of the Spirit at Pentecost, Paul began to interpret for the church the significance of the Jesus of History as the Christ of Faith. At the time of Paul's ministry, Christians believed that the risen Jesus would return soon, certainly in their lifetime, to complete the work of his Father.

The four Gospels were written to preserve and pass on the story and message of Jesus. Only when it became evident that Jesus was not returning soon did the early Christians realize the need for preserving the life and message of Jesus in some written form. It was out of that need that the four Gospels emerged.

Tensions increased between Christians and Jews. As the proclamation about Jesus took root in small Christian communities throughout the Roman Empire, tension steadily deepened between Christians and Jews. The Gospel was first proclaimed to Jews, and the Jerusalem Council's decision that Gentile converts to Christianity did not have to first convert to Judaism represented a major turning point, even a breaking point, in the

2
In a paragraph, describe some area of your life in which you have had to struggle for balance —for instance, in schoolwork versus other activities. What helped you find the right balance?

From Proclamation to Explanation

As the church moved into the second century, and away from the influence of Judaism, one of the most significant steps in the development of its understanding of Jesus took place. This was the move to not only joyfully proclaim the Good News but also to deepen the church's intellectual understanding of Jesus and his message.

A New Way of Thinking

By the end of the second century, theologians trained in Greek philosophy of the time dominated the church's thinking. These theologians tried to translate the experiences of the Apostles and earliest Christian communities into a language and mind-set that made sense to themselves and suited their audiences. These men—today referred to as the fathers of the church—tried to re-evaluate the New Testament in terms of their own way of thinking about and understanding the world.

This move toward a Greek philosophical approach seems to have been a reasonable, even a necessary, step to take if people from various cultures were to understand Jesus at all. Some church historians suggest that it is only because of this development that the church was able to survive as it spread beyond its birthplace in Palestine.

From the Concrete to the Abstract

What eventually resulted from the influence of Greek thought was that many Christians began talking about Jesus in more technical and complex terms. Words like *God-man, substance, person, nature,* and hotly debated definitions of each word entered into discussions about Jesus and his identity. These were Greek philosophical terms of the time, and their use amounted to a major shift in the church's way of thinking about Jesus—a shift

relationship between Christians and Jews. Around the year 70 C.E., the Romans destroyed the Jewish Temple, and the Jews were then forced to use the synagogues as their central gathering places. As tensions between Christians and Jews increased, Jewish Christians were banned from the synagogues, and the break between Christianity and Judaism was virtually complete.

The canon of the Hebrew Scriptures was set. In a related development, around the year 90 C.E., Jewish leaders made a final decision about the canon, that is, which books were to be officially recognized as the Jewish Bible. This was done partly to ensure that the writings then emerging in the Christian community—that is, the letters of Paul and others, as well as the Gospels—could not be included in the Jewish Bible. From that point until this day, Judaism survived largely because of its faithful commitment to its Scriptures and to synagogue worship. Christianity, after its initial break from Judaism, began its own fascinating journey through history.

■
The early Christian community's understanding of Jesus was rooted in his Crucifixion and Resurrection.
Photo: The Via Dolorosa, the route believed to have been taken by Jesus on his way to the Crucifixion.

■

In the second century, the church began using more abstract and technical Greek philosophical concepts to deepen its understanding of Jesus' divinity.

Photo: A more abstract depiction of the risen Jesus.

from a concrete, tangible, and somewhat simple approach to a more abstract, complex, and technical approach. In addition to the joyous proclamation of the Gospels, a whole new language began to develop; for example, the church began to try to explain Jesus philosophically, describing him as "one person with two natures sharing one substance."

The Great Christological Heresies and Councils

Three major heresies, or false teachings, arose out of the debates over how to explain Jesus. Each one of these heresies resulted in the calling of a church council, or official gathering of church leaders, to respond to the false teachings and clarify the church's statement of who Jesus is.

Jesus: More than Human, Less than Divine?

About the year 300 C.E., a priest named Arius began teaching that Jesus was not one with God, as the early church claimed him to be. Rather, Arius saw Jesus as a special creature of God, a being of a very high order created by God at a particular point in time. In other words, he viewed Jesus as more than human but less than divine. Arius's false teaching became known as the **Arian heresy**, or **Arianism.** This teaching led to the calling of the first ecumenical, or worldwide, council of the church: the **First Council of Nicaea**, in the year 325. This council solemnly declared that in Jesus, God had truly appeared on earth in the person of God's own Son.

The **Nicene Creed**, the profession of faith that is commonly recited in eucharistic celebrations, was first drawn up by this council. This creed, on page 298, articulates the church's belief about Jesus.

Jesus: Two Different Beings?

About the year 400 C.E., a theory was proposed that Jesus was two different persons—one who was divine and one who was human—rather than one person who was both divine and human. This was an attempt by some to uphold a false and unbiblical notion of God's "purity." That is, they wanted to establish a complete separation between divinity and humanity. Their notion of God's purity was threatened by an understanding of Jesus as both human and divine.

At this time, a debate also flared up about the mother of Jesus, Mary, and her role in God's plan of salvation. One side argued that Mary could not be given the title *Mother of God* because, among other reasons, a human mother could not be said to give birth to a divine being who already existed from eternity. The other side argued that if Jesus were truly to be recognized as both God and human and yet one person, then Mary could rightly be called Mother of God, because she gave birth to one who was both human and divine.

In response to these disagreements, the **Council of Ephesus** was convened in 431. This council proclaimed that despite the differences between his divine and human natures, there is but one person in Jesus. The council also formally and officially gave Mary the title **Mother of God,** though this title was more an attempt to make a statement about Jesus than an attempt to describe the nature of Mary herself.

F • O • C • U • S
The Nicene Creed

Out of the debates about Jesus at the First Council of Nicaea evolved one of the great creeds of the church. A religious **creed** is an official statement of belief issued by the church, which attempts to find words to express realities that are truly beyond words. The Nicene Creed was initially drawn up by the First Council of Nicaea in the year 325 C.E. and then later reaffirmed by a council convened in Constantinople in 381. Since the seventh century it has been officially known as the Nicene-Constantinopolitan Creed, but this is often shortened in common usage to simply the Nicene Creed.

   This creed is often recited by the community of faith—both Roman and Eastern Orthodox Catholics and members of all the major Protestant denominations—during liturgies. Unfortunately, this central statement of belief is often said too quickly and without much thought by many worshipers. Here you are asked to read the creed slowly, reflectively, even prayerfully. As you do so, recall the hundreds of years of church history, the numerous arguments and discussions by devout Christians, and the profound expressions of faith and prayer that led to its development. Recall as well not only the historical situation that gave birth to this statement of the faith but also the portrait of Jesus that has been presented in this course. In doing so, you will recognize in this creed the basic Gospel proclamation of Jesus and also the effects of the history of the church as it tried to come to terms with the man and his message.

I believe in one God,
the Father almighty,
maker of heaven and earth,
of all things visible and invisible.
I believe in one Lord Jesus Christ,
the Only Begotten Son of God,
born of the Father before all ages.
God from God, Light from Light,
true God from true God,
begotten, not made, consubstantial with the Father;
through him all things were made.
For us men and for our salvation
he came down from heaven,
and by the Holy Spirit was incarnate of the Virgin Mary,
and became man.

For our sake he was crucified under Pontius Pilate,
he suffered death and was buried,
and rose again on the third day
in accordance with the Scriptures.
He ascended into heaven
and is seated at the right hand of the Father.
He will come again in glory
to judge the living and the dead
and his kingdom will have no end.

I believe in the Holy Spirit, the Lord, the giver of life,
who proceeds from the Father and the Son,
who with the Father and the Son is adored and glorified,
who has spoken through the prophets.

I believe in one, holy, catholic and apostolic Church.
I confess one Baptism for the forgiveness of sins
and I look forward to the resurrection of the dead
and the life of the world to come. Amen.

Jesus: Only Pretending to Be Human?

At about the same time, another group of devout people proposed that Jesus possessed a divine nature only, and that despite all the apparent indications of his humanity while on earth, he was not truly human. Jesus, according to this belief, only played the role of a human person; he only acted human for our benefit. In the year 451, the **Council of Chalcedon** was called to deal with this heresy. This council solemnly declared that Jesus was not only divine but also fully human. **3**

A Decisive Time for the Church

In many ways, the first five to six centuries of the church's history were some of its toughest and most exciting. It was during this early period that critical decisions had to be made about what Christians believed and did not believe about Jesus. Though other church councils have dealt with the identity of Jesus, the three councils of Nicaea, Ephesus, and Chalcedon—often referred to as the Great Christological Councils—were by far the most formative.

Illustration: The bishops who debated the Arian heresy at the Council of Nicaea in 325 C.E. came from a variety of cultures and regions of the spreading Christian world.

3
Which, if any, of the three christological heresies dealt with by the early church do you think might still exist today? Express your opinion in writing.

- The Council of Nicaea defended Jesus' divinity.
- The Council of Ephesus defended his unity as both God and man.
- The Council of Chalcedon defended his full humanity.

These conclusions about Jesus literally laid the foundation of the church's understanding of Jesus. In effect, these conclusions set the parameters for nearly all future discussions of Jesus by Christians, making the later discussions more like elaborations on these earlier teachings rather than whole new teachings about Jesus.

For Review

- What significant things were happening in the early church about the time it began searching for a full understanding of Jesus?
- What role did the fathers of the church play?
- Identify the three Great Christological Councils and briefly explain what each council decided about Jesus' identity.
- Why did the church officially give Mary the name *Mother of God?*

Understanding Jesus in the Middle Ages

The Rise of Scholasticism

The influence of Greek philosophy on the church's understanding of Jesus continued through the centuries and reached its peak in the Middle Ages with the rise of **Scholasticism.** This was a form of philosophy based on the concepts of the Greek philosopher Aristotle, and it relied greatly on order and logic. As a philosophy, or way of understanding reality, it has endured to this day. Its primary advocate in the church was **Saint Thomas Aquinas** (1224–1274), almost without question the greatest and most influential theologian in the entire history of the church.

An Emphasis on Order

Scholastic philosophy, as applied to Christian faith by Thomas and others, became the basis for the thinking and teaching employed by the church for nearly seven hundred years. It was the approach used in the religious education of many of today's adult Catholics, especially those who were formally taught in either Catholic schools or parish religious education programs before the 1970s.

Scholasticism involves a very ordered and organized approach to reality. Just as the adoption of Greek ways of thinking early in the church's history may have saved the church from disappearing altogether, so Scholastic theology broadened and therefore strengthened the church's understanding of Jesus. As the foundation of Catholic teaching for centuries, particularly in seminaries

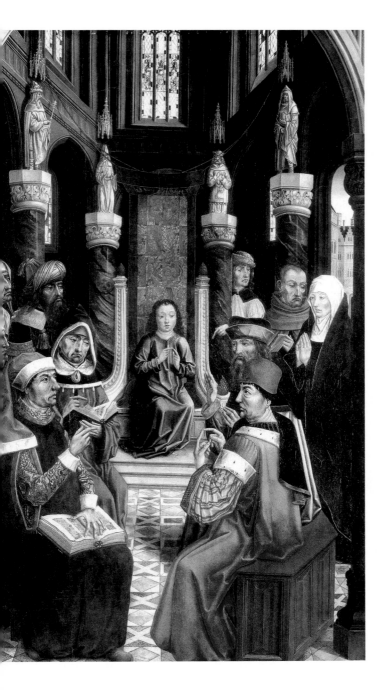

and universities, this approach has no doubt strengthened the faith of many millions of Christians.

Balancing the Mind and the Heart

The Scholastic approach to understanding Jesus and matters of Christian faith can be useful, but it is not the only approach—nor should it be. Scholasticism's intellectual approach needs to be balanced with a "heart" emphasis. In other words, we need to grasp the meaning of Jesus not only with our mind but also with our heart. And what matters most, as the Gospels repeatedly show us, is a believer's personal, heartfelt response to Jesus and his message. The church is always challenged to try to balance the intellectual and the emotional in its understanding of the mysteries of Christian faith.

Rediscovering the Common Touch

Earlier in this chapter, it was stated that whenever the church begins to lose its bearings, the Spirit of God leads it back to a balanced view of Jesus. During the Middle Ages, the Spirit worked through a strong reaction by "the common folk" against the image of Jesus presented by theologians who relied heavily on Greek philosophy in their teachings about Jesus. For example, people like **Saint Francis of Assisi** (1181–1226) recognized the need for a more personal and human understanding of Jesus, and they started a popular movement based on imitating the Jesus of the Gospels and performing other acts of piety.

A New Problem

Despite the great benefits of the popular movement, however, a new problem gradually evolved:

The understanding of Jesus in the Middle Ages was affected by the orderly, logical approach of Scholastic philosophy.
Photo: A fifteenth-century painting, *Christ Among the Doctors,* depicts the story of Jesus as a child in the Temple.

sion in the church is reflected in its celebrations of major liturgical feasts. For example, Christmas as a celebration of the birth of Jesus emerged as a major Christian feast only in the fourth century. Before that time, Easter, the celebration of Jesus' Resurrection from the dead, was recognized as the central Christian feast. Christmas became the major focus of popular devotion during the medieval period, when many of the traditions that surround the Christmas season today originated.

In recent years, the Catholic church has attempted to recover the sense of Easter as the central Christian feast. Unfortunately, some Christians try to emphasize Easter by criticizing the cultural celebration of Christmas. Certainly, much of the commercialism and materialism associated with Christmas seems to conflict with the message of Jesus. But perhaps the chief lesson of this tension is that the struggle to find balance in the church's understanding of Jesus continues to this day. **4**

The Protestant Reformation

Rooted in a Desire for Renewal

Toward the end of the Middle Ages, the kind of philosophical analysis and discussion of Jesus that had characterized the church for centuries began to fade somewhat. The church became increasingly concerned about itself—its own identity, purpose, and role in the world. New teachings and ideas challenged the church's accepted traditions, and scandalous behavior among the clergy became commonplace.

These factors, combined with a rise in an awareness of the Scriptures and a heightened personal spirituality among some members of the church, led many people to yearn for a renewal of the

the danger shifted from overcomplicating to oversimplifying the person of Jesus and his message. When the approach to understanding Jesus is governed by a need for emotional experiences or when people seek artificial experiences of the sacred or mysterious dimensions in life, they can be open to superstition, distortion, and even magical understandings of Jesus. This happened in the Middle Ages as legends about Jesus began to develop, art forms began to reflect false notions about him, and people initiated popular practices that were out of touch with the Jesus of the Gospels.

The Struggle for Balance Continues

Of course, nonscriptural notions about Jesus have not been confined to the church of the Middle Ages (500–1500 C.E.). This recurring ten-

---

■

Illustration: **Many of the traditions that surround the Christmas season today—such as the Christmas crèche or manger scene—originated in the Middle Ages.**

4

Ask an adult Catholic fifty years old or older to describe her or his religious education. Write a report on your interview and note any connections with the

material discussed on pages 300–302.

church, the pope, and the questionable practices by some leaders in the church.

For the next three centuries, Catholics and Protestants were caught up in debates about who was right and who was wrong in the church, about proper forms of church government, about the number and nature of the sacraments, and so on. Often the debates seemed to be more important to the church than following the way of Jesus and the God he revealed. The church was dangerously close to losing touch with the Jesus of the Gospels. **5**

For Review

- Define the term *Scholasticism.* Why is Scholasticism alone inadequate for understanding Jesus and Christian faith?
- What popular response did the extreme use of Scholasticism evoke during the Middle Ages? What were the dangers of the new movement?
- What factors led Christians such as Martin Luther to yearn for a renewal of the church?
- What was the central conflict of the Protestant Reformation? What was in danger of being lost because of the conflict?

church. Out of this climate of great tension and desire for change, the **Protestant Reformation** was born in the sixteenth century, and Protestant churches (the name given those who "protested" against the Roman church) gradually formed.

Conflicts over the Church, Not Jesus

During the Protestant Reformation, ideas and teachings about Jesus were discussed more in the context of disagreement about the nature of the church than as points of contention about Jesus. **Martin Luther** (1483–1546), for example, revolted not against the church's teachings about Jesus but against the Roman understanding of the

---

■

Photo: **During the Middle Ages, popular piety sometimes distorted or clouded a clear understanding of the Jesus of the Gospels.**

5

Using an encyclopedia or other sources, write a brief report on one of the following leaders of the Protestant Reformation: Martin Luther, Huldrych Zwingli, John Calvin. Include a discussion of the main denomination and its major characteristics that grew out of the efforts of the person you choose.

Understanding Jesus in the Modern Age

An Antireligious Cultural Climate

Though the study of science and technology as we know it today had its start in the sixteenth century, the scientific approach exploded during the eighteenth and nineteenth centuries. This period is often referred to as the Age of Enlightenment. With this explosion came a completely new set of problems for the church. Chief among these problems was that religious beliefs and practices began to be looked down upon as "unenlightened" and obsolete. **6**

Explaining Away Jesus and God

During the Age of Enlightenment, some people tried to prove that Jesus had never even existed or, more commonly, that he had just been an ordinary person with no special relationship to the Divine. The Apostles' belief in and reaction to the Resurrection were explained away by some people as symptoms of psychological disorders. From this perspective, human beings were increasingly seen as self-sufficient, and God was explained as a "projection of people's minds," a kind of psychological "father figure" created by people through the years to explain the mysteries of the world. **Atheism**, or the rejection of a belief in any God, was proposed as a philosophical position. **7**

Defending the Faith

The Catholic church was already in a defensive posture from its experience with the Reformation. The increasingly scientific mentality of the mod-

ern age, with all the doubts and questions it raised, only strengthened the church's commitment to defend the faith against all attacks. Christian education, for example, became recognized as the process of preparing Catholics to become "soldiers of Christ," ready to stand in defense of the faith. For that role, students were expected to memorize answers to basic questions about Catholic belief.

For some Catholics, the approach of knowing correct answers intellectually did not easily lend itself to developing a love relationship with God in and through Jesus. This approach was predominant until just the last few decades in the church, but it is clearly not so today. What happened to change things so much?

The Contemporary Church

The Catholic church of today, particularly since the **Second Vatican Council** in the early 1960s, has responded to its long history in a variety of

6
Over the ages, the church has withstood periods of severe attack and ridicule. Today, many people simply ignore the church. Which do you think is the greater threat to the church and why?

7
Write your reflections on the following: *Some young people claim they do not believe in God. What factors account for this claim? What factors might move a young person from disbelief to belief?*

■
Photo: Catholics today read and study the Scriptures more, sometimes in Bible study groups, to gain a better sense of the Jesus of the Gospels.

studying the Gospels. The result is that more and more Catholics are getting a better sense of the Jesus of the Gospels.

A different understanding of church. A different perception of the church itself has emerged—a movement away from the sense of it as a defensive protector of the faith and toward an image of a faith-filled "People of God." With this new image has come the desire to get in touch with Christianity's roots in the early church of the New Testament. The idea that the church is on a journey guided by the Spirit toward the Reign of God is emphasized as well.

A decreased tension between religion and science. Finally, the modern faith community has experienced a new awareness of the relationship between science and religion, and a decrease in tension between the two. To a great extent, the breaking down of the division has made a renewed understanding of the Scriptures possible by opening us to the real contributions that can be made by the sciences. For example, without the help of archaeology, it would be difficult to know much about the world in which Jesus lived.

ways, many of them dramatic, and nearly all of them touching on its understanding of Jesus. **8**

What's New in the Church Today

Just a few of the more significant changes that have had the greatest effect on current Catholic understandings about Jesus are outlined below. These changes have taken place within the Catholic church, in large part, as a result of the Second Vatican Council.

A return to the Scriptures. For many years, lay Catholics were not encouraged to read the Scriptures as part of their private devotions, at least not nearly to the extent that Protestants were. As a result of the Second Vatican Council, however, a tremendous renewal has taken place in the church's interest in and study of the Scriptures. Today, many more Catholics are reading and

With the Impact of a Boulder

With these new developments in the church's understanding of both Jesus and itself, Catholic Christians have witnessed a dramatic change in all their expressions of faith—in their sacramental worship, in their discussions of theology and the meaning of Jesus, and in their relationships with Christians in other churches and denominations.

Recall the analogy made earlier in this chapter between the effects of changes in the church's life and understanding of Jesus and a stone being thrown into a pool of calm water. The Second

---

■

Photo: **Catholic bishops of the world at Saint Peter's Basilica during the Second Vatican Council; this council made significant changes that affected the church's understanding of Jesus.**

8
Using resources suggested by your school librarian and teacher, write a report on the Second Vatican Council. Why was it convened? In what ways did it change life in the church? What

impact does it have on the church today?

Vatican Council, and the increase in biblical scholarship that was so much a part of it, struck the deceptively calm body of water that was the church of the eighteenth, nineteenth, and early twentieth centuries with the impact of a huge boulder. The resulting waves of change have amounted to a tidal wave for some adult Catholics, at times completely shaking them from their roots in the past. But for many others, the effects of this monumental period in the church have only served to cleanse and purify the community of faith, thrusting members not into chaos but back to their deepest roots in the Gospel proclamation of the early community of faith.

A Shift in Starting Points

A significant change brought about by all this recent history is a shift in the starting point of the Catholic church's understandings and teachings about Jesus. Those who seek to understand Jesus may do so by beginning either with his divinity or his humanity. The approach that starts with Jesus' divinity and then moves to his humanity is known as a Christology from above. (**Christology** is the branch of theology that studies the person, role, nature, and message of Jesus.) The approach that starts with Jesus' humanity and moves to his divinity is known as a Christology from below. In both cases, the goal is to recognize the full humanity and divinity of Jesus; the difference is in where we first focus our attention.

Christology from Above

In Christology from above, Christians begin their discussion and understanding of Jesus with a recognition of his special eternal relationship with God. This approach rightly affirms Jesus as the divine Son of God, sent by God to take on our humanity in order to save us from our sins and lead us to salvation. By starting from this point of view, great weight is logically given to the Incarnation (the formal term for the teaching that the Son of God took on human nature in Jesus). Jesus is seen as freely accepting death as a perfect offering to his Father, thereby satisfying our debts to God and opening the gates of heaven to us once again. For the most part, this understanding of Jesus from above has been the dominant emphasis in the church's teachings about Jesus throughout its history.

A Christology from above greatly stresses Jesus' divinity. If it is not balanced with an appreciation of Jesus' humanity, however, it can give the sense

■
The approach of understanding Jesus "from above" begins with a recognition of Jesus' special eternal relationship with God—his divine sonship.

Photo: A fifteenth-century painting, "Madonna of Humility," by Fra Angelico, approaches Jesus "from above" by focusing on his divinity.

that the Jesus of the Gospels is more a superman of sorts than human like us. He can seem removed from our human experience and not truly in touch with life as we experience it.

Christology from Below

Today many Christian scholars and teachers increasingly refer to an understanding of Jesus that starts at the other end, so to speak—a "Christology from below." A renewed interest in the Scriptures and the Jesus presented in the Gospels came about in the latter half of this century. That interest is largely behind the shift from one Christology to the other. In this approach to understanding Jesus, Christians begin not with his divinity but with his humanity—his historical life as a faith-filled Jewish preacher of first-century Palestine. Primarily through studying and reflecting on the Gospels, Christians gradually come to terms with Jesus' message about the Reign of God and its profound implications for their understanding of both God and Jesus.

Following the disciples' lead. Many contemporary Christians now consider how the disciples only slowly grew to a full awareness of the identity of Jesus. Then they reflect on how they, as

■
The approach of understanding Jesus "from below" begins with a recognition of Jesus' humanity and his historical life as a Jew born and raised in Palestine.

Photo: A modern "madonna and child" in Lebanon.

A Word of Encouragement to Young Catholics

Young Catholic Christians sometimes express confusion, even alienation, over what seems to be disagreement and anger among adult Catholics regarding some of the issues about Jesus discussed in this chapter and throughout this course.

For example, in a homily during Mass, the priest may interpret a scriptural passage in a way that conflicts with what a parent may have previously believed, and that becomes a topic for conversation on the car ride home. Or some adult Catholics may appear to disagree with the church leaders on an issue. Naturally, young people exposed to such conflict might begin to wonder who they should listen to in the church—or whether they should care enough to listen at all.

Those who find themselves in such circumstances might find some consolation in the following two points:

First, young Catholics today, especially those who have the opportunity to take religion courses like this one, may well be better informed and have access to more information than any previous generation of Catholics.

Second, the church today is experiencing tremendous growth in its understanding of many dimensions of Christian faith—not only Christology but also the understanding of sacraments, prayer, and spirituality. While times such as these can be quite frustrating and confusing for almost everyone, they can also be times of great excitement. The times that Catholic Christians are currently experiencing give witness to the richness of the message of Jesus as well as the depth of insight gained through the church's history. Understood in this way, times of growth and change can be seen as opportunities to make one's faith come alive.

■
Young Catholics today are witnessing tremendous growth in the church's understanding of Christ, as well as other dimensions of Christianity.

Photo: Hundreds of thousands of young Catholics from around the world gather for an overnight prayer vigil during the 1997 World Youth Day celebration in Paris.

Christians of today, can follow the disciples' lead. Such Christians see Jesus not as a superman but as a marvelous person who, while being divine, also truly shared in their humanity, with all its fear, loneliness, confusion, and pain; and they discover deep consolation in that knowledge. In this view of Jesus, everything about him comes together and makes sense, not just in his death on the cross but even more so in the event that followed it—the Resurrection of Jesus by God.

A different path to the same truths. Christology from below is not about the discovery of "new" truths. On the contrary, what an understanding of Jesus that begins with his humanity can offer is another path to precisely the same essential truths the church has always professed.

The strength of this approach is that it follows the common journey of humans more closely. Therefore, what were before perhaps only mysterious teachings to be memorized and accepted as truths now become far more understandable realities that can touch the hearts of believers as well as their minds.

One Without the Other Doesn't Work

An idea expressed previously in this chapter can be repeated here: the church must constantly strive for balance as it searches for a sound and truthful understanding of Jesus. In other words, neither a Christology from above nor one from below is particularly helpful when taken to an extreme or followed exclusively.

An understanding of Jesus that emphasizes his divinity and ignores his humanity results in a viewpoint that can seem so "spiritual" that it is disconnected from the daily life of believers. Likewise, an approach that emphasizes Jesus' humanity and ignores his divinity can lead to an image of the church as a kind of "self-help group," with an image of Jesus as just a particularly good man who was its founder and model.

In the centuries preceding the Second Vatican Council, the church was in danger of losing touch with Jesus' humanity. Some have cautioned that in the decades since the Second Vatican Council, the church has overreacted to its past and is in danger of losing touch with Jesus' divinity as Lord. The constant attempt in this course has been to strive for a healthy balance in its portrait of Jesus, but one clearly rooted in an understanding of Jesus from below. **9**

For Review

- Define *Age of Enlightenment* and describe its attitude toward religion. How did the church respond to the Age of Enlightenment?
- In the early part of the twentieth century, how did many Catholics view Jesus?
- Name three significant changes resulting from the Second Vatican Council that have had great impact on current Catholic understandings about Jesus.
- Briefly compare the major characteristics of an approach to Jesus "from above" with an approach "from below"—including the benefits and limitations of both.

9
Respond in writing to this statement: *"Christology from above" and "Christology from below" are simply two different paths to the same truth.*

The Journey of Faith in Jesus

Heir to a Rich History

As a young person born into the Christian community, you are heir to a deeply rich history of some two thousand years of struggle by Christians to come to terms with the Jesus of History, whom they recognize as the Christ, their Lord and Savior.

The Decision Is Yours

The invitation and the challenge to come to your own recognition of Jesus—offered to you by the larger church community and in this course—is an intensely personal one. No one can make you accept faith in Jesus. What must be asked of you, however, is that you take the person and message of Jesus seriously and recognize the questions he posed about the meaning of life as central to your own struggle to become a mature person. What you ultimately decide about him is for you to determine with honesty, openness, and integrity. That you must decide is a reality that can be postponed but not permanently avoided.

In the Company of Others

The history of the church has demonstrated that one's personal search for a response to Jesus seems to take place best in communion with other believers. The question posed by Jesus in the Gospels almost two thousand years ago is put to each of us today: "Who do you say that I am?" Those who seek to know, follow, and celebrate Jesus the Christ gather together in the community of the church as its members constantly renew and deepen their response to that question. In gathering together to live out his message, they trust that the Spirit of Jesus is alive among them, always guiding, encouraging, and saving. As you search out your own answer to Jesus' question, you are invited to do so with others in the church who can share that journey with you. **10**

A Concluding Prayer

The prayer of Paul for the Christian community at Ephesus is also meant for you as you contemplate embarking on the marvelous journey of a life lived with faith in the God revealed by Jesus:

For this reason I bow my knees before the Father, from whom every family in heaven and on earth takes its name. I pray that, according to the riches of his glory, he may grant that you may be strengthened in your inner being with power through his Spirit, and that Christ may dwell in your hearts through faith, as you are being rooted and grounded in love. I pray that you may have the power to comprehend, with all the saints, what is the breadth and length and height and depth, and to know the love of Christ that surpasses knowledge, so that you may be filled with all the fullness of God.

Now to him who by the power at work within us is able to accomplish abundantly far more than all we can ask or imagine, to him be glory in the church and in Christ Jesus to all generations, forever and ever. Amen. (Ephesians 3:14–21)

For Review

- Why is it important for a person to be in community with other believers as he or she seeks to make a personal decision about Jesus?

10
Imagine that right now Jesus confronts you with the question, "Who do you say that I am?" Write your honest response to that question. Then compare it with the response you gave at the beginning of this course. What did you learn about Jesus during this course that you will most likely remember several years from now?

■

Photo, facing page: As you search for your response to Jesus, you are not alone; the whole church joins in that journey with you.

Glossary

Abba. An Aramaic word used by Jesus to address God. It is an affectionate and intimate term for "Father," equivalent to our "Dad" or "Daddy."

Acts of the Apostles. A book of the New Testament written by Luke as a continuation of his Gospel. It is concerned with the early Christian communities after Jesus' Resurrection and Ascension, recording the church's development under the leadership of Saint Peter and the spread of the Good News throughout the Roman Empire by Saint Paul. Acts is sometimes referred to as the Gospel of the Holy Spirit.

Age of Enlightenment. The historical era when the study of science and technology that had begun in the sixteenth century exploded in the eighteenth century, bringing about an emphasis on reasoning as the dominant way of viewing reality. One result of this period was that the church came to be viewed as "unenlightened" and obsolete.

"amen" statements. A way of speaking that was unique to Jesus in his time. He used *amen* at the beginning of statements to confirm or give weight to what he was saying. *Amen* is a Hebrew word meaning "truly" or "it is true."

Apocalypse. *See* **Book of Revelation.**

Apostles. In the New Testament, primarily the twelve men chosen by Jesus to be his closest followers and to play a central role during his ministry and in the future. The title *Apostle* is also applied to Saint Paul, who never met Jesus during his earthly life.

Ascension. After the Resurrection, the event in which Jesus passed totally into the presence of his Father.

Babylonian Exile. The period from 597 to 538 B.C.E., when citizens of the kingdom of Judah were held captive in Babylon. This period of captivity tested the faith of the Jews, and though many lost faith in God, others (the remnant) began to live with a much deeper faith and trust. *See also* **remnant.**

baptism. In many religious traditions, the act of bathing in water as a sign of spiritual purification. Jesus was baptized by John the Baptist at the beginning of Jesus' public life. In the Catholic Tradition, Baptism is a sacrament that celebrates a person's initiation into the church, the forgiveness of sins, and the conversion to a new life in Christ.

Beatitudes. A series of statements found in Matthew's Sermon on the Mount and in Luke's Sermon on the Plain. The Beatitudes summarize the attitudes of people whose lives are grounded in and focused on Jesus' vision of the Kingdom of God. These statements are among the most familiar and popular passages of the Christian Scriptures.

Body of Christ. Saint Paul's favorite image of the church, one that suggests an intimate connection between the risen Jesus and the believing community. The church is understood as the visible manifestation of the risen Jesus on earth.

Book of Revelation. The last book of the New Testament, which deals with the expectation among Christians that Jesus will return again in glory at the end of time to fulfill God's work on earth. Characterized by symbolic language and imagery, Revelation was probably written to encourage continued faithfulness in late-first-century Christians, who were suffering persecution for their beliefs. The Book of Revelation is often called the Apocalypse, from the Greek word for "revelation."

canon. The authoritative list of sacred writings accepted officially as the scriptures for a religion. The word *canon* is based on a Greek word for "rule" or "standard." The church organized and approved the canon of the New Testament—that is, the twenty-seven books now contained in the New Testament—at the end of the fourth century.

catholic epistles. In the New Testament, a collection of seven letters: one attributed to James, two to Peter, three to John, and one to Jude. These letters are called catholic (meaning "universal") or general because they are addressed to believing Christians as a general audience rather than to specific individuals or communities.

Christ. The title the early Christians used for Jesus in order to confess their belief that he was the Messiah, the One sent from God, who would save them from all oppression. The word *Christ* is based on the Greek word *Christos,* meaning "the anointed one." *See also* **Christ of Faith; Messiah.**

Christianity. The religion based on Jesus' life and teachings.

Christian Scriptures. The entire Christian Bible, composed of both the Old Testament and the New Testament.

Christ of Faith. A title for Jesus that recognizes the Christian conviction that he was raised from the dead by God and that he truly was and is forever Lord and Savior. *See also* **Christ; Jesus of History; Messiah.**

Christology. The branch of theology that studies the person, role, nature, and message of Jesus.

Christology from above. An understanding of Jesus that begins with the recognition of his special eternal relationship with God. A Christology from above first emphasizes Jesus' divinity and then moves toward an understanding of his humanity.

Christology from below. An understanding of Jesus that starts with an attempt to grasp his humanity and his historical roots in first-century Palestine, and then moves toward a comprehension of his divinity.

church. The gathering of baptized persons who profess faith in the risen Jesus and his message and who, through the power of the Holy Spirit, strive to live that message in their daily lives.

conversion. The point at which someone who has had no faith at all comes to believe in God, or the experience of someone who has had a radical change in, or deepening of, their attitude toward God and religion.

covenant. A special agreement between two parties, either as individuals or as communities. In Jewish history, such a special relationship between the Jews and their God was established during an encounter between God and Moses on Mount Sinai. There, God promised to care for the people of Israel, and they in turn promised to follow the dictates of the Law—in particular, the Ten Commandments. This event came to be known as the Sinai Covenant. Christians believe that a new Covenant between God and people was established through the life, death, and Resurrection of Jesus.

cross. A symbol based on the wooden structure on which Jesus was executed. The cross has taken on profound and complex significance for Christians, representing both sacrifice and victory.

crucifixion. At the time of Jesus, a method of execution reserved for non-Roman citizens and slaves. The person being executed was nailed to or hung on a wooden cross and eventually died from bleeding, choking, the inability to breathe, or attacks by wild animals.

Damascus event. Paul's profound encounter with the risen Jesus on the road to Damascus, which brought about Paul's conversion and radically changed his life. This event is described in the Acts of the Apostles 9:1–22.

Day of Atonement. A major, solemn Jewish feast when the Jews repent of their sins. This day involves ceremonies, fasting, prayer, and ritual bathings.

Diaspora. The Jews who settled in regions outside of Palestine during or after the Babylonian Exile. The word *diaspora* is derived from a word meaning "dispersion" or "those who have been dispersed."

disciple. In the New Testament, any follower of Jesus' teaching. The word *disciple* is derived from a Latin word meaning "pupil" or "follower."

discipleship. Common among the ancient Jews, a style of teaching and learning in which a rabbi would attract disciples who would then study his teachings through lengthy discussion, memorization, and so on. In contrast, Jesus called his disciples to a personal, lasting relationship of love with God, and Jesus then sent his followers out to share in his mission of proclaiming the Kingdom.

ecumenical council. A worldwide official gathering of church leaders. The first was the First Council of Nicaea, in 325 C.E., and the last was the Second Vatican Council, in the early 1960s. *See also* **Jerusalem Council; Second Vatican Council.**

epistle. The common method of written communication in Paul's era. The word *epistle* means "letter." *See also* **catholic epistles; Pauline epistles.**

Essenes. A faction of ancient Jews who withdrew from Jewish society in order to observe strict religious traditions.

Eucharist. The sacrament in which Christians recall and enter into the mystery of Jesus' life, death, and Resurrection through a sacred meal, sharing Jesus' body and blood under the signs of bread and wine. The Mass is a celebration of the Eucharist. The word *eucharist* is based on a Greek word meaning "to give thanks."

Evangelists. A title given to the authors of the Gospels—Matthew, Mark, Luke, and John. The word *evangelist* is derived from the Greek word *evangelion,* meaning "the proclamation or announcement of good news."

Exile. *See* **Babylonian Exile.**

exorcism. The act by which evil is driven out of the person whom it "possesses."

faith sources. Documents written by believers prompted by the Holy Spirit for the purpose of proclaiming the work of God evident in all aspects of their life.

fathers of the church. Theologians trained in Greek philosophy who, at the end of the second century, explained the faith handed down by the Apostles. Their theological developments had profound effects on the church and its teachings.

general epistles. *See* **catholic epistles.**

Gentile. Any person who is not of the Jewish faith.

Gospels. The major sources of information about Jesus, written under the inspiration of the Holy Spirit and contained in the New Testament, attributed to Matthew, Mark, Luke, and John. The word *gospel* is derived from the Middle English word *godspell,* meaning "good news."

grace. God's total, unconditional, and unmerited love for people, which has the power to transform and save those who accept that love.

Great Sanhedrin. The official governing body of the ancient Jews, recognized as such by the Romans. It consisted of representatives of the priestly families, the scribes and doctors of the Law, the elders (outstanding Jewish laymen), the Pharisees, and the Sadducees. In the trial of Jesus, the Great Sanhedrin acted like a kind of supreme court.

Hebrews. A collective group of ancient tribes that made up the earliest ancestors of the Jewish people. Abraham, Isaac, Jacob, and their families were Hebrews.

heresies. False teachings about matters of faith, officially rejected by the church.

high priest. At the time of Jesus, the influential head of the priestly caste and, often, president of the Great Sanhedrin. He held a special kind of authority, like that of a king, and was appointed by the political masters of the country. During the trial of Jesus, Caiaphas was the high priest.

"I am" sayings. A distinctive literary feature of John's Gospel, in which Jesus expresses his identity and role by comparing himself to another reality. For example, "I am the living water."

Incarnation. The official church teaching that God took on human nature in Jesus.

infancy narratives. Stories about the birth of Jesus and his early life. These are found in the Gospels of Matthew (1:1–25; 2:1–23) and Luke (1:5–80; 2:1–52).

inspired texts. Texts whose authors, prompted by the Holy Spirit, convey God's revealed truth using their own abilities, words, and styles. For Christians, these Scriptures comprise the Bible, God is their ultimate author, and the truth in them is reliable.

Israel. Any one of the following: (1) the political and religious group of people with whom God made the Sinai Covenant, that is, those descended from the twelve tribes named for the twelve sons of the patriarch Jacob, who was called *Israel* by God; (2) after the death of Solomon, the northern kingdom, consisting of the ten northern tribes, which split off from the two southern tribes of Judah to form a separate nation and would later be destroyed by the Assyrians; and (3) more generally, the People of God, regardless of what land they occupy or their national or political status.

The modern state of Israel is seen by many Jews around the world as the political and national descendant of the ancient people of Israel. *See also* **Judah.**

Israelites. The descendants of Jacob, the patriarch who was given the name *Israel* by God. Later they would be known as Jews.

Jerusalem Council. An important meeting of Paul and his coworkers with Peter, James, and John in Jerusalem. The meeting's purpose was to ensure that all the church leaders were preaching the same Good News. The meeting resulted in the decision that the mission to the Gentiles could continue without demanding that the Gentiles become Jews before being accepted into the church.

Jesus. A popular Jewish name of Jesus' day. It means "Yahweh saves" or "Yahweh is salvation."

Jesus of History. The term for the divine Son of God who walked the earth in the person of Jesus, up to and including his death. *See also* ***Christ of Faith.***

Jew. A follower of Judaism.

Jewish Law. A statement of the Israelites' responsibility in their Covenant with God, the cornerstone of which was the Ten Commandments, given to Moses by God on Mount Sinai. More broadly, the Law is the first five books of the Old Testament, or the Torah. *See also* **Torah.**

Judah. The southern kingdom of the Jews (the northern one was Israel), formed by two of the original twelve tribes of Israel. This kingdom was eventually destroyed by the Babylonians, and its citizens were exiled. But a remnant, or group of the exiles, survived and returned to resettle the area under foreign domination. *See also* **Israel** (2).

Judaism. The religion based on the remnant, who survived the destruction of the southern kingdom of Judah and later returned to rebuild it. *Judaism* is the word from which the term *Jew* is derived.

Judea. At the time of Jesus, the region of central Palestine formerly known as Judah. It had been dominated in succession by the Persians, the Greeks, and the Romans.

Kingdom of God. Jesus' description of the rule, or reign, of God over the hearts of people. The Kingdom is an ideal future but also a present reality that is communal in nature and implies a new relationship between God and people and among people themselves. It therefore connotes the development of a new social order based on unconditional love.

Lamb of God. An image of Jesus that links him with the paschal lambs, which were slaughtered and sacrificed by the ancient Jews during Passover. This image is used in John's Gospel and in the Book of Revelation. *See also* **paschal lambs.**

Last Supper. A supper during Passover that was the last meal Jesus shared with his disciples before being handed over for crucifixion. It is remembered by Christians as the occasion of the first Eucharist and commemorated by them on Holy Thursday.

Law. *See* **Jewish Law.**

legalism. An overemphasis on rules and regulations. In the Jewish society of Jesus' time, it tended to dominate many aspects of life.

Letter to the Hebrews. A book in the New Testament that is a kind of extended sermon to a group of Christians who are in danger of falling away from their belief in Jesus. This book has often been attributed to Paul, but scholars today generally believe it was written by someone else whose identity is unknown.

Lord. A title commonly used in the Old Testament as a substitute for God's name. Jews believed that calling God by name was sacrilegious, because doing so implied that people had control over God. Often the word *Lord* is presented in all capital letters in the Old Testament.

In the New Testament, the title is applied to Jesus in two ways: (1) as an Aramaic form of address comparable to "Sir" and (2) after the Resurrection, as a way of acknowledging that Jesus is divine and one with God. *See also* **Yahweh.**

Magi. Non-Jewish members of the priestly caste of the Persians, serving as chaplains to and representatives of the royalty. The Magi were known for their understanding of astrology and the occult. They appear in Matthew's infancy narrative.

matriarchs. Women who played key roles throughout Jewish history. In the era known as the patriarchal period, *matriarchs* refers to Sarah, Rebekah, and Rachel—the women who, with the patriarchs, founded the religion we now know as Judaism. The word *matriarch* literally means "mother." *See also* **patriarchs.**

Messiah. The title given to the saving leader who was hoped for by the Jews. Later the title was applied to Jesus, who Christians believe fulfilled the hope of the Jews. The word *messiah* is derived from a Hebrew word meaning "anointed." *See also* **Christ; Christ of Faith.**

miracles. Works of wonder or extraordinary occurrences revealing divine intervention. As performed by Jesus and written about in the synoptic Gospels, miracles were intended to show God's power over all creation and, in a special way, over the forces of sin and evil.

nationalism. Allegiance to a nation. In Jesus' society, an excessive sense of nationalism led some Jews to believe that "love your neighbor" referred to Jewish neighbors only.

New Testament. The section of the Christian Bible pertaining specifically to Christian faith and containing twenty-seven books: the Gospels; the Acts of the Apostles; various epistles, or letters; and the Book of Revelation.

Nicene Creed. The profession of faith commonly recited in eucharistic celebrations, declaring the church's beliefs about Jesus. It was written at the First Council of Nicaea, in 325 C.E., as an official statement of the faith that was handed down by the Apostles.

Old Testament. The first part of the Christian Bible, containing, in the Catholic canon, forty-six books of the Scriptures that originated with Judaism. Christians believe the Old Testament is fulfilled by Jesus Christ in the New Testament.

oral tradition. The sharing of carefully selected and highly polished recollections primarily by word of mouth. The early Christians' oral recollections of Jesus became the basis for the Gospels.

Palestine. The former name of a country on the eastern shore of the Mediterranean Sea. Jesus was born and lived in Palestine, which was part of the Roman Empire at the time.

papyrus. The material on which letters were written in Saint Paul's day. It consisted of thin slices of the papyrus plant glued horizontally onto a backing formed by thin slices of the plant placed vertically.

parable. A special form of storytelling, used by Jesus in the synoptic Gospels. A parable usually builds from a simile, where two very different things are compared to each other in order to illustrate a point. The word *parable* comes from a Greek word meaning "comparison."

paschal lambs. In Jewish history, the lambs sacrificed in the Temple during the feast of Passover, as part of the ritual of a special meal recalling the one eaten by Moses and the Israelites before the Exodus. The word *paschal* is derived from a Hebrew word meaning "to pass over." Jesus is often referred to as the new paschal lamb because of his sacrificial death on the cross.

paschal mystery. The whole series of events by which Jesus saved humanity—from his giving the Eucharist at the Last Supper, through his death and Resurrection, to the outpouring of the Holy Spirit at Pentecost. Together, those events constitute a "new Passover," a way that passes through death to life. The paschal mystery is the Christian belief that ultimately God brings life and goodness out of suffering and death.

Passion. The arrest, trial, and Crucifixion of Jesus, recorded in all four Gospels in a detailed and generally consistent way.

Passover. The holiest and most celebrated Jewish feast, memorializing the miraculous liberation of the Israelites from Egypt, or the Exodus. In Jesus' time, Passover lasted for a week and included the ritual sacrifice of lambs in the Temple. This feast played a central role in the events surrounding the Last Supper and the Crucifixion of Jesus.

patriarchs. The key historical men who, with the matriarchs, founded the religion we now know as Judaism. The word *patriarch* literally means "father and leader of a family or a people." It is commonly used to identify three special Hebrew leaders—Abraham, Isaac, and Jacob. *See also* **matriarchs.**

Pauline epistles. In the New Testament, thirteen letters either written by or attributed to Saint Paul. These were intended to support and further educate individual Christians or small communities who had been brought to belief in Jesus through the missionary work of Paul and others.

Pentecost (Christian). The event in which the gift of the Holy Spirit was poured out on the disciples, transforming them into courageous witnesses to the risen Jesus. This is described in the Acts of the Apostles (2:1–13).

Pentecost (Jewish). The Jewish celebration of the giving of the Law to Moses. It is also called the Feast of Weeks. The word *pentecost* is derived from the Greek word for "fiftieth" and reflects the belief that fifty days after leaving Egypt Moses received the Law on Mount Sinai. Historically, this feast also celebrated the Jews' harvest season, a time for experiencing the wonderful gifts of God and expressing gratitude for them.

Pharisees. An influential and respected group within ancient Judaism. The Pharisees were conservative in politics in that they refused to compromise their strict faithfulness to the Covenant in order to gain political power. They were liberal in matters of religion in that they accepted new developments in Jewish thought. They also accepted the elders' oral traditions regarding the Jewish Law, and this often added significantly to what was required by the written Law. The Pharisees' tendency toward legalism put them in conflict with Jesus. Their chief political and religious rivals were the Sadducees. *See also* **Sadducees.**

priests. A group of leaders within the ancient Jewish community who were responsible for offering sacrifices in the Temple.

pronouncement stories. A form of storytelling used in the Gospels. The stories act as setups for "punch lines" containing the main lessons Jesus wanted to get across.

prophets. Special figures in Jewish history who continually challenged the people to live in accordance with their Covenant with God. The word *prophet* literally means "one who speaks out."

Protestant Reformation. The movement, begun in the sixteenth century by Martin Luther, that protested the Roman Catholic understanding of the church, the papacy, and questionable practices by some leaders in the church.

rabbi. In the time of Jesus, a scribe who taught in a synagogue. The word *rabbi* means "master" or "teacher."

Reign of God. *See* **Kingdom of God.**

religious truth. The deeper meaning that God intends to reveal to people through historical events.

remnant. The group of faithful Jews from the southern kingdom of Judah who survived the destruction of Jerusalem and the Babylonian Exile and later returned to rebuild Jerusalem and the Temple.

Resurrection. The event in which Jesus was raised from the dead by God.

Revelation, Book of. *See* **Book of Revelation.**

Sabbath. A weekly day of rest and prayer, based on the Creation story in the Book of Genesis. The Jewish Sabbath lasts from Friday evening to Saturday evening. The Christian practice of Sunday worship has its origins in the Jewish Sabbath.

Sadducees. The priestly aristocracy within ancient Judaism. The Sadducees were willing to compromise with the Romans in politics, but they were conservative in religious matters (that is, they were not open to new developments in Jewish thought or to the oral traditions of the elders). The Sadducees' chief political and religious rivals were the Pharisees. *See also* **Pharisees.**

salvation. God's work that frees humanity from the evils of sin. Salvation is a gift from God and not something achievable by human effort. Paul used the term *salvation* somewhat synonymously with the terms *redemption, righteousness, justification,* and *reconciliation.*

Sanhedrin. *See* **Great Sanhedrin.**

Scholasticism. A form of philosophy based on the concepts of the Greek philosopher Aristotle and relying to a great extent on order and logic.

scribes. Within the ancient Jewish community, leaders and scholars who were responsible for teaching the Law of Moses. They were given the title *rabbi*. In the Gospels, scribes are often portrayed in conflict with Jesus, because they imposed such heavy burdens on people by their righteous interpretations of the Law. Most of the scribes were Pharisees.

Second Vatican Council. An official worldwide gathering of leaders of the Roman Catholic church from 1962 to 1965. Its teachings brought about tremendous changes in the Catholic church, including a return to the Scriptures, a different understanding of church, a decreased tension between religion and science, and a renewal of the liturgy, especially the eucharistic celebration.

signs. *See* **miracles.**

sin. Most commonly thought of as a personal, freely chosen action that has negative effects on the sinner as an individual and on his or her relationships with others and with God. Sin can also be understood as a social evil that affects all people simply because we live in community with one another.

Son of God. A term used by Israelites to refer to the kings of their nation, or any particularly good man. Later the term's use was fundamentally changed in the New Testament to signify Jesus' divinity.

synagogue. In communities outside of ancient Jerusalem, a Jewish center where worship and the study of the Scriptures were conducted. After the Romans destroyed the Temple and Jerusalem in 70 C.E., these institutions became the principal places of Jewish religious activity.

synoptic Gospels. The Gospels of Matthew, Mark, and Luke. They are called synoptic because their authors often seem to have used the same sources or one another's work in writing their accounts. The word *synoptic* means "to see together."

tax collectors. Jewish agents hired by the Romans to attain a quota of taxes from the Jewish people. After reaching their quota, the tax collectors could keep whatever "extra" money they managed to collect. They were a despised group of men.

Temple. The magnificent house of God built by Solomon in Jerusalem. It became the center of Jewish life and worship. In 587 B.C.E., the Temple was destroyed by the Babylonians, but decades later it was rebuilt by the Jews returning from the Babylonian Exile. A new, much more grand Temple was built by Herod the Great before the birth of Jesus, but it was destroyed by the Romans in 70 C.E.

Ten Commandments. The cornerstone of the elaborate system of Jewish Law given to Moses by God on Mount Sinai and contained in the Old Testament. The Commandments are followed by Jews and Christians alike, guiding ethical conduct in everyday life.

testimonies of faith. *See* **faith sources.**

Torah. The written version of the Jewish Law contained in the Old Testament. Also, *Torah* is the name given to the first five books of the Old Testament.

Tradition. Among Christians, the teachings believed to have been handed down by Jesus and the Apostles; among Roman Catholics, the essential teachings and practices that have emerged from the ongoing, lived faith of the Christian community. Roman Catholic Tradition includes the official decrees of church councils and popes. These decrees are considered true and authoritative.

Trinity. The Christian doctrine that three divine persons—the Father, the Son, and the Holy Spirit—exist in the one God.

vocation. The call from God for a person to fulfill a specific and significant purpose. The word *vocation* is based on a Latin word meaning "call."

Yahweh. The Hebrew name for God, translated as "I am who am" or "I am the One who is always present." It signifies that God is the Creator and Ruler of nature and history. The Jews of Jesus' time held this name in such reverence that they refused to pronounce it, even when reading their Scriptures. *See also* **Lord.**

Zealots. In the time of the New Testament, a Jewish faction dedicated to achieving Jewish independence from the Roman Empire through a military overthrow of the Romans.

Index

Italic numbers are references to maps, photos, or illustrations.

Acknowledgments *(continued)*

Unless otherwise noted, the scriptural quotations herein are from the New Revised Standard Version of the Bible. Copyright © 1989 by the Division of Christian Education of the National Council of the Churches of Christ in the United States of America. All rights reserved.

The quotation of Josephus on page 16 is from *Jerusalem and Rome: The Writings of Josephus,* selected and introduced by Nahum N. Glatzer (New York: Meridian Books, 1960), page 145. Copyright © 1960 by Meridian Books.

The excerpts from an account by Tacitus on page 17 are quoted from *The Jesus Event and Our Response,* by Martin R. Tripole, SJ (New York: Alba House, 1980), page 42. Copyright © 1980 by the Society of Saint Paul.

The quotation of Suetonius on page 18 is quoted in *The New Encyclopaedia Britannica,* Macropaedia, fifteenth edition, under "Jesus."

The excerpt on page 37 is based on *How to Read the New Testament,* John Bowden's translation of Etienne Charpentier's *Pour lire le Nouveau Testament* (New York: Crossroad, 1982), page 19. English translation copyright © 1981 by John Bowden. Permission applied for.

The quotation on page 80 is from *Daily Life in the Time of Jesus,* Patrick O'Brian's translation of Henri Daniel-Rops's *La vie quotidienne en Palestine au temps de Jesus* (New York: Hawthorn Books, 1962), page 15. Copyright © 1952 by Hawthorn Books.

The information on page 83 is adapted from *Harper's Introduction to the Bible,* by Gerald Hughes and Stephen Travis (New York: Harper and Row, 1981), page 104. Copyright © 1981 by Lion Publishing, Oxford, England. Used with permission from Chariot/VICTOR Publishing/Lion Publishing.

The article on pages 132–133 is adapted from "World Youth Day '97: Pilgrimage to Paris," by Jerry Daoust, *Saint Anthony Messenger,* December 1997, pages 17–21.

The modern parable on page 161 is from *Fables for God's People,* by John R. Aurelio (New York: Crossroad, 1988), page 7. Copyright © 1988 by John R. Aurelio.

The miracle story on page 180 is based on *Making Saints: How the Catholic Church Determines Who Becomes a Saint, Who Doesn't, and Why,* by Kenneth L. Woodward (New York: Simon and Schuster, 1990), pages 209–210. Copyright © 1990 by Kenneth L. Woodward.

The scriptural quotation on page 210 is from the New American Bible with revised Psalms and revised New Testament. Copyright © 1991, 1986, and 1970 by the Confraternity of Christian Doctrine, 3211 Fourth Street NE, Washington, DC 20017. All rights reserved.

The scriptural quotations on pages 223, 226, and 272 are from the Jerusalem Bible. Copyright © 1966 by Darton, Longman and Todd, London, and Doubleday and Company, New York.

The creed on page 298 is from the English translation of *The Roman Missal* © 2010, International Commission on English in the Liturgy (ICEL). All rights reserved.

Photo Credits

Michael Agliolo, International Stock Photo: pages 6–7

Art Resource, NY: pages 41, 126, 218

Michael Bisceglie: page 186

Daniel Blatt: pages 22–23, 23 (inset), 24 (inset), 45, 79, 84, 100, 103, 121, 169, 203, 205, 214 (inset), 234–235, 256, 290, 295

Mike Carr, Index Stock Photography: page 291

Celcelio de Lora, SM: page 210

CLEO Freelance Photography: pages 145 (inset), 283

J. P. Colligan, Maryknoll Missioners: front cover (top); pages 1, 128–129

Copyright © Corbis, David Lees: page 305

Corbis: Annie Griffiths Belt: pages 82, 250; Bojan Brecelj: pages 264–265; Richard Cummins: page 213; Dennis di Cicco: page 222; Ric Ergenbright: pages 170–171; Owen Franken: page 296; Chris Hellier: pages 192–193; Robert Holmes: page 75; Jeremy Hormer: page 142; Dave G. Houser: page 220 (inset); John Swope Collection: page 180 (inset); Library of Congress: pages 17, 236–237; Caroline Penn: page 254; Pablo San Juan: page 270; Ted Spiegel: pages 48–49

Corbis-Bettman/Agence France Presse: front cover (middle); pages 2–3 (inset), 308

Jerry Daoust: pages 132 (inset), 133 (right), 144

Gail Denham: pages 13, 157 (inset), 273, 274

Duke University, "Amulet" permission granted by Rare Book, Manuscript, and Special Collections Library: pages 15 (right), 16, 20, 24–25, 29, 37, 39, 53, 61, 64, 72, 83, 87, 96, 98, 106, 110, 124, 132–133, 135, 140, 145, 155, 156–157, 160, 161, 168, 172–173, 178, 180–181, 185, 190–191, 198, 200, 204, 206–207, 220, 228, 239, 240, 243, 248–249, 252–253, 258–259, 268, 286, 298, 308

Editorial Development Associates: pages 11, 65, 244, 251, 257, 285, 293

Chad Ehlers, International Stock Photo: page 130

Gianni Giansanti, SYGMA: page 181 (inset)

Tom and Michele Grimm, International Stock Photo: page 87 (inset)

Tim Haske, Index Stock Photography: page 135 (inset)

Jack Hoehn Jr., Index Stock Photography: page 147

Norma Holt, Impact Visuals: page 91

Index Stock Photography: page 136

Phil Lauro, Index Stock Photography: page 275

Jean-Claude Lejeune: page 303

Erich Lessing, Art Resource, NY: cover (background); pages 2–3, 48 (inset), 58, 73, 111, 148 (inset), 174, 177, 188, 195, 260

Barry Levy, Index Stock Photography: page 156 (inset)

Maria Antoinette Evans Fund, Courtesy of Museum of Fine Arts, Boston: page 227

Mary E. Messenger: page 266

NASA, Jorge Scientific Corporation: page 106 (inset)

National Gallery of Art, Washington, D.C.: pages 107, 301, 306

Tom Nebbia: front cover (bottom); pages 15 (left), 28, 33, 34, 93, 110 (inset), 114, 116, 122, 166, 232, 307

Richard T. Nowitz: back cover (middle); pages 4–5, 6, 19, 26, 42, 44, 52, 67, 78, 96 (inset), 127, 131, 152, 170 (inset), 191, 192 (inset), 200 (inset), 238, 262–263

Paul A. Pavlik: pages 159, 211, 261

Gene Plaisted, The Crosiers: pages 57, 104–105

Z. Radovan, Jerusalem: pages 35, 50, 66, 76 (inset), 79 (inset), 86, 95, 99, 104 (inset), 115, 117, 128 (inset), 160 (inset), 163, 164, 173 (inset), 175, 183, 236 (inset), 241, 258 (inset)

Martin Rogers, Tony Stone Images: page 153

Ellen Rooney, International Stock Photo: pages 288–289

Saint Mary's Press: pages 267, 276, 284

Ron Sanford, International Stock Photo: pages 214–215

James L. Shaffer: pages 29 (inset), 76–77, 207 (inset)

Vernon Sigl: pages 280, 288 (inset)

Skjold Photographs: pages 27, 47, 268 (inset), 304

Sonia Halliday Photographs: pages 31, 32, 248 (inset), 264 (inset), 287

Staatliche Glyptothek, Munich, Germany/ET Archive, London, SuperStock: page 63

Stearn Publishers: page 37 (inset)

C. Takagi, Impact Visuals: page 278

Jane Taylor, Sonia Halliday Photographs: page 194

Olney Vasan, Tony Stone Images: pages 148–149

Wheater, Maryknoll Missioners: page 271

Bob Winsett, Index Stock Photography: page 311

W. P. Wittman Limited: page 12

Illustration Credits

Evy Abrahamson: pages 10, 38, 40, 71, 80, 83, 88, 108, 134, 137, 150, 151, 162, 176, 189, 196, 204, 216, 223, 224, 245, 246, 277, 279, 292, 302

. . . *And All Ate and Were Satisfied,* by Pablo Mayorga, on page 184 is used by permission of Peter Hammer Verlag on behalf of Fr. Ernesto Cardenal.

Ken Call: pages 9, 36, 56, 90, 101, 102, 119, 138, 154, 182, 197, 231, 242, 282, 299

Head of Christ on page 199 is from l'Eglise Saint-Sauveur de Beauvais (destroyed), Beauvais, Musée Départemental de l'Oise (Photo copyright © Patrice Diaz).

World of the Hebrews on page 228 is from *St. Joseph New American Bible* (New York: Catholic Book Publishing Company, 1991). Copyright © 1991 by Catholic Book Publishing Company. Used by permission. All rights reserved.